John Marshall's Achievement

Recent Titles in
Contributions in Legal Studies

JOHN MARSHALL'S ACHIEVEMENT

Law, Politics, and Constitutional Interpretations

EDITED BY
Thomas C. Shevory

Contributions in Legal Studies, Number 51
Paul L. Murphy
SERIES ADVISER

Greenwood Press
NEW YORK
WESTPORT, CONNECTICUT
LONDON

Library of Congress Cataloging-in-Publication Data

John Marshall's achievement : law, politics, and constitutional
  interpretations / edited by Thomas C. Shevory.
     p.   cm. — (Contributions in legal studies, ISSN 0147-1074 ;
  no. 51)
    Bibliography: p.
    Includes index.
    ISBN 0-313-26477-5 (lib. bdg. : alk. paper)
    1. Marshall, John, 1755-1835—Congresses. 2. United States—
  Constitutional history—Congresses. I. Shevory, Thomas C.
  II. Series.
  KF8745.M3J625 1989
  342.73'029—dc19
  347.30229   88-38554

British Library Cataloguing in Publication Data is available.

Library of Congress Catalog Card Number: 88-38554
ISBN: 0-313-26477-5
ISSN: 0147-1074

First published in 1989

Greenwood Press, Inc.
88 Post Road West, Westport, Connecticut 06881

Printed in the United States of America

The paper used in this book complies with the
Permanent Paper Standard issued by the National
Information Standards Organization (Z39.48-1984).

10 9 8 7 6 5 4 3 2 1

For Lane Davis and John Nelson

Contents

Preface

I must say that I might never have taken more than passing interest in the thinking of John Marshall had I not worked for four years in West Virginia. West Virginians, like others in that region of the country, are very conscious of their connections to the forming and founding of the American union, and it is difficult to spend time there without having that interest rub off. Marshall University, where the groundwork for the publication of this collection of essays was laid, was founded not long after the Chief Justice's death by his friend and great admirer, John Laidley. The university has done much since to preserve its namesake's legacy in a fine library collection devoted to works by and about him. I found that collection quite useful in the preparation of my contributions to the present work. More importantly, I found the interest of my colleagues and students in early American political thought to be quite contagious. I would have to say that serious consideration of this period of constitutional history began for me in conversations with one of my brightest and most contentious students, Kent Keyser. His Jeffersonian perspective gave me much food for thought and did much to shape my thinking about Marshall.

This collection of essays is the result of a John Marshall symposium, a week-long celebration, held at Marshall University, in November 1987, in conjunction with its sesquicentennial and the state of West Virginia's celebration of the bicentennial of the U.S. Constitution. The activities associated with the Marshall symposium were jointly sponsored by Marshall University and the Humanities Foundation of West Virginia. I would like to express my sincerest thanks to Charles Daugherty, executive director of the Humanities Foundation, and the entire foundation board, for having faith in the project and providing the requisite funding. Others at the foundation who deserve thanks include Robert Weiss and Linda Lewis.

The participants in the Marshall University John Marshall celebration deserve the credit for making it work. Some contributed essays to this collection, and all worked hard to develop and communicate new insights into the important contributions of Justice Marshall to American constitutional and political history. I would very much like to thank the following: John Brigham, Richard Brisbin, Robert Faulkner, Dick Howard, Herbert Johnson, Kent Keyser, James Lennertz, Joseph McCoy, Richard Matthews, Clair Matz, Simon Perry, John Stookey, Ira Strauber, George Watson, and Michael Zuckert.

Brian Smentkowski and Beth Adkins chipped in with help in a variety of ways for which they deserve thanks as well.

I would also like to thank the secretary of Marshall University's Political Science Department, Charlene Anteman, whose help with typing made for the expeditious preparation of the manuscript that became this book.

Last but not least, the moral support and encouragement for this project provided by the entire Marshall Political Science Department will not soon be forgotten.

John Marshall's Achievement

Introduction

Thomas C. Shevory

"[H]is opinions live almost as if they were a part of the Constitution itself," wrote George Haskins in his contribution to a John Marshall symposium published some thirty years ago in commemoration of the Chief Justice's two hundredth birthday.[1] Much has occurred since then with regard to scholarship on the period of America's founding. New techniques have been developed in the pursuit of historical understanding, and positivist notions of political science have flowered and to some extent declined. Legal scholarship has been forever altered by its attention to the literature of criticism, which has encouraged a more sophisticated understanding of the problems of interpretation. Yet much has remained the same. We have essentially the same Constitution, and Supreme Court decisions still make reference to the great decisions promulgated by the Marshall Court "almost as if they were a part of the Constitution itself."

Given the ongoing celebration of the Constitution's bicentennial and the upcoming celebration of the ratification of the Bill of Rights, it seems timely to consider once again the contributions of John Marshall and the early Supreme Court. This collection examines Marshall from a variety of political and methodological perspectives encouraged by current approaches to constitutional theory and history. The collection, we hope, fills a gap in analysis of the constitutional foundations laid by the Marshall Court. It reflects the continuities and changes that have transpired in legal scholarship and political philosophy over the last three decades. The chapters represent a strong and healthy diversity of opinion as to Marshall's contribution to American political and legal development, along with contention over the question of how Marshall's reasoning can be best applied to the continuing process of interpreting our national charter. John Marshall's contributions become thus the starting point for an exercise in political engagement. While often celebrating Marshall's achievements, we have attempted to move beyond celebration toward critical analysis of constitutional meaning and political philosophy.

That America was intended by its founders to be one long grand experiment in Lockean liberalism is a thesis that has been subject to more than a little dispute by recent critics of American culture and history. Gordon Wood's pioneering work on the republicanism of the Federalists, while not specifically a reinterpretation of the intentions of the framers, encouraged scholars to consider the founding period in new ways.[2] Wood rediscovered the republican elements extant in the revolutionary period and found them reactionary. They reached, he argued, backward toward an idealized period of small republics where a virtuous citizenry lived in harmony with natural order. Republicanism thus supported a mythology for nostalgic Federalist idealists. Whether this characterization of republicanism is entirely accurate and complete is not settled. But Wood's contribution, beyond the generation of an original historical understanding, was to encourage consideration of the period as a complex of ideologies, rather than an unambiguous expression of the *Second Treatise on Civil Government*.

Republicanism has not been the only nonliberal ideology discovered. Garry Wills's *Inventing America* cast considerable doubt on the conventional view of Jefferson as a careless Lockean, who considered "happiness" and property so entwined as to be virtually synonymous.[3] Jefferson, Wills argued, was a child of the Scottish Enlightenment, a communitarian who, like the early Adam Smith, saw property as a social good only insofar as it grew from and strengthened the natural bonds of human affection and sympathy. Recently, countering Wills, John Diggins has argued that the search for an optimistic communitarianism, stressing the empathetic aspects of human nature, was directly contrary to the Puritan origins of the American experiment.[4] It was Calvin who inspired Hume, Adams, and Madison. And it is recognition of the darkness of the human spirit that must be the governing principle behind the organization of civil society. If Jefferson was a communitarian whose optimism outreached Locke's, then, Diggins contends, he was a philosophical renegade. Richard Matthews's radical reconstruction of the Jefferson persona in his *Radical Politics of Thomas Jefferson* thus completes the picture by placing Jefferson in the service of the democratic critique of liberalism.[5] Matthews sharpens and extends the picture of Jefferson as representative of a lost egalitarian and radically democratic tradition. And he invites consideration of other figures of the period in terms of his insights.

John Marshall's contribution deserves rethinking in light of reevaluations of Jefferson and other founders. His life and thought have not been a central focus of historical reinterpretations. There are reasons for this. While Marshall served as a colonel in the war, he was a generation younger than the instigators of independence, and thus he did not contribute to the authorship of the founding documents. His most lasting and important contributions to the definitions of the American republic came after the beginning of the new century and thus were, in a sense, more reformative than formative. Moreover, his contributions are recognized as more significant in the domain of law than of politics or political philosophy, although that distinction, as several of our authors suggest, may be overdrawn (thanks in part to Marshall's determination to keep these spheres separate, expressed early on in *Marbury v. Madison*). Yet while Marshall's influence on the shape of the new republic may be secondary to that of Jefferson, Madison, or Washington, it is just barely so. His successful attempts to shape American conceptions of separation of powers and federalism attest to his importance as a figure in American political thought. He deserves attention.

Marshall, not unlike Jefferson, has often been considered as a kind of liberal, largely because of his contributions as Chief Justice to the protection of property and other vested rights in cases ranging from *Marbury* to *Dartmouth College v. Woodward* and *Sturges v. Crowninshield*. Marshall's liberalism is a theme of significance for each of our contributors. His liberal credentials are not seriously questioned by any of them, although varying degrees of approval are expressed.

Robert Faulkner's work was among the first to suggest that Marshall was not a simple liberal. *The Jurisprudence of John Marshall* remains the standard by which subsequent analyses of Marshall's jurisprudence and political theory must be measured.[6] Faulkner developed a strong and approving sense of Marshall's liberalism, while suggesting that it was tempered by republican values—a regard for and acceptance of virtue in the life of a republic. In his earlier work, Faulkner's sympathy for Marshall's natural rights liberalism is clear. Central to it is the distinction between simple democracy and constitutional or liberal democracy, between political power and the preservation of right. His fine chapter in this collection portrays Marshall as perhaps the most important impediment to the Jeffersonian and Jacksonian challenges, which entitles him to be considered as among the most significant figures of the nineteenth century for the preservation of constitutional democracy. Faulkner, at times drawing from the interpretations of Henry Adams and Charles Warren, provides a sense of the sweep of Marshall's decisions, which often attempted to preserve the division between legal rights and democratic prerogatives.

Faulkner's breadth of perspective is complemented by Herbert Johnson's careful analysis of Marshall's approach to contracts as developed in the Supreme Court bankruptcy cases, *Sturges v. Crowninshield* and *Ogden v. Saunders*. Johnson shows how the private contract cases illustrate Marshall's concern for the economic life of the union and the direction that it took. Johnson suggests that Marshall's legal practice in the service of debtors and his

involvement in speculative land schemes may have influenced his views on the
necessities and dangers of accruing debt in the service of personal profit and national economic development. Through an exceptionally close reading of the
opinions, Johnson is able to develop the connections between Marshall's
natural rights views on contractual relations and his positions in these two important debt cases. Johnson distinguishes Marshall's position in *Sturges* in relation to the context provided by the views of his fellow justices. Marshall,
Johnson concludes, preferred the exercise of federal power in this arena, but,
given Congress's unwillingness to act on bankruptcy, he was satisfied to draw
reasonably close boundaries around state prerogatives.

In *Ogden*, Marshall's only dissent, Marshall unsuccessfully maintained that
the right of contract existed before men entered into civil society and could
thus not be altered by such entry. Marshall's natural law perspective connected
with his desire for a uniform national bankruptcy law, which would prevent
states like New York from obtaining unfair commercial advantage and which
would provide for a stable system of agreements that was, it can be argued, the
economic justification for the origination of the federal union. Yet Johnson
questions the wisdom of relying upon natural law considerations to annul state
economic regulations given the abuses of subsequent courts.

A collection of works on jurisprudence and judicial decision would be incomplete without consideration of the contributions of analytical decision
theory. From the pioneering work of Glendon Schubert and C. H. Pritchett
has developed an approach to judicial decision making that emphasizes outcomes of the judicial process as the result of the interaction of an assortment of
variables. While this style of research has been extremely fruitful in the evaluation of contemporary Supreme Court decision making, its application to
historical periods prior to the Roosevelt era has barely commenced. John
Stookey and George Watson develop guidelines and suggestions useful to
future inquiry.

While jurisprudence must be viewed as a primary determinant of a justice's
voting record, other factors must be considered as well. Stookey and Watson
suggest examination of the justice's role perceptions, group dynamics operating
within the court, and the social background characteristics of the judge.
Stookey and Watson review appropriate techniques useful to analysis of the
jurisprudential positions of members of the Marshall Court, while noting
special features of the Court that pose problems. They envision content
analysis as a potentially fruitful mode of inquiry. Substantively, they consider
Marshall's "activism" and the effect of his leadership upon the Court's unity. A
suggestive bloc analysis of the Marshall Court's voting illustrates the operation
of certain group dynamics.

Marshall's presence as a historian, while perhaps minor, does serve to illuminate his political thinking. Thus, my analysis of Marshall's *Life of*

Washington portrays Marshall as something of a disturbed republican. My interpretation of Marshall's republicanism thus differs from Robert Faulkner's. I
argue that it evidenced deep suspicion of attempts at self-governance. Marshall,
like previous republicans such as Machiavelli, desired civic virtue but despaired
of its perpetuation without the presence of a great republican leader, such as
Washington. His survey of the republic's history finds much conflict, instability, and vice. Marshall's historical interpretations are thus deeply foreboding.
While he viewed the Constitution as a dike, the strength of which might hold
back the forces of dissolution in a democratic polity, without Washington's
presence its endurance became less assured. Marshall, at least as author of *The
Life of Washington*, expressed the pessimism of classical republicanism, rather
than the optimism of John Locke.

Richard Brisbin, also concerned with the relationship of republicanism and
liberalism in Marshall's thought, perceived the Chief Justice as a transitional
figure on the road from republican idealism to liberal pragmatism. Brisbin examines Marshall's political ideas regarding history—or "time"—and virtue and
legality—or "space." According to Brisbin, Marshall held a republican's fear of
the corruption of political institutions in time, and sought to teach the lessons
of civic virtue through historical analysis. Yet unlike less diluted republicans,
he regarded commercial activity as a means to stave off potentially corrupting
forces in history. Marshall's liberal aspect moved him to consider commercial
activity as civilizing. Marshall placed republican historical understanding in the
service of justifying liberal political institutions.

Marshall's concern with virtuous political leadership was also a republican
concern. He viewed leadership as the means to control the politics of interest,
but with no guarantee of wise leadership in political life, Marshall felt the
necessity of instituting legal institutions to check what he considered the
unscrupulous demagoguery of men like Jefferson. *Marbury* epitomized
Marshall's use of liberal legality to contain what he considered democratic
despotism. Legality thus carried forward where virtue failed. Liberal institutions would substitute for republican leadership. Thus, Marshall's federalism
was transitional and progressive in the sense that he was able to transcend the
nostalgia of the reactionary "high federalists" and see the future of the republic
in the institutional ordering of conflicting interests.

Examination of Marshall's political theory would be incomplete without
critical appraisal from a Jeffersonian perspective. Richard Matthews's "radical"
perspective, drawn as it is from a revisionist interpretation of Jefferson, concedes Marshall's liberalism and finds little to commend in it. Marshall, Matthews suggests, while he was not as steeped in the wickedness of liberalism as
Hamilton, lacked the humane, democratic, and egalitarian sensibilities of Jefferson. Marshall's defense of property rights is consistent with his suspicion of participatory and other rights recognized by Jefferson as essential to the pursuit of

human happiness. Jefferson resisted the Supreme Court as an antidemocratic institution. Marshall served for more than three and a half decades from its powerful station, where he was protected from the exercise of the people's franchise. The genuine personal antipathy that existed between the two was thus firmly grounded in strong divergences on issues of political principle. Marshall's abilities are not questioned by Matthews. Able, as he often was, to win political battles with Jefferson, as in *Marbury*, he deserves a considerable amount of the credit (or blame) for America's liberalism. He institutionalized the Hamiltonian outlook for generations during his service on the Supreme Court. America, Matthews implies, must reject Marshall to fulfill the ideals of the Declaration of Independence.

The idea that interpretation might itself be problematic would be foreign to Marshall's jurisprudence. Marshall's was a life of thought wedded to political enterprise. His judicial temperament, shaped as it was by the politics of his time, entailed an unself-conscious view of the Constitution as a necessarily and imminently interpretable document. Marshall, as has often been observed, announced judicial decisions as though they were destiny. He never expressed doubt in his interpretive capacities or the knowability of the Constitution. He had a "knack for making his conclusions appear to follow inevitably from his initial premises."[7] Such a feat seems quite unimaginable in our milieu of postdeconstructionism.

The authors herein most centrally concerned with interpretation, while very much aware of its difficulties, are uniformly determined to save at least some vestige of its possibility. Marshall, in a sense, shows the way. His faith and political determination exemplify not only that interpretation is imaginable, but that it can be political without being arbitrary.

The Critical Legal Studies movement has subverted interpretive complacency in legal scholarship. Ira Strauber relies upon the sophistication of Marshall's legal reasoning to clarify difficulties with Mark Tushnet's critical legal analysis. Marshall's *McCulloch v. Maryland* opinion is grounded in a highly complex federalism and is laced with a necessary and admirable regard for political ambiguity. In Strauber's significant reinterpretation of *McCulloch*, he cogently argues that Marshall's decision hinged on considerations of "plain politics," tied to the desire for stability, security, and peace extant in his conception of federalism. *McCulloch* is an exercise in demonstrating the inevitable indeterminacy of liberal political life. Strauber's meticulous reading of *McCulloch* offers it as an argument still relevant to recent attempts on the part of Critical Legal Studies scholars to characterize liberal politics as ambiguous to the point of arbitrariness. Strauber presents the somewhat startling argument that Marshall's processes of argumentation in *McCulloch* were more important than its particular result. And CLS, unable to appreciate liberalism's complexities, still suffers from the linguistic dilemmas for which it reproaches liberal constitutionalism.

John Brigham is more than a little suspicious of the tendency of Americans to interpret the founding period through a set of standard texts of American jurisprudence designed, as he sees it, to fit current conceptions of institutional authority. Why is it, he wonders, that constitutional law texts always start with *Marbury* and follow it inevitably with *McCulloch*? Surely this habit should be considered in light of its implied political meanings. (There was more than a little pre-Marshall American constitutional law.) Marshall, we now take for granted, supplied us with the "givens" of constitutional government. But neither Marshall's path nor our interpretations of it are political necessities. Unfortunately, we are so prone to see Marshall's decisions as inevitable (as George Haskins did) that we no longer perceive them as political, as Edward Corwin and Albert Beveridge did.

Marshall clearly understood the relationship of the political and the interpretive, in Brigham's view. To accept Marshall's rhetoric of inevitability with a false legal finality can result in interpretive narrowness, such as is reflected in the constitutionalism of Christopher Wolfe and Robert Bork. Marshall is only partly responsible for the homage that we pay him. Much of it derives from and is sustained by the tendency of scholars and members of the legal community to interpret his opinions without question. Reliance upon him has become, in essence, a substitute for attention to our own political and judicial experiences.

James Lennertz, like Strauber and Brigham, believes that Marshall has something important to tell us about constitutional interpretation that transcends the substantive implications of his decisions. Like Strauber, Lennertz sees the processes of argument as at least as important, if not more important, than the particular results. Lennertz begins with two of the most important figures in current controversies of interpretation, Robert Bork and Ronald Dworkin. Bork's emphasis on neutral principles is contrasted with Dworkin's commitment to creative interpretation and the virtue of political integrity. In the search for general standards by which the practices of interpretation can be analyzed and judged, Lennertz explores scientific epistemologies. He is able to utilize Marshall's opinions in two areas, federalism and the contract clause, as evidence of the connection between scientific and legal perspectives. Lennertz's examination of seven major Marshall Court decisions in terms of orientation toward text, precedent, natural law, and legal intentionality leads him to an evaluation of Marshall's views as closer to Ronald Dworkin's than Robert Bork's.

Michael Zuckert does not concede Lennertz's presentation of Marshall as a Dworkinian noninterpretivist. Marshall's view of the role of the judiciary as interpreter of the law, eloquently stated in *Marbury*, provides ample evidence of that. And whereas Brigham and Lennertz are hostile to Christopher Wolfe's defense of interpretivism via Marshall, Zuckert, sympathetic to Wolfe's enterprise, defends a version of the interpretivist John Marshall and in the process extends, and perhaps even reconstitutes, interpretivist conceptions.

As words are not always clear nor meanings complete, a constitution cannot be entirely inclusive. We thus must ask how something "can not be in a text and yet be in it." Zuckert's reading of *Marbury* features a John Marshall who creatively *mis*interprets the Constitution as he moves from "pretext," through "text," "context," "transtext," and "pantext" in an evolving, expanding, hermeneutic circle. Zuckert questions the ultimate defensibility of the interpretivist/noninterpretivist distinction as he argues that interpretation is indeed possible and that Marshall's example is still highly relevant to those who consider the text worth saving.

The enterprise of constitutional interpretation, by linguistic and political necessity, remains always incomplete. Marshall's accomplishment was nothing less than to create a ground of meaning from which future arguments and conflicts could be considered and judged, if not always settled. Political arguments, to paraphrase de Tocqueville, almost always become constitutional arguments in the American context. This was not foreseen by the participants at the Philadelphia Convention, nor could it have been. To create a national constitution was a brand new enterprise, a political leap into the dark. History could offer but the most incomplete precedents for a human action of such magnitude. Even if the Constitution was in some sense "good" or "correct," containing elements of justice, what its force would be for governance could be a matter of only the most indistinct speculation.

John Marshall, a person of fairly modest educational attainment, entered his long tenure as Chief Justice with what seems in retrospect to have been an almost instinctual understanding of what a written constitution might mean as a force for the shaping of American history. Without the force of his argument or his political determination, the evolution of the republic would certainly have been different. This is not to say that Marshall's accomplishments were unambiguously good. Marshall, as much as any single individual, shaped our practices of limited government. But a limited government is a government not fully and completely democratic. Marshall saw clearly the constitutional tension between political authority and notions of right. Strong democracy collapses the distinction, putting full faith in the decisions of the majority. This was not Marshall's faith. The sphere of rights must, he felt, be protected from the sphere of democratic rule. Steeped in the English tradition, he viewed this separation as nothing less than the rule of law.

His arguments and rulings, compelling and important as they were, have infused our views of legitimate constitutional authority to the point that it is very difficult to evaluate critically and objectively our current culture of constitutional discourse. The following chapters make some step in that direction. Significantly, it is virtually impossible to consider Marshall without attention to his great nemesis, Thomas Jefferson. And Jefferson, it is worth recalling, the author of America's "declaration of right," also considered rights as paramount. Yet

Jefferson saw the rule of Marshall's constitutional law as both an impediment to the full exercise of democratic prerogatives and indeed a violation of right. Thus Marshall's accomplishment may be in some sense our loss. Our faith in the Constitution as an ageless and permanent ark shapes our political culture and justifies our self-important faith in our status as a constitutional democracy. But it also limits our ponderings on alternative constitutionalisms and other versions of democracy. Marshall deserves credit, but we must not abandon the imaginative consideration of possibilities that may have been forgotten or lost because of his convincing rhetoric of constitutional politics.

NOTES

1. Haskins, *John Marshall and the Commerce Clause*, 104 U. PA. L. REV. 37 (1955).
2. G. WOOD, THE CREATION OF THE AMERICAN REPUBLIC, 1776–1787 (1969).
3. G. WILLS, INVENTING AMERICA: JEFFERSON'S DECLARATION OF INDEPENDENCE (1978).
4. J. P. DIGGINS, THE LOST SOUL OF AMERICAN POLITICS (1984).
5. R. MATTHEWS, THE RADICAL POLITICS OF THOMAS JEFFERSON: A REVISIONIST VIEW (1984).
6. R. FAULKNER, THE JURISPRUDENCE OF JOHN MARSHALL (1968).
7. THE PAPERS OF JOHN MARSHALL 488 (C. Hobson ed. 1987).

PART I JUDICIAL DECISION

1

The Marshall Court and the Making of Constitutional Democracy

Robert K. Faulkner

The Supreme Court has done much to make and keep the United States a constitutional or liberal democracy, not a simple democracy. The Marshall Court of 1801–35 did the most, and in face of the powerful democratizing movements led by Thomas Jefferson and then Andrew Jackson.[1] Chief Justice John Marshall and his associates raised the Supreme Court from erratic obscurity to semipolitical eminence as the voice of the semisacred fundamental law. When, in 1833, five years into the Jacksonian era, Alexis de Tocqueville examined the new world of American democracy, he concluded that "a more imposing court was never constituted by any people."

Five principal tasks engaged Marshall's Court during its thirty-four years. Defying Jefferson's plans and protests, first, it established general judicial authority to construe the Constitution (and to restrict Congress, President, and states accordingly). Second, it held the executive branch to the rule of law, to its duties as defined by statute and Constitution. Third, it upheld and expounded federal legislative powers, especially extensive discretion as to implied powers. Fourth, it secured creditors' rights and land titles despite virulent protests, several times verging on rebellion, from the states and from debtors. Last, it upheld an international law that prescribed strict fidelity to treaties, equal sovereignty of other governments, and rights and duties necessary for free trade and mutual agreement.

DANGEROUS BEGINNINGS

Marshall took over a court that, although respectable, had failed to establish its authority before confronting powerful enemies. From its start the Court's tasks were weightier than they seemed. The Constitutional Convention of 1787 had seldom discussed the judiciary, but relegated much to it. The "judicial power" extended to "all Cases, in Law and Equity, arising under this Constitution, the Law of the United States, and Treaties . . . made under their authority." But even this sweeping legal language hid the sweeping political implications. In particular, federal courts had been left as a decisive barrier to the two domestic forces most opposed to the new constitution, state governments and democratic legislatures. The convention rejected a legislative or executive veto of state laws (Virginia and Hamilton plans) and instead authorized judges to enforce upon the states "the supreme Law of the Land." Also, the Court was tacitly expected to hold the executive and the popular legislature to the Constitution's mandates, and, by construing law, to lessen an unfair impact, as No. 78 of *The Federalist* put it, upon the "private rights of particular classes of citizens." Such checks upon democratic inclinations would affect the very "character of our governments."

President George Washington had taken care to nominate as justices prominent citizens from each section of the new nation, choosing especially those who had helped draft or defend the Constitution. His appointees made an immediate and favorable impression, and their decisions, together with their charges to grand juries while on circuit, helped the new government to win popular acceptance. In its first eleven years the Court passed upon the constitutionality of an act of Congress, upheld federal treaties and laws against challenges from state legislatures and courts, and held unconstitutional a state law relieving debtors.

Nevertheless, the judges' early role was largely untested and ceremonial; no cases reached the Court during the first few terms, and only about seventy were heard during all eleven years prior to Marshall's appointment. Also, the public was at first ignorant of the potential conflict between the distant new judiciary and familiar old powers. When realization and resentment arrived, the Republican party was at hand to inflame the old antifederal animus of debtors, states, and legislatures. In *Chisholm v. Georgia* (1793), the Court disregarded the express assurances of the Constitution's advocates, to states burdened with unpaid war debts, and held that a citizen of a state might sue another state for breach of contract. This venture was promptly reversed by the Eleventh Amendment, which was introduced next day into the House of Representatives.

The early Court's voice was often muffled. The judges inclined to write individual opinions, which were not much noticed. There was no opinion for the Court and no reporter of decisions. Hardly any opinions were even partially reprinted by newspapers. Also, the Court had three chief justices in eleven years, and with an odor of partisanship. Chief Justice John Jay absented himself to negotiate with Britain, signed a hotly disputed treaty, and then resigned in

1795 to become governor of New York. For opposing Jay's treaty the Federalist Senate rejected John Rutledge as Jay's successor, even after Rutledge had served a term in a recess appointment. Less than three years after Oliver Ellsworth succeeded Jay, in March 1796, he was appointed to negotiate with France and so resigned as chief justice in December 1800 while still abroad.

Meanwhile, federal judges conspicuously challenged some favorite Republican doctrines. Circuit courts decided that France might be considered an enemy with whom the United States was engaged in partial war: that a citizen had no inherent rights to expatriate himself (to fight, as the case would have it, for revolutionary France); that the Court (and government) had common law jurisdiction to punish subversive acts; and, worst of all, that the Federalists' abhorrent Alien and Sedition Acts were constitutional. The Republican reaction pointed toward rebellion and disunion. Madison and Jefferson themselves fathered the Virginia and Kentucky Resolutions of 1798, which maintained that the states retained the last word as to constitutional construction. The radical Republican paper *Aurora* urged that judges be impeached for political heresies. Popular enmity toward the court was one cause of Jefferson's "revolution," his electoral triumph of 1800.[2] Meanwhile, the Court became more embroiled. Justice Samuel Chase proclaimed against Jeffersonian "mobocracy" and absented himself to electioneer for Federalist candidates in Maryland. The Federalists appointed Marshall as Chief Justice in January 1801, on February 13 pushed through a judiciary act that eliminated the rigors of riding circuit by adding sixteen circuit judgeships, and promptly filled them, during the dying hours of Adams's presidency, with good Federalists. Jefferson complained bitterly: defeated at the polls, the Federalists "have retired into the judiciary as a stronghold . . . and from that battery all the works of republicanism are to be beated down and erased."[3]

The Republicans brought their own batteries to bear. The new Congress repealed the Judiciary Act of 1801 and replaced it with the Circuit Court Act of 1802, which eliminated the new courts and restored Supreme Court justices to circuit duty. This act also postponed the next term of the Supreme Court for fourteen months, so that the Court could not overrule, as violating Article III, Section 1, either the cancellation of judicial offices or the joining of the duties of circuit courts to one supreme court. Meanwhile, Jefferson and his chiefs awaited an opportunity (which Chase eventually provided) to transform the Court through a series of impeachments.

The sixteen judges who in turn made up the Marshall Court displayed extraordinary unity. At first all six justices were Federalists, antipathetic to Jefferson's designs and secure after the decisive failure of the Chase impeachment in 1805. Beginning in 1804, with Jefferson's appointment of the spirited William Johnson of South Carolina to replace Alfred Moore, however, nine appointments lay with Republican and then Democratic presidents (and but one with the Whig John Quincy Adams). The majority tipped in 1811 when Madison appointed the great Joseph Story of Massachusetts to replace William Caleb Cushing. Yet, surprisingly, the Court's balance tipped only slightly. Justice Johnson followed Marshall's lead in essentials. Story became a protégé (but not a rubber stamp), and so it went until Marshall's final years. Then Marshall feared that the Court would fall to the states' rights school, and he dissented in crucial cases affecting creditors' rights. On the other hand, Justice Henry Baldwin almost resigned in 1831, warning that Marshall's Court was extending its authority beyond "subjects clearly with the judicial power."[4]

Various factors caused the unity that Marshall cultivated and Jefferson deplored. The Court was threatened from without. The judges were imbued with a certain jurisprudence. Justices such as Johnson, Story, and Thomas Todd were Republicans never fully devoted to the quixotic Jeffersonian creed. John McLean and James M. Wayne were far from clones of Jackson, who appointed them. Besides, Jefferson and Jackson were themselves constitutionalists as well as democrats. Also, the justices lived in congenial association with one another and with leading lawyer-statesmen of the time. Until 1845 Supreme Court justices lived and ate together, a practice begun because of skimpy accomodations in the District of Columbia and promoted by Marshall after necessity passed. The Court's deliberations were aided by a Supreme Court bar chiefly composed of senators and representatives and led by gifted public men such as William Pickney, William Wirt, and Daniel Webster.

Probably the most unifying influence was Marshall's superior prudence and reasoning. Indeed, the six justices appointed by Jefferson, Madison, and Monroe entered not a dissent to the Court's key affirmations of federal power. Marshall filed dissenting opinions in but six of the 1,100 opinions decided with opinions between 1801 and 1835, fewer dissents than any chief justice since. He wrote the opinion for the Court in 519 cases. Jay had written three opinions: Ellsworth wrote five. In his first five years Marshall wrote the opinion in every case in which he participated; in the next seven years he delivered 130 of the Court's 160 opinions. From the start he established the custom of one opinion for the Court; concurring opinions and dissents were discouraged. Jefferson fought this "engine of consolidation" until he died; he would restore opinions seriatim.[5] Jefferson pressed additional schemes, including easier modes of impeachment and a six-year term for federal judges with reappointment by the President after consent of both houses of Congress.

CONSTITUTIONAL REGULATOR OF GOVERNMENTS

The Marshall Court's crucial achievement was to establish the Supreme Court's authority to limit other federal branches and to limit state governments. This effort was never free of dangerous challenges, not least because of

.d: the general government "shall not be the final
Three law cases resolutely ventilated these issues:
), *Martin v. Hunter's Lessee* (1816), and *Cohens v.*

.a in *Marbury* is the classic judicial formulation of the
.aw. It appears beneath an ingeniously politic cover. *Marbury*
.ation of Supreme Court predominance over executive and
.vers—without much exacerbating the enmity of the suspicious
Rep.. ...s that controlled both. The secret is the creed of rights and effectual
provision, prudently managed. The Court held first that Marbury had a right
to his commission, and second that he might appeal from executive to courts
for vindication of his right. It finally denied a remedy, however, holding that
the law authorizing the right for which he asked violated the Constitution.
Marshall took the engaging position, as E. S. Corwin put it, of denying a certain judicial power while using the occasion to assert the transcendant power to
void legislation as unconstitutional. Jefferson grasped immediately the implications and fought all his life to discredit the decision. But his party did not
follow. Even the most zealously Republican papers refrained from denying the
necessity of judicial review for perpetuating a written constitution.

Yet Jeffersonians charged that other parts of the opinion were partisan hec-
toring as to Jefferson's duties and the judiciary's authority. In fact, Marshall
sought and hit bigger game. He set forth a comprehensive ranking of federal
powers and laws to govern all presidents, legislators, and judges. Law, not executive decree, determines a citizen's rights when the executive is engaged in
"ministerial" execution of law (not the discretionary exercise of his "political"
powers). To enforce a legal right the citizen may appeal to the judiciary. Else
there would not be "civil liberty" nor "a government of laws." He may finally
appeal from legislature's law to Constitution. The doctrine that a law violating
fundamental law is void is "essentially attached to a written constitution and is
consequently to be considered, by this court, as one of the fundamental principles of our society." If fundamental, the doctrine must govern courts as well as
Congress. Otherwise, the "very foundation of all written constitutions would
be subverted" because the legislature, limited in words, would enjoy "a practical
and real omnipotence."

The Court prospered by means other than telling argument. The justices
returned to circuit duty under the Republican Circuit Court Act of 1802, in
light of precedent and despite their constitutional doubts, and then affirmed
the act's constitutionality in *Stuart v. Laird* (1803). The Chief Justice was
cautious, even timid, while testifying before the Senate during Samuel Chase's
impeachment trial. "Had Marshall been a man of less calm and certain judgment," Henry Adams concluded, "a single mistake by him might easily have
prostrated the judiciary at the feet of partisans."[7] Instead impeachment became,

Jefferson said, "a mere scarecrow" that the judges "fear not at all."[8] Meanwhile, Jefferson's party and power ebbed. Immediately after the Senate's vote to acquit on all counts, John Randolph, leader of the House and of the impeachment, proposed a constitutional amendment for removal of judges by the President on joint address of both houses. An ally in the Senate proposed an amendment such that the legislature of any state might recall a senator and vacate his seat. These writhings further divided the imperious Randolph's radical and aristocratic Virginians from the ordinary northern democrats and the moderates of both parties. While Jefferson's personal popularity burgeoned during his first term, with the acquisition of Louisiana and the decline of the Federalists, it shriveled during the second. His pet embargo brought ruin and sedition at home, reinvigorated the Federalists in commercial and Francophobic New England, and reaped disdain abroad. Congressional Republicans had split; Jefferson left office discredited.

In reviewing the Jeffersonians' failure to reduce the federal judiciary, Henry Adams blamed Jefferson's own direction and caution. At the flood of his power, his new Judiciary Act removed only the new Federalist judges and left intact the old core. It did not democratize judicial appointment, shorten judges' terms, or restrict the courts' protection and definition of federal powers. The Virginia Republicans had thought the general government not the supreme judge of its powers; they also thought, as Congressman William Branch Giles put it, "a permanent corporation of individuals invested with ultimate censorial and controlling power over all the departments of government" to be "in direct hostility with the great principle of representative government."[9] When Jefferson finally fomented the impeachment of Chase, which might have politicized the judiciary, he remained in the background and allowed the erratic Randolph to hang himself with his own rope. Adams was not sure whether Jefferson's hesitations stemmed from love of popularity, which led Jefferson to instigate but to withdraw from execution, or complexity of principles, which mixed states' rights and democracy with acknowledgment of governmental power and a fixed separation of powers.[10] Marshall and the Court outlasted Jefferson's hesitant initiatives and meanwhile diffused the principles that appealed to the constitutional side of the Republican creed.

In *Martin v. Hunter's Lessee* and *Cohens v. Virginia* the Court confronted challenges by the states. If the national democratic party was cautious and divided, individual states were direct and decided. In 1803 a Pennsylvania law defied a federal district court decision and directed the governor "to protect the just rights of the State from any process issued out of any Federal Court." The governor and legislature united to forbid compliance with the Supreme Court decision, in *United States v. Judge Peters* (1809), that the district judge enforce his order. Only when armed conflict threatened, between state troops and a United States marshal's posse of two thousand, did the state back down.

Disobedience was widespread to federal court orders enforcing the hated embargo in New England and South Carolina; enforcing the security of certain property rights and land claims in Pennsylvania, Georgia, Kentucky, and Virginia; and protecting the national bank in Kentucky, Ohio, and elsewhere. The worst crisis came in the Marshall Court's last years. Georgia was near rebellion. It defied the Court's order, in *Worcester v. Georgia* (1832), to free missionaries whom the state had imprisoned for violating its rules governing valuable Cherokee territory. Georgia's seizure of the Cherokee lands violated the Constitution, the Court announced in an opinion by Marshall, because federal jurisdiction over the Cherokee, as an independent nation, was exclusive. Georgia's governor threatened "the most determined resistance" to such a decision. The legislature denied the Supreme Court's jurisdiction in any proceedings interfering with a state court's criminal decision. The state's highest court refused to change its decision or free missionaries. Georgia backed down only at President Andrew Jackson's proclamation against nullification, of December 10, 1832, and the subsequent Force Bill to enforce federal laws. Jackson's acts were directed against South Carolina's ordinance nullifying the tariff of 1832. The state ordinance specifically forbade appeal to the Supreme Court of questions concerning the ordinance, state laws carrying it out, or the federal tariff law.

The Court's enforcement of federal supremacy twice provoked Virginia to challenge its appellate authority and elicited two classic opinions. The twenty-fifth section of the original Judiciary Act of 1789 had authorized appeal to the Supreme Court from judgments of state courts when federal treaty, law, or Constitution was drawn into question. The Court had taken jurisdiction in this manner sixteen times between 1789 and 1813, and had invalidated a state statute, all without serious opposition. In *Martin* a state for the first time asserted the unconstitutionality of such jurisdiction. The case involved title to extensive and valuable lands and growing determination on the part of Virginia's Jeffersonian leaders, such as Judge Spencer Roane, to counter the Court's nationalism.

The Virginia courts decided according to Virginia law, and the Supreme Court according to the superiority of the federal treaty with Britain. The Virginia Court of Appeals then declared invalid the Supreme Court's decision; while controversies may arise between state and federal governments, one Virginia judge wrote, "the constitution has provided no umpire, has erected no tribunal, by which they shall be settled." Justice Story's response for the Supreme Court was elaborate but firm. According to Article III of the Constitution, jurisdiction extends to all cases arising under the Constitution, laws, and treaties of the United States—whether the court of first instance is state or federal. If state courts and state sovereignty are impaired, accordingly, that is the necessary result of the Constitution's erection of an effectual national government. The Court's power, Justice Johnson added, is the government's "power of protecting itself in the exercise of its constitutional powers."

Feelings had been further inflamed by 1821 when the Court decided *Cohens v. Virginia*. The defense of implied powers in *McCulloch v. Maryland* (1819), already anathema to the South, had become entangled in the fiery debate over Congress's power to limit slavery. Northerners tried to prevent Missouri's admission as another slave state, and, despite the Missouri Compromise (1820), the coincidence of sectional division with principled division was an ominous portent—Jefferson's famous "alarm bell in the night." Southerners feared that *McCulloch* tacitly authorized further congressional conditions upon the admission of new states.

Jefferson and Roane were now joined by the fiery publicist John Taylor of Caroline, who took specific aim at the Court's doctrine of "ample means" and its supervision of state decisions. The Supreme Court may not construe fundamental law when "the Constitution operates upon collision between political departments." Taylor argued, but only when it operates upon "collisions between individuals."[11]

A Virginia court had convicted the Cohens brothers of selling a lottery ticket in Virginia, the sale being forbidden by state law and the lottery being authorized by the federal District of Columbia. When Cohens sought to appeal, the state denied also that Congress might authorize what the state law forbade. When the Supreme Court took jurisdiction, the Virginia legislature denied federal jurisdiction and resolved that counsel for the state were to argue only the question of jurisdiction, not the merits of the case. Although Marshall eventually construed the statute to authorize a lottery only within the District, his opinion was attacked bitterly for its elaboration of federal authority. The people of the United States had made a "supreme government" to which "ample powers are confided." Virginia is subordinate to that government, and to the judiciary that protects it, to the extent the Constitution requires. If courts of the Union cannot correct courts of the states in such a case, the government will be no better than the league it replaced: "Each member will possess a veto on the will of the whole."

The *Cohens* opinion, widely circulated in the press, was followed within two weeks by *McClung v. Silliman* (1821), which denied the right of a state court to issue a writ commanding a federal official. The Court's opponents were furious. Jefferson redoubled his efforts, and Roane composed a series of attacks that were reprinted in full in many southern and western papers. Various proposals percolated, in addition to Jefferson's continuing crusade for judicial opinions seriatim: to give the Senate appellate jurisdiction whenever a state might be a party to a federal case, to provide for concurrence of five judges or even all seven judges when a state law was declared invalid, to repeal Section 25 of the Judiciary Act. None of these attacks succeeded, but neither did attempts to relieve the judges of circuit duty and to provide an additional judge and circuit for the ten new states of the West and Southwest. Although in 1807 a judge had been added to the original six, and assigned to the circuit encompassing Kentucky, Tennessee, and Ohio, subsequent bills all foundered on congressional distrust of the Court and partisan distrust of presidents from the other party.

As the doctrine of nullification took hold in the South, and Georgia came close to rebellion in 1830, congressional animosity erupted again. Senator Robert Hayne of South Carolina, defending nullification in January 1830, justified state veto of laws deemed unconstitutional, even laws validated by the Supreme Court. On January 24, 1831, a majority of the House Judiciary Committee reported favorably a bill to repeal Section 25 of the Judiciary Act. Yet the full House rejected the bill, virtually without debate, and a subsequent attempt to limit terms of federal judges also lost. The congressional attacks had failed, and Jackson's rebuff of nullification secured the Marshall Court's last two years against the vengeance of jealous states.

THE COURT AND THE PRESIDENCY

The Marshall Court's first sharp fights involved judicial limitation of executive actions. In *Marbury* the Court divided executive authority into that directed by law (ministerial) and that involving executive discretion (political). An individual had a right to something due by law but denied by executive, and the judiciary might vindicate such a right.

Little v. Barreme (1804) held an officer liable for civil suit for an action beyond statutory authorization, even if prescribed by presidential instruction. President Adams's order could not "legalize an act which, without these instructions, would have been a plain trespass." The doctrine was soon turned against two of President Jefferson's favorite projects, punishment of Aaron Burr and the embargo of 1807.

Two trials over which Marshall presided halted prosecutions of Burr and his coconspirators. Finally convinced that Burr was plotting to separate the Southwest from the Union, Jefferson had ordered arrests, transfer of the prisoners from the West, and trials for treason; he proclaimed their guilt and sought temporarily to suspend the writ of habeas corpus. *Ex parte Bollman and Swartwout* (1807) held that a writ of habeas corpus might issue to free Burr's associates Bollman and Swartwout and that they could not be tried for treason; the evidence did not show levying of war, and the crime, if any, could not be tried in the District of Columbia because it had not occurred there. Jefferson's worst fears were realized when Marshall on circuit defined treason so strictly that a jury reluctantly freed Burr himself. The trial was sensational. Jefferson, in effect the prosecutor, became in effect the defendant, skewered by the contemptuous rhetoric of Burr and his band of lawyers. To convict for treason the

Constitution had required either confession or testimony by two witnesses "to the same overt Act" of "levying War." Without a confession, Marshall would allow conviction only for an open act of levying war or, if for procuring the overt act charged, then only by testimony of two witnesses to the procuring. While the prosecution had witnesses to Burr's movements and forces, it had none to prove either that Burr was present at the armed gathering specified, on the Ohio, or that he procured the gathering. After the verdict Marshall was hanged in effigy, charged with partisan bias, and savagely attacked by the Republican press. Yet the framers of the Constitutional provision seem to have aimed to limit partisan abuses by defining treason strictly and requiring unequivocal evidence.[12]

Jefferson designed the Embargo Laws of 1807 and 1808 to halt attacks on American trade by halting trade with the predators, imperial Britain and the France of Napoleon. Their purpose went beyond particulars, however. The embargo was a Jeffersonian experiment in humane reform, in conquering conquerors by peace. Immediately upon his election he would, Henry Adams said, "legislate as though eternal peace were at hand, in a world torn by wars and convulsions and drowned in blood."[13] The courts affirmed the embargo's constitutionality even as they limited some extensions of executive power.

The sharpest rebuff was unexpected. It came in Republican South Carolina from Jefferson's appointee Justice William Johnson. The President had ordered customs-fees collectors in the ports to detain all vessels containing provisions, whereas the authorizing statute ordered collectors to detain only those loaded vessels that, in the collector's opinion, intended to evade the embargo. In *Ex parte Gilchrist* (1808), on circuit, Johnson held the instruction void as unwarranted by statute. Jefferson, furious, circulated a contrary opinion, to which Johnson replied with a stinging public defense of the primacy of law over executive order and of the primacy of judicial exposition of law. "You can scarcely elevate a man to a seat in a Court of Justice," wrote Attorney General Rodney glumly to Jefferson, "before he catches the leprosy of the Bench."[14]

To impress the citizenry, Rodney ordered treason trials for the murderers of three Vermont militiamen killed while enforcing the embargo. Justice Brockholst Livingston, on circuit, distinguished a general levying of war from willful opposition to a particular statute, and would not sustain the indictment (*U.S. v. Hoxie* [1808]). Similarly Marshall, on circuit, quashed criminal indictments for violations of an embargo act that mentioned only civil penalties. Also, he refused to follow the example of Virginia, amidst the distress caused by the embargo, in easing federal court enforcement of civil judgments such as compulsory sale or garnishment of property.

Still, Jefferson won the great judicial victory. District Judge John Davis of Salem, Massachusetts, rebuffed an almost treasonous Federalist establishment to hold the Embargo Acts constitutional (*U.S. v. Brigantine William* [1808]). He held the embargo to be a valid regulation of commerce under the commerce power, a valid preparation for war under the war power, and a valid exercise of discretion for both purposes under the "necessary and proper" clause of the Constitution. Years later, in *Gibbons v. Ogden* (1824), Marshall noted "the universally acknowledged power of the Government to impose embargoes."

THE COURT AND NATIONAL POWERS

In defending great national powers of war, taxation, and commerce, Marshall's Court was controversial not because it overturned legislation, but because it did not: it affirmed congressional powers that many states and many Republicans would have denied. While President Jefferson took Louisiana without an explicit constitutional warrant, imposed an embargo that even Justice Story thought went to the very edge of constitutional power, and recommended internal improvements, he preached before and after his Presidency the virtues of states' rights and the vices of implied federal powers. His preachings found ready ears, especially in the South. In the North the old Federalists had long ago turned against a general government controlled by Jefferson and agrarian democrats. What became the Essex Junto's conspiracy to break up the Union was influential in New England and dominant in Massachusetts. The causes were several: the embargo on New England's trade, Madison's degrading alliance with the atheistic tyrant Napoleon, a drain of men and money for war against the mother country, spotty war effort that mixed an occasional exhilarating success with humiliating failures. The beginning and end of the War of 1812 found the federal government decisively unprepared in men, money, and will. The end arrived just in time. The country was almost a confederation, dependent upon state banks and even state armies. The Hartford Convention was meeting to consider a New England Confederation.

Amidst the indecisive weaknesses of the political branches, and the recalcitrance of people and states before the demands of war and governance, the Marshall Court remained a nationalizing court. *McCulloch v. Maryland* (1819) is the classic case. The Bank of the United States had been the special object of Jefferson's and then Jackson's attacks on implied powers, monopoly, governmental patronage of the unproductive rich, and judicial construction. It was a federal power, but not explicitly prescribed, and a central power that reached into daily life, encroached on local establishments, and made state banks and bankers pay off its loans and redeem their circulating paper. The "monster bank" could be strict with credit in a time of democratic laissez-faire and populist envy. National banks seemed a distant financial elite that pressed an industrious and honest majority. The stockholders were often eastern or British, and as often antipathetic to democrats. While the Second Bank was outfitted with Republican stockholders, its crucial first years were tainted with fraud and mismanagement. The new directors expanded credit with the boom and then abruptly contracted. They reaped blame, partly deserved, for a whirl-wind of bankruptcies and foreclosures. By 1819 eight states had passed legisla-tive or constitutional penalties to drive out the Bank. The Baltimore branch had led all others in inflating credit, and cashier J. W. McCulloch proved the ringleader in a sensational scheme of embezzlement. The state sued McCulloch for refusal to pay Maryland's tax. After losing in the state courts he appealed to the Supreme Court.

Marshall's opinion ignores all mitigating circumstances, and concentrates on Congress's power to charter a bank and on the supremacy of Congress's power when exercised. The United States is a government and not a league, derived from the people and not dependent on the state governments. While limited to enumerated powers, it is supreme within its sphere. Unlike the Articles of Con-federation, the Constitution does not require that all its power be expressly stated. No government could have its incidental powers enumerated, unless its constitution were to have the "prolixity of a legal code." "Great outlines" can be marked; subordinate powers must be implied. "We must never forget that it is a constitution we are expounding." Marshall was not advocating unlimited government. Congress may not exercise a major power not enumerated, or "under pretext of executing its powers pass laws for objects not entrusted to the government," or exercise a subordinate power merely because it is secondary. Nevertheless, a government must have ample latitude to provide for its legitimate objects. "The power being given, it is the interest of the nation to facilitate its execution." Accordingly, Congress had even been granted an ex-plicit power to go beyond explicit powers: to "make all Laws which shall be necessary and proper for carrying into Execution" the explicit powers. Maryland's counsel insisted that "necessary" meant "absolutely necessary." Marshall insisted that "necessary" can and must mean "convenient" or "useful," if the Constitution is not to be a "splendid bauble." Congress may select a "vast mass of incidental powers," and in particular a bank to assist in war, taxation, and regulation of commerce. What the supreme government may constitutionally do, no state may undo or hinder. The Court declared void not only a tax aimed at destroying the national bank but any state tax on a federal function.

There was ferocious indignation in the South and West, and then defiance. "If Congress can select any means which they consider 'convenient,' 'useful,' 'conducive to' the execution of the specified and granted powers" said the *Rich-mond Inquirer*, "if the word 'necessary' is thus to be frittered away, then we may bid adieu to the sovereignty of the States; they sink into contemptible corpora-tions; the gulf of consolidation yawns to receive them."[15] Virginia's legislature recommended a new tribunal to judge conflicts between states and the Union. Four states ratified a constitutional amendment to confine national banks to the District of Columbia. Ohio, which had suffered badly from inflation and bank failures, refused to abide by the decision.

Osborn v. Bank of the United States (1824) confirmed *McCulloch* while refuting Ohio's claims, but it also emasculated the Eleventh Amendment in a revealing manner. The amendment had prohibited federal courts from deciding suits against a state by citizens of another state (or of a foreign state). Marshall held that the amendment applied only to a state as a party of record—and not to an agent of the state, such as Osborn the state auditor. This bit of reasoning follows a "pause" to reflect on "the relative situation of the Union with its members" if the Court decided otherwise. Each state might attack at will "while the nation stands naked, stripped of its defensive armor, and incapable of shielding its agent or executing its laws." Nevertheless, the Court had to repudiate this doctrine four years later in *Governor of Georgia v. Madrazo* (1828).

In the steamboat case, *Gibbons v. Ogden* (1824), Marshall boldly set forth a broad commerce power interpreted so as to promote a national free market. New York had granted a monopoly in New York waters, under which Ogden's steamboat sailed. The Court held for Gibbons, saying that the grant violated a "right to trade," which the court derived from a simple federal coasting license. The opinion begins and ends with attacks on those who would construe the Constitution artificially, so that "the original powers of the states are retained." In turn Marshall defines commerce expansively, so as to include navigation and all intercourse involved in buying and selling, authorizes Congress to regulate all commerce within the states except that which does not "extend to or affect other states," holds Congress's supreme power not to be limited by the states' powers, and supposes that the laws of civilized man authorize a right to trade, a right presumed by Congress's grant of the coasting license. Marshall's argument contrasts with opinions such as President Monroe's, while vetoing the Cumberland Road Act in 1822: the federal power over commerce can merely impose duties and imposts on foreign trade and prevent such taxes on trade among the states. *Brown v. Maryland* (1827) applied the Court's reasoning to foreign trade; a Maryland tax on importers was held in conflict with federal law. The federal law seemed merely to levy duties on imports. But the Court held that payment of the duty indicated a reciprocal and pervasive "right to sell" the goods imported. Any other construction would "break up commerce" with other nations.

Gibbons's liberation of trade among the states had striking consequences. Within a year steamboats working out of New York City increased in number from six to forty-three. The effect extended farther, since the monopoly had granted franchises in four other states, which, in retaliation, had often authorized their own monopolies. Steam transport and exploration swelled on coastal waters and on inland rivers and lakes, notably in the distant West. *Gibbons* was "the emancipation proclamation of American commerce," according to Charles Warren.[16] It was the most popular of the Marshall Court decisions, welcomed by all but monopolists and leading Republican strict constructionists—who feared consolidation and in particular a federal commerce power that could reach slavery within the states.

In 1823, on circuit in his native South Carolina, Justice Johnson hit the South's raw nerve. To maintain servility among the slaves, South Carolina and Virginia had enacted laws to prevent free blacks from entering and to detain them in custody until their ships departed. Johnson held South Carolina's law to violate the "exclusive and paramount" federal authority over commerce among the states and with foreign nations. State officials resolutely ignored the decision, and ignored less than a year later the implications of *Gibbons* as well.

Yet the Court left a place, albeit residual, for state independence, a place for state regulation of health, police, and safety. This residual power was the larger because the chief federal power over internal affairs, the commerce power, was limited to the encouragement of commerce. If embargoes were allowed, they were, per *Gibbons*, to be retaliatory measures for the sake of future commerce or, at most, instruments of the enumerated powers of war. Also, ample implied powers did not mean unlimited implied powers. In Marshall's own opinion, as expressed in a letter, the Court would not under the commerce power authorize general patronage of such internal improvements as roads and canals, but only internal improvements "for military purposes or for the transportation of the mail."[17] In *Willson v. Black Bird Creek Marsh Company* (1829), the Court tolerated a Delaware dam, erected to promote health and the value of property, across a small navigable stream in tidewater, despite a contrary claim on behalf of a sloop holding the same coasting license that had freed Gibbons's steamboat. The toleration is clear, although the principle is not.

In one important respect the Marshall Court retreated from the nationalism of its predecessors. The pre-Marshall Supreme Court allowed indictments under common law despite the absence of a statute or a constitutional provision, as for perjury in federal court. Republicans had been appalled. All of the federal government's "other assumptions of ungiven powers have been in detail," said Jefferson: the doctrine "of the common law being in force and cognizable as an existing law in their courts, is the most formidable."[18] But in *United States v. Hudson and Goodwin* (1812), the Court denied a federal common law jurisdiction as to crimes, throwing out an indictment of certain Federalist publicists for libeling Jefferson while president. Story and Marshall seem to have dissented.

COURTS AND THE SECURITY OF RIGHTS

Perhaps the distinctive function of all modern courts remains the protection of individual rights. Marshall and his fellow justices also elaborated this function for the federal courts, although in a spirit different from contemporary judicial protection of free expression, minimum human needs, and the welfare of disadvantaged minorities. The Marshall Court afforded judicial remedies to protect personal security under law and to protect property obtained by contract. In relying principally upon statute, treaty, and Constitution, it differed sharply from the modern judicial orientation by a vision of progressive social equality—although the old Court's view of law was conditioned by an earlier view of progress, inherent in the "general principles" of civilized or common law. The Court protected Marbury's right to a commission according to statutory conditions of appointment. Burr's rights as a defendant in light of the prescriptions in Article III for treason prosecutions, and creditors' rights in light of common "rules of property" and Article I's prohibition to any state of a "Law impairing the Obligation of Contract."

The judicial mixture of law and right is a mixture of obvious subordination with subtle direction. In applying law to the rights of individuals in particular cases, courts "are the mere instruments of the law," Marshall once said, "and can will nothing." Yet the Constitution and all law are instruments of rights, and by their interpretations judges determine which rights exist by action of law. "The question whether a right has vested or not," *Marbury* said, "is in its nature, judicial, and must be tried by the judicial authority." Judges define much of the sphere of individual liberty, often in limitation of political branches and purposes.

Only a minor part of the Marshall Court's protection of rights involved the Bill of Rights, the first ten amendments that dominate modern constitutional litigation. It decided no cases under the First Amendment, whose provisions against establishing religion and for protecting free speech have come to seem preeminent, nor under the next two amendments, which guarantee a right to bear arms and limit civilians' duty to board soldiers. It specified only a few details of the next five amendments' regulation of criminal and civil proceedings. The vast bulk of legislation and litigation took place in the states, while the Bill of Rights was obviously intended, the Court held in *Barron v. Baltimore* (1833), to restrict federal powers alone. During the nation's early years the federal government passed rather few laws, federal courts allowed large discretion to the political branches, and federal judges passed on comparatively few cases. Besides, the judges inclined to observe the civil and criminal procedures derived from the common law and to interpret the amendments to require no more.

The Marshall Court is famous for its protection of property rights, especially rights vested under contract. It characteristically overruled state attempts to take back land grants, to revise corporate charters, and to ease the burdens of debt through bankruptcy or stay laws. Favoring investors, corporations, and creditors, while checking state legislatures, state courts, and the many debtors, the Court was plunged into bitter controversies. However we view such controversies now, the justices then thought their procedures legal, right, and politic. They supposed that an individual had a right to the fruits of his labor and to dispose of his property. To protect this right was to encourage industry, commerce, and prosperity, and to discourage class conflict. The Court's protection of rights vesting through exchange complemented its patronage of trade through the commerce power. In effect it was the nation's authoritative political economist.

Fletcher v. Peck (1810) gave to state grants the obligation of sacrosanct contracts and to grantees the security of creditors. The Georgia legislature of 1795 had granted millions of Yazoo acres; the next, elected in a burst of popular indignation at the fraud and bribery that had greased the transaction, revoked the grant. Those whose titles were thus impaired pressed for compensation. The dispute was long and bitter, partly caused the crucial split of the Republican party (Randolph accused Jefferson and his ministers of toadying to speculators), and was pursued in the courts as well as through Congress and the presidency. *Fletcher* declared the Georgia revocation unconstitutional. While a court might not question law because of the legislators' motives, it might hold a law invalid for meddling with a judicial function—that is, for divesting property without following "those rules of property which are common to all the citizens of the United States" or "those principles of equity which are acknowledged in all our courts."

Dartmouth College v. Woodward (1819) held that a state grant of a corporate charter was a contract not to be subsequently impaired. A New Hampshire legislature had rechartered Dartmouth College at the behest of a new board of trustees, and in so doing enlarged the board, gave to the governor the additional appointments, and subordinated the trustees to new overseers all appointed by the governor. The governor and legislature were Republican, and Jefferson personally approved the changes: the security of private trust for public use "may perhaps be a salutary provision against the abuses of a monarch, but it is most absurd against the Nation itself."[19] The Court held otherwise. The charter is a contract of a sort that the framers would protect. A corporation need not be a governmental body even if its purpose, education, is public, of the sort patronized by government. To arguments from public policy Marshall replied that the framers had their own policy incentives. If the giver's wishes are respected, giving is encouraged. Charitable foundations no less than economic enterprises are served by withdrawing contracts from "the fluctuating policy and repeated interferences" of legislative bodies. The Dartmouth College case encouraged the American system of foundations and educational institutions privately endowed, privately governed, and constitutionally protected from a popular majority. The sanctity provided to corporate charters secured economic corporations as well. Yet the Marshall Court was somewhat tentative as to the economic corporation. It refused to infer from the mere grant of a charter an exemption from state taxation, even destructive taxation (*Providence Bank v. Billings* [1830]). It delayed federal protection of corporations as independent persons at laws, holding that shareholders of corporations suing in a circuit court (which held jurisdiction only by virtue of the parties' diverse citizenship) must be all citizens of a state different from that of the opposite party (*Bank of the United States v. Deveaux* [1810]). Few corporations were parties before the Marshall Court. Eventually, however, the Court decided over Marshall's dissent that a corporation's approval of its agents' acts may be shown by presumptive evidence without a written record and vote of the shareholders (*Bank of the United States v. Dandridge* [1827]).

Marshall also dissented from the Court's eased stance as to bankruptcy laws. *Sturges v. Crowninshield* (1819) had been strict: a state bankruptcy law, which discharges the debtor from a debt, unconstitutionally impairs the obligation of contracts. Beset by laws delaying payment of debts and allowing payment in inflated currency, the framers had favored "the inviolability of contracts" to "restore public confidence completely." *Sturges* shocked the states that had moderated or canceled the debts of bankrupts: the opinion restricted its holding to the circumstances of that case. In *Ogden v. Saunders* (1827), a bare majority of four justices held bankruptcy laws constitutional if prospective, for contracts to follow, and construed *Sturges* to exclude only a retrospective application.

The Marshall Court's most poignant decisions as to property rights concerned slaves and Indians. Although slavery violated a person's "natural right to the fruits of his own labor" (*The Antelope* [1825]), and the Indian tribes had been deprived of their original natural rights to their land, the Court held that the country's civil laws establishing slavery and subordinating Indian tribes had to take precedence over natural right. Justice Story, on circuit, had held that the slave trade was contrary to the law of nations, because "a breach of all moral duties." In *The Antelope*, the Supreme Court decided otherwise. It would adhere to international law as then formulated and not treat slave traders as pirates even if the trade was "unnatural." Similarly, the Court held that slavery was built into the country's laws. Courts, whose first duty was to apply the laws, whatever their sympathies with liberty, had to maintain the general policy of laws securing property.

The great cases on Indian claims first affirmed that the laws and titles of a conqueror would control the conqueror's courts and then ordered that the conquered Indians be allowed their property, and a certain independence, until their own "voluntary cession." *Johnson v. Graham's Lessee* (1823) confirmed a title derived from a grant by Virginia, in preference to a title derived from Indians who lived there. Titles turn on "the law of the nation in which they lie," Marshall argued, not merely on "abstract justice." Nor might Indian tribes sue as foreign nations: if "distinct political societies," they were nevertheless "domestic dependent nations" (*Cherokee Nation v. Georgia* [1831]). Still, the court supposed that the justification for further conquest had passed as danger from the Indians had passed. The conqueror should encourage "minglings" of the peoples, or at least toleration of the Indians as "a distinct people." The Cherokee had an "unquestionable" right to their lands until they ceded them. In *Worcester v. Georgia* (1832), the Court declared void various Georgia laws that sought to abolish Cherokee independence and appropriate the tribe's Georgia territory. While the Cherokee territory was guaranteed by federal treaty, the federal government had also promised Georgia what it had not provided, extinguishment of the Indian claims. The Marshall Court came down on the side of the Indians and, in effect, the more humane national policy followed, if never successfully enforced, by every president from Washington through the Virginia Republicans and up to Andrew Jackson.

THE COURT AND THE LAW OF NATIONS

Like its predecessor, the Marshall Court held the "law of nations in its modern state of purity and refinement" to be part of the supreme law of the land (*Brown v. United States* [1814]). In particular, the Court was disposed to defer to the determinations of other nations' courts as decisions of equal sovereigns, to enforce stringently the obligations of treaties, and to be solicitous, where possible, of commercial rights, especially the rights of neutral traders during wartime.

During the Court's first dozen years the United States lived in the shadow of the Titans—of the epochal struggle between old Europe, led by Britain, and revolutionary France, captured by Napoleon Bonaparte. That changed. There occurred the Louisiana Purchase from France in 1803, the semivictory over Britain in the War of 1812, Britain's final defeat of Napoleon at Waterloo in 1815, the Rush-Bagot agreement of 1817 to limit British and American naval vessels on the Great Lakes, and the United States's acquisition of the Floridas from a decaying Spain in 1819. The restless new nation was free to extend its trade and enlightenment into the Americas. During the first period, the Court chiefly upheld treaties with Great Britain and France and condemnations by their prize courts, even when these contradicted American advantage and violated the law of nations. It insisted upon strict observance by American traders of their duties as neutrals. During the second period, the Court repeatedly enforced treaties as to the Floridas and Louisiana, and duties of neutrals, so as to provide for Spanish land grants and protect the Spanish and Portuguese from marauders and partisans of independence for the Latin colonies.

Croudson v. Leonard (1808) upheld the condemnation of an American ship by a British prize court for penetrating Britain's blockade of Napoleon's continental empire. That the British orders-in-council ignored the traditional conditions of a blockade, that decisions of British and French courts were self-serving and oppressed neutral traders, and that the administration was in a kind of war using its Embargo and Nonintercourse Acts, did not sway the court from respecting the finality of another sovereign's court. *Schooner Exchange v. McFadden* (1812) involved an American ship captured by the French, converted into a public ship of France, and seized while visiting this country. That the emperor constantly seized U.S. ships, and violated neutral rights, was irrelevant: matters rather "of policy than law." Still, sovereignty had its other face. The court would enforce its nation's sovereign authority. *The Rapid* (1814), one of the many cases in which the Court enforced the Nonintercourse Acts against dissident New Englanders, held illegal the importation during the war of goods purchased from England before the war and stored in Nova Scotia. "Every individual of the one nation must acknowledge every individual of the other nation as his own enemy—because the enemy of his country."

Where governmental actions were unequivocal, however, the court inclined to limit them by a concern for individual rights. *Murray v. Schooner The Charming Betsey* (1804) put the point succinctly: "An Act of Congress ought never to be construed to violate the law of nations if any other possible construction remains, and consequently, can never be construed to violate neutral rights, or to affect neutral commerce, further than is warranted by the law of the nations as understood in this country."

The Court's solicitude for neutral commerce stretched far. *The Nereide* (1815) decided that a Spanish neutral cargo was not good prize for an American privateer, even when carried aboard an armed British ship—this despite a declared war with Britain and a Spanish law that allowed confiscation. Yet American traders might not parade as neutrals while aiding belligerents. A series of cases punished American privateers that masked the freighters and preyed on Spanish and Portuguese commerce. These decisions opposed both the greed of adventurers and patriotic sympathy with rebels seeking self government. In a series of cases, notably *The Santissima Trinidad* (1822), the Court held invalid prizes taken by ships fitted out in violation of the United States's neutrality. Many Portuguese and Spanish ships were restored, as were relations with the two countries. Similarly, mutineers and privateers often prowled under one patriotic flag or another. The lower courts, sympathetic or intimidated, inclined to acquit of piracy. A number of decisions in 1820 held that an American citizen, sailing under the flag of a revolutionary government unrecognized by the United States, might be convicted of piracy for attacking a Spanish vessel. There ensued two executions in each port city where convictions had been obtained, which ended for the United States the fashion of piracy in South and Central America.

During 1832 and 1834 the Marshall Court required scrupulous respect for Spanish grants of land protected by the Adams-Onis Treaty of 1819 and by the

Louisiana Treaty of Cession of 1803. Fraudulent titles abounded, often assigned to financiers and speculators in New York and abroad. Jackson was indignant. Nevertheless, the Court held that a grant made by an official was to be presumed an official act unless the United States proved lack of authority (*United States v. Arredondo* [1832]). Charles Warren concluded that the Court's decision significantly reduced America's public lands and unjustly enriched many private speculators. An alternative determination would have shaken land titles in all older quarters of the United States and thereby put into question the sanctity of treaties and law.

NOTES

1. This paper draws on my *The Marshall Court and Era*, in 1 Encyclopedia of the American Judicial System (R. Janosik ed. 1987).

2. *See* Henry Adams, 1 History of the United States of America during the Administration of Thomas Jefferson 96 (1986). I rely on Adams's accounts, extensively on Charles Warren's invaluable The Supreme Court in United States History (1926), and also on my The Jurisprudence of John Marshall (1968).

3. Letter from Jefferson to John Dickinson (Dec. 19, 1801) in 9 The Writings of Thomas Jefferson 302 (A. Bergh ed. 1907) [hereinafter cited as Writings].

4. Quoted by 1 Warren, *supra* note 2, at 797–98 (1926).

5. Letter from Jefferson to Nathaniel Macon (Nov. 23, 1801), in 15 Writings, *supra* note 3, at 341.

6. 1 Adams, *supra* note 2, at 175.

7. 1 Adams, *supra* note 2, at 454.

8. Letter from Jefferson to Thomas Ritchie (Dec. 25, 1820) in 15 Writings, *supra*, note 3, at 297–98.

9. Quoted by 1 Adams, *supra* note 2, at 196.

10. 1 Adams, *supra* note 2, at 186ff., 585 (1986).

11. J. Taylor, Tyranny Unmasked (1822).

12. Note Adams's judgment in *supra* note 2, at 925; also Hurst, *Treason in the United States*, 58 Harv. L. Rev. 246–72, 395–444, 806–57 (1944–45).

13. 1 Adams, *supra* note 2, at 101.

14. Letter from Caesar Rodney to Jefferson (Oct. 31, 1808), in 1 Warren, *supra* note 2, at 336.

15. *See* 1 Warren, *supra* note 2, at 516.

16. Warren, *supra* note 2, at 616.

17. Letter from J. Marshall to T. Pickering (Mar. 18, 1828) in R. Faulkner, The Jurisprudence of John Marshall 83 (1968).

18. Letter from Jefferson to E. Randolph (Aug. 18, 1799) in 10 Writings, *supra* note 3.

19. Jefferson to William Plumer (July 21, 1816) in 15 Writings, *supra* note 3, at 46.

2

Federal Union, Property, and the Contract Clause: John Marshall's Thought in Light of *Sturges v. Crowninshield* and *Ogden v. Saunders*

HERBERT A. JOHNSON

The contract clause of our federal Constitution has played a significant role in American government and constitutional development.[1] This was particularly true in the years before the Fourteenth Amendment introduced the much more flexible concepts of substantive due process, equal protection, and procedural due process, as grounds upon which federal supervision could be exercised over the economic legislation of the various states. Chief Justice John Marshall is credited with having made the contract clause into a preeminent instrument of federal power. His fundamental contributions are exemplified by the four major contract clause decisions: *Fletcher v. Peck, Dartmouth College v. Woodward, New Jersey v. Wilson,* and *Sturges v. Crowninshield.*[2] On the other hand, in *Ogden v. Saunders,* Marshall uncharacteristically fielded a dissent from the decision of his brother justices.[3] *Ogden* was the only major constitutional decision in which the Chief Justice openly dissented.[4] In doing so he differed from Bushrod Washington, the fellow Virginian who had been so closely identified with Marshall's jurisprudence that they were, by some, considered to think as one judge.[5]

Three of the four opinions that Marshall wrote for the Court's majority involved contracts entered into by a state, rather than private contracts between individuals. For this reason Marshall's majority opinion in *Sturges* and his dissent in *Ogden* deserve special attention. They provide material for a careful analysis of the Chief Justice's attitudes toward private property and private contractual rights. Better than the public contract cases, they demonstrate his concern for the economic well-being of the federal union. And they highlight the Chief Justice's view, soon to be discredited posthumously, of the role that the federal government should play in protecting private property rights against state legislative power.

MARSHALL AND PRIVATE DEBTS BEFORE 1801

Marshall did not approach *de novo* the problems of insolvency laws, imprisonment for debt, and debtor relief through bankruptcy. His professional life as a Richmond attorney involved him in representing both creditors and debtors in the Virginia courts. And the major concern of the day was the substantial amount of debt Virginians owed to British merchants by virtue of prerevolutionary transactions. These had been sequestered by a Virginia state statute passed in 1777, which discharged Virginians who paid the amount due into the state treasury. However, the 1783 Peace Treaty with the mother country specifically provided that obligations entered into prior to the Revolution were to be freely collectible, and it was unclear whether this stipulation revived the British merchants' claims.[6] As a member of the Virginia legislature Marshall favored reopening Virginia courts to these cases, but a series of state statutes, coupled with adverse decisions by the courts, made it virtually impossible for a British creditor to bring a case to trial.[7]

As a member of the Virginia Ratifying Convention in June 1788 Marshall was selected to quiet anti-federalist fears that the new federal government might provide an additional prop for the treaty rights claimed by the British creditors. Stressing that the law of the place of making a contract would still govern rights and remedies—even under the new constitution—he helped to quiet Virginia's misgivings. Significantly his speech did not discuss the British debt question in light of the peculiar phraseology of the supremacy clause, which made all treaties entered into by the United States (even those prior to the ratification of the Constitution) the supreme law of the land.[8]

With ratification by the states and the establishment of federal courts in Virginia, the British debt issue became a matter of professional concern to Marshall. His account book and the federal circuit court dockets evidence his active participation in the defense of Virginia debtors against British claimants. Well over 100 cases were answered by Marshall as defense counsel and the sheer pressure of litigation compelled him to print "boiler plate" answers to be used in pleading. Those answers contained the usual defenses, pleaded discharge under the Virginia sequestration laws, and then asserted that since Britain had refused to surrender the Northwest territory military posts to the United States, the United States was not obliged to perform its undertakings in regard to debts owed to British merchants.[9]

Arguing before the Virginia federal circuit court, and subsequently in the Supreme Court of the United States, Marshall made a valiant attempt to prevent, or at least delay, collection of these debts. When *Ware v. Hylton* was decided against him at the February 1796 Supreme Court term, there was no further doubt that Virginia debtors (if they could be found) would have to pay their obligations a second time. Ironically Marshall's only appearance as an attorney before the United States Supreme Court was in defense of Virginia debtors and in opposition to federal supremacy under the 1783 Peace Treaty.[10]

The future Chief Justice was also involved in two land speculation schemes, any one of which could have resulted in financial embarrassment. Immediately after the American Revolution he began to purchase Virginia treasury warrants for the acquisition of land in Kentucky. In this endeavor he was associated with and counseled by his father, Colonel Thomas Marshall, who was surveyor of the rich lands in Fayette County. As the Richmond operative Marshall purchased warrants covering nearly 300,000 acres. Entries were made on slightly more than 225,000 acres, and final surveys covered somewhat more than 200,000 acres. Colonel Marshall was assigned over 100,000 acres of this surveyed land, and John Marshall received over 40,000 acres. Because of Colonel Marshall's ability in avoiding conflicting entries or overlying surveys, no caveats were entered against any of these acquisitions. Incomplete records make it impossible to determine John Marshall's ultimate profit from these speculations in Kentucky land, but subsequent events would suggest that the high risk was richly rewarded. By 1792 and 1793 Marshall was in a financial position to join with his brother, James Markham Marshall, in forming a syndicate to purchase from the family of Lord Fairfax the manor of Leeds (160,000 acres) and the South Branch Manor (55,000 acres). These manor lands were areas reserved by the proprietor of the Northern Neck for his personal use. Not only were they rich and arable, but they also were the least likely to be affected by Virginia revolutionary laws causing the escheat of lands passing at death to nonresident alien enemies. In February 1793 the Marshall syndicate committed itself to pay £20,000 to the Fairfax heirs for the two manor land tracts. Not until 1802 was the debt extinguished and title to the vast territory secure.[11]

Marshall's economic activities also involved him in the purchase of claims against Virginia and the federal government, arising from the war. Among these were military half-pay certificates, purchased from their original holders and surrendered for United States stock in connection with federal assumption of state debts in February 1792. Marshall received $7,142.24 in six percent stock certificates as a result of this transaction.[12]

As a debtor throughout his entire precourt career, Marshall was acutely aware of the risks one took in pursuit of speculative profit. Professional practice acquainted him with the hazardous position debtors occupied in an unstable economy, and he undoubtedly applied that wisdom to his circumstances. His argument in *Ware v. Hylton* supporting Virginia's sequestration law may well have represented the position he adopted in connection with his own heavy indebtedness:

Property is the creature of civil society, and subject in all respects, to the disposition and control of civil institutions. There is no weight in the argument founded on what is supposed to be the understanding of the parties at the place and time of contracting debts; for, the right of confiscation does not arise from the understanding of individuals, . . . but from the nature and operation of government.[13]

Marshall's financial vulnerability was dramatically underscored by the insolvency and imprisonment of Robert Morris of Philadelphia. Long a professional client of Marshall, Morris and his family became close friends of the future chief justice in the course of his visits to Philadelphia in 1794 and 1795. When in 1795 Marshall's brother, James Markham Marshall, married Morris's daughter, affectionate social relations were cemented by intermarriage of the two families.[14] Marshall's biographer, Leonard Baker, suggests that Morris's long imprisonment for debt caused Marshall's advocacy of the 1800 bankruptcy law in the House of Representatives.[15] Documentation for the causal relationship is not very persuasive, but the official records leave little doubt that Marshall was an active force in drafting, and gathering votes for, the short-lived federal bankruptcy act of 1800.[16]

When John Marshall took his place on the Supreme Court he already had wide professional and personal experience with debtor relief laws, and his sympathies may well have favored the relief of honest insolvents. His argument in *Ware v. Hylton* demonstrates his awareness of the manner in which contractual rights might be subordinated to statutory regulation in the name of public policy. The interesting question is how Marshall was educed to abandon this view in favor of a positivist interpretation of contract rights in *Ogden v. Saunders*.

BANKRUPTCY PRIOR TO *STURGES*

Before the ratification of the federal Constitution, American colonial and state legislatures had taken steps to extend humanitarian relief to honest debtors unable to settle their accounts. Initially this consisted of schemes for assignment of assets to trustees for the creditors, in return for which the debtor would be freed from the rigors of debtor's prison. This release from imprisonment was widely available throughout New England and the middle colonies, and with the exception of the relatively new frontier colony of Georgia, it was also available in the South.[17]

By way of contrast, bankruptcy legislation not only released the debtor from prison, but also discharged his indebtedness, leaving him free to begin a new financial life without burden of having to repay his past obligations. Within the imperial system where most debts were payable to British merchants, colonial bankruptcy laws were ephemeral things. The 1757 Massachusetts bankruptcy act survived until its disallowance by the Privy Council in London a year later. Thereafter it was perpetuated by a series of short-term bankruptcy laws, designed to expire and to be replaced by new legislation prior to the disallowance by the Privy Council.[18] After independence Massachusetts did not enact a bankruptcy law until 1838. A temporary bankruptcy law enacted by Rhode Island in 1756 provided relief for three years, but thereafter the danger of disallowance shifted bankruptcy relief to the colonial assembly. Through private bills passed at the petition of insolvent debtors, the Rhode Island assembly authorized the courts to hear evidence concerning the transactions of the petitioner and to grant settlement and discharge in appropriate cases.[19]

Among the middle colonies New York was first and most generous with bankruptcy relief. Following a quarter century of permitting relief from debtor's prison through insolvency proceedings, New York's legislators enacted a statute permitting discharge in bankruptcy upon any assignment acceptable to three quarters of the creditors based upon the value of their credits. The colonial bankruptcy law remained in effect from 1755 through 1770, maintained by a series of reenactments as temporary laws expired. The colonial law, known as the Three Quarter Act, was revived in 1788 and remained the law of New York State until repeal by an 1813 revision known as the Two Thirds Act because of the reduced amount of concurrence required of creditors.[20]

Among the southern colonies South Carolina by an early statute permitted discharge of debts by a debtor's property assignment. The 1744 act discharged obligations owed to all creditors living in the colony and all who had agents in the colony. However, in 1745 the discharge was limited and made available only against those who accepted the dividend paid in bankruptcy. By way of contrast Virginia, which throughout the eighteenth century was heavily indebted to British mercantile firms, steadfastly refused to enact a bankruptcy law. North Carolina, widely reputed to be a haven for absconding debtors, enacted a bankruptcy law in 1749 only to have it negatived by a royal disallowance. The state legislature renewed bankruptcy relief in 1777, substantially on the same basis as the colonial statute.[21]

Colonial bankruptcy legislation, while unpopular with the imperial authorities, made humanitarian relief available to debtors who were honest in their dealings and wished an opportunity to rebuild their fortunes on a solid basis. On the other hand, the extension of debt discharge within a colony created difficulties for British merchants already uneasy concerning debt collection in the American colonies. A 1732 parliamentary statute provided an expeditious procedure for collection of debts accrued in the colonies.[22] In 1766 English bankruptcy rulings were amended to provide that the American assets of British debtors could be attached in English bankruptcy cases.[23] There were also complicated intercolonial legal issues, and the New York moot (a debating society of lawyers) in 1768 studied the troublesome question of whether discharge in one colony was effective to protect a debtor's assets from seizure in another colony.[24]

Economic as well as legal factors influenced the history of bankruptcy law in the American colonies. A province such as South Carolina, blessed with a positive balance of trade with the mother country, provided attractive business opportunities that offset any risk of a British merchant losing his trade balances in a colonial bankruptcy case. Massachusetts Bay, with its burgeoning ship-building economy, its lumber industry, and its preeminence as a leading commercial and cultural center, also enjoyed some of the same advantages. But Virginia, deeply in debt and sinking further into economic servitude to London, Bristol, and Glasgow trading houses, could not venture into discharge of trade debts for fear of precipitating an immediate panic among her many creditors. Ever sensitive to colonial economic initiatives, the British Board of Trade regularly advised the Privy Council to disallow American bankruptcy acts.

Emerging from the restrictions of British mercantilism, newly independent American states took advantage of their full sovereignty under the Articles of Confederation. Virginia's maneuvers to avoid debt collection under the terms of the 1783 peace treaty with Britain have been briefly traced; while the magnitude of the Virginia debt entitles it to special attention, it was by no means the only foreign debt and in nearly all aspects it was typical of other situations throughout the former British colonies. Additionally, as Peter Coleman points out, even among American merchants the variety of bankruptcy laws in the American states made it difficult for a merchant to conduct interstate trade.[25] Although this did not necessarily discourage business, it could easily add to its complexity and might, in extreme cases, protect intrastate markets from external competition. It was this balkanized economic situation that formed part of the impetus toward the Philadelphia Constitutional Convention of 1787. The final draft of the Constitution provided that Congress might enact a uniform bankruptcy law; it also provided that no state might pass legislation that impaired the obligation of contracts.[26] Except for the temporary bankruptcy law passed in 1800 and repealed in 1803, no federal legislation on the subject occurred until the controversial and short-lived bankruptcy act of 1841.[27]

Congressional failure to act, coupled with the short life of the 1800 and 1841 bankruptcy acts, created confusion among the various state courts and federal circuits. And it also provided general encouragement for the exercise of state legislative initiative in the area. While presiding over the Pennsylvania circuit in 1814, Justice Bushrod Washington found a state bankruptcy statute to be unconstitutional, based upon his conclusion that the bankruptcy power conferred on Congress by the federal Constitution was exclusive; he also viewed the state statute as impairing the obligation of contracts.[28] Three years later Justice Brockholst Livingston in the New York circuit sustained the validity of the 1811 New York bankruptcy statute. An unreported South Carolina circuit decision by Justice William Johnson held that authority to legislate concerning bankruptcy was shared by the states and the federal government, but subject to federal preemption in the event of conflict.[29] Sustaining their state's bankruptcy statute's validity and denying an exclusive power in Congress, Pennsylvania judges supported state action as did their South Carolina colleagues shortly before *Sturges v. Crowninshield* was argued in the United States Supreme Court.[30] These judicial contradictions and inconsistencies demanded a definite statement by the federal Supreme Court. So did the economic impact of the depression following the War of 1812, which generated a flood of bankruptcy petitions in state courts. New York courts during the five-year period 1814–19 heard no less than 6,000 bankruptcy cases, in the last three years averaging approximately 1,300 petitions per annum.[31]

STURGES: A TIME FOR COMPROMISE AND DISCONTENT

The opinion in *Sturges* arose from litigation over two promissory notes drawn in New York on March 22, 1811, one payable on August 1, 1811, and the other on August 15, 1811. On April 3, 1811, the New York legislature passed the bankruptcy act that would form the basis of the maker's defense. An action was brought by the payee in the United States Circuit Court for Massachusetts, and the maker demurred that he had been discharged under the April 3, 1811, statute. The circuit judges divided in opinion concerning the demurrer, and four questions were certified to the Supreme Court.[32] They were as follows:

1. Whether, since the adoption of the constitution of the United States, any State has authority to pass a bankrupt law, or whether the power is exclusively vested in the Congress of the United States?
2. Whether the Act of New York, passed the third day of April, 1811, and stated in the plea in this case, is a bankrupt act, within the meaning of the constitution of the United States?
3. Whether the act aforesaid is an act or law impairing the obligation of contracts, within the meaning of the constitution of the United States?
4. Whether the plea is a good and sufficient bar of the plaintiff's actions?[33]

For the plaintiff (payee of the notes) it was argued in the Supreme Court by Joseph Hopkinson and David Daggett that Congress has exclusive power under the Constitution. Since the Constitution referred to providing a "uniform bankruptcy law," action by the federal government was clearly presupposed, since a multitude of state laws would spawn diversity rather than uniformity. The fact that Congress had not acted since repealing the first federal bankruptcy law could not be construed as its acquiescence in state intrusion into the bankruptcy field.

Moving to the operation of the New York statute, counsel urged that the 1811 law plainly resulted in discharge of debts, and thus was distinguishable from insolvency proceedings traditional in colonial America. Insolvency merely released the debtor from prison upon the surrender of his assets for the benefit of creditors.[34] It did not discharge the debt nor free subsequently acquired assets from seizure by creditors. Operating as "an absolute discharge of the body of the debtor and his future acquisition of property . . ." the 1811 statute was a true bankruptcy law, and in Hopkinson's phrase it constituted a "legislative interference with the ordinary and regular course of justice; . . ."[35] Bankruptcy was not a mere remedy, such as a statute of limitations, but rather it went to the very heart of contractual obligations. Thus it changed or impaired obligations created by contract and violated the contract clause of the federal Constitution.

The defendant outlined the historical evolution of insolvency and bankruptcy in England and the American colonies and states, demonstrating that state usages were well established by the time the federal Constitution was ratified. Congress in enacting the 1800 bankruptcy law specifically provided that it should not negative prior state insolvency legislation, or any such legislation to be subsequently enacted.[36] In effect the federal Congress recognized and acquiesced in state legislative authority. David B. Ogden picked up the argument for defendant by demonstrating that the power to enact insolvency and bankruptcy laws was not expressly prohibited to the states by the Constitution. Since it was not absolutely necessary that bankruptcy authority be vested in a national government, the states and federal government might exercise it concurrently, subject of course to the rule that in the case of conflict federal power would prevail. Thus "until Congress does legislate, and in such a way as to preclude the States, the States retain their power to legislate. . . ."[37] With the certified questions ably briefed and fully argued, the Supreme Court was in a position to clarify many of the constitutional issues that had beclouded debtor relief law for the preceding twenty years.

What transpired in the Supreme Court conference chamber will probably never be known, but eight years later Justice Johnson wrote that

the judgment in *Sturges* partakes as much of a compromise, as of a legal adjudication. The minority thought it better to yield something than risk the whole. And, although their course of reasoning led them to the general maintenance of the State power over the subject, . . . yet, as denying the power to act upon anterior contracts, could do no harm, but, in fact, imposed a restriction conceived in the true spirit of the constitution, they were satisfied to acquiesce in it, provided the decision were so guarded as to secure the power over posterior contracts, as well from the positive terms of the adjudication, as from inferences deducible from the reasoning of the Court.[38]

Given pre-*Sturges* decisions issued by some of the sitting Supreme Court justices we know that Justices Livingston and Johnson already had sustained state bankruptcy statutes against charges of unconstitutionality.[39] In his opinion in *Ogden v. Saunders* Justice Washington stated that he was "now inclined to come" to the view that a state bankruptcy law that operates prospectively does not violate the Constitution.[40] He reached that conclusion even though

I have always thought that the power to pass such a law was exclusively vested in the legislature of the United States. But it becomes me to believe that this opinion was, and is, incorrect, since it stands condemned by the decision of a majority of this Court, solemnly pronounced.[41]

The minority in *Sturges* (which supported concurrent powers in state and federal bankruptcy and which acquiesced in holding the 1811 statute unconstitutional based upon its retroactive application) was composed of Justices Livingston and Johnson. Justice Thomas Todd was absent from the Court for the entire term.[42] The majority consisted of Chief Justice Marshall, Justices Story and Duvall (both of whom joined with Marshall in the *Ogden* dissent)[43] and Justice Washington, who was destined to alter his opinion between 1819 and 1827. The *Sturges* vote was thus four to two, and the Chief Justice delivered the opinion for the Court.

Regarding the issue of an exclusive congressional bankruptcy power Marshall observed that the reference to uniformity in the Constitution created the strong inference of an exclusive federal power.[44] However, since Congress did not exercise the power, the lack of constitutional prohibition against partial state laws was determinative.[45] The states might act when Congress failed to exercise the constitutional power since then the federal power remained dormant. Enactment of the 1800 bankruptcy act did not permanently extinguish state bankruptcy power, nor did repeal of the national bankruptcy act confer a power upon the states. Rather it removed a disability from state exercise.[46] Another reason the Chief Justice advanced for not declaring the New York statute unconstitutional was the fact that the definition of insolvency and bankruptcy overlapped, and on a mere semantic similarity of terms one could not condemn a state legislative act.[47] As he pointed out, it was unnecessary to decide whether the New York law was a bankruptcy act or not; that in turn rendered unnecessary consideration of the exclusive character of Congress's authority to act.

This deft avoidance of comment upon the controversial issue of exclusive federal power was the material about which the minority silently acquiesced rather than risk the whole—that Marshall and his majority would hold the bankruptcy power to be exclusive and invalidate the 1811 New York statute on that basis, as well as on the ground of contract impairment. The question remained unanswered until 1827—after the death of Brockholst Livingston, the resignation of Thomas Todd, and the appointments of Smith Thompson and Robert Trimble to replace them.

Having mollified the minority, Marshall moved on to the contract clause issue, which he termed "the great question on which the cause must depend."[48] Indeed, it was the issue upon which he permitted the case to be decided. He had recourse to theory firmly established by the doctrine of vested property rights and supported by the traditional rule that the law of the place in which a contract is made governs its meaning and legal consequences. Drawing upon historical events between the Revolution and the Philadelphia Convention, Marshall recalled that there existed a "general dissatisfaction with that lax system of legislation"[49] permitting among other things the discharge of debtors by means other than those stipulated in their contracts. To restore public confidence the convention felt that contracts should be made inviolable. On the other hand, statutes of limitation and usury laws passed subsequent to the negotiation of a contract might alter the remedies available under its terms, and not violate or impair its obligations.[50] Marshall conceded that his opinion for the Court was confined to the precise case under consideration—where an existing contract was altered by subsequent legislative action.[51]

Simplicity and brevity are not always virtues in writing constitutional law opinions. Marshall's quest for unanimity in the *Sturges* appeal resulted in a narrowly based precedent. Simply put, the Court held that regardless of whether New York had authority to enact the 1811 bankruptcy law, any application of the statute to contracts already in being at its effective date resulted in an unconstitutional impairment of vested rights accrued under that contract. The Chief Justice's dicta concerning statutes of limitation and usury laws suggested that laws altering remedies available to the contracting parties would not necessarily impair the obligations of contract. However, the distinction between impairment of obligation and alteration of remedies was far from distant. Similarly the discussion of confusion between insolvency laws and bankruptcy legislation did more to complicate than to clarify the issue. Given the Delphic aspects of the *Sturges* opinion, it is not surprising that most legislatures and many state courts remained uncertain of state ability to afford relief to honest debtors. At the federal level Congress, despite several attempts, did not succeed in passing a federal bankruptcy law until six years after Marshall's death, leaving it to the Supreme Court to police state infringements upon what many came to believe was an exclusive federal bankruptcy authority.

A companion case to *Sturges*, entitled *M'Millan v. M'Neill*, illustrated the most obvious disadvantage of bankruptcy in state courts.[52] The gravamen of the case was a customs bond issued in South Carolina, upon which M'Millan was the surety. The bond was defaulted, but by that time M'Millan had moved to Louisiana and secured a discharge in bankruptcy from Louisiana state courts. His commercial firm had also obtained a discharge under an English commission of bankruptcy, and he pleaded it and the Louisiana discharge in defense against M'Neill's action. Although the Louisiana statute had been passed well before the bond was executed, it was unclear whether a foreign discharge (either from England or Louisiana) could be pleaded in South Carolina. In a brief memorandum opinion for the Court, Marshall pointed out the English rule, adopted in American insolvency and bankruptcy cases, that a discharge under foreign law might not be pleaded in the jurisdiction that gave rise to the transaction.[53]

THE MAJORITY OPINIONS IN *OGDEN* v. *SAUNDERS*

The Supreme Court's 1827 opinions in *Ogden v. Saunders* were based upon bills of exchange drawn upon defendant Ogden while he was resident in New York. After Ogden accepted the bills they were protested for nonpayment. But then Ogden moved to Louisiana and Saunders, a citizen of Kentucky, brought suit in the federal district court for Louisiana (exercising its circuit court jurisdiction). The bills were both drawn and accepted subsequent to the enactment of the New York bankruptcy act of April 3, 1801, which Ogden pleaded in discharge. Following a jury verdict for plaintiff Saunders below, the district court entered judgment and Ogden took his appeal by writ of error to the Supreme Court. Argument began in the February 1824 term, and was adjourned to February 1827.[54]

For the appellant Henry Wheaton contended that the bankruptcy power was exclusive to Congress, and thus the New York statute was invalid. And, second, that the law impaired the obligation of a contract, even though it was in force at the time the bills were issued and accepted.[55] In shaping the contract clause, the Philadelphia Convention had in mind the circumstances of economic life in 1787: "One of the great objects of the constitution was to restore violated faith, and to raise the country from that state of distress and degradation into which it had been plunged by the want of a regular administration of justice in the relation of debtor and creditor."[56] The convention, he contended, wished to include all contracts within the protection of the constitutional provision. And contracts derived not only from municipal law, but also "from a higher source; from those great principles of universal law, which are binding on societies of men as well as on individuals."[57] The contract clause was intended to ensure to American citizens, to foreign merchants, and to interstate traders, that obligations would be performed as stipulated.

In opposition, a virtual battery of lawyers including William Wirt, Edward Livingston, and Henry Clay claimed that any state in the Union was empowered to enact a bankruptcy statute, subject to limitations that it not violate the contract clause and that no act of Congress conflicted with the state enactment. The federal government had permitted state legislation to cover debtor relief, and when it briefly executed the terms of the bankruptcy law of 1800, Congress provided that the federal statute should not be considered a revocation of existing or future state insolvency laws.[58] Historians writing of the period of constitutional drafting and ratification concur that the economic evil was legislative acts affecting vested rights or past transactions.[59] Thus the contract clause protected from state action only those obligations created by contracts executed prior to enactment of the impairing statute. To be impaired an obligation had to exist. And obligations as well as remedies must be relative to the municipal law of the place of contracting.[60] "There is nothing of mere human institution . . . which binds to the performance of any contract, except the laws under which that contract is made, and the remedies provided by them to enforce its execution."[61]

The replying argument by Daniel Webster looked first to the "great political design" of the Constitution, which was to "give security to all contracts, stability to credit, uniformity among all the States in those things which materially concerned . . . foreign commerce . . . and their own credit, trade and intercourse among themselves."[62] The obligation of contract was created not by municipal law, but by the assent of the parties and through the operation of a universal law. It would be inconsistent with the other grants of power to the federal government for the convention to have left the control of bankruptcy law with the several states.[63]

On February 19, 1827, the justices began to deliver their opinions seriatim, the senior associate justice, Bushrod Washington, speaking first. After retreating gracefully from his prior position that the bankruptcy power was exclusive in Congress,[64] Washington stated forcefully his position that contracts should be construed to effectuate the intention of the parties. While some universal or natural law might arguably impel performance, it is the municipal law of the place of contracting that controls validity, construction, remedy, evidence, performance, and discharge. All laws in force at the time and in the jurisdiction of contracting continue to govern the agreement regardless of the travels of the parties or subsequent changes in law. Since the operation of the New York statute was prospective only it was valid and the bankruptcy of Ogden might properly be pleaded in bar.[65]

After casting considerable light on the Court's division in *Sturges*, Justice William Johnson indicated his concurrence with Washington's view that all contracts must be given a relative interpretation, based upon the municipal law at the place of making. In his opinion the Constitution conferred concurrent power on Congress to enact a bankruptcy statute, since a federal bankruptcy discharge would supplement the more limited relief available under already well-established state procedures.[66] Contract rights were not absolute, for even in the state of nature there were limits beyond which a creditor could not go in exacting payment.[67]

Smith Thompson, who joined the Court subsequent to the *Sturges* decision, felt no compulsion to defend earlier judgments. Instead he adopted a straightforward view that the Constitution left the regulation of civil contracts to the states, and that in a commercial community a bankruptcy law was essential. The states might validly enact such bankruptcy provisions as did not offend the contract clause, provided those laws were only prospective in operation.[68] The other justice appointed since *Sturges* was Robert Trimble of Kentucky. His opinion makes short work of the exclusivity of congressional bankruptcy power, pointing to *Sturges* as binding precedent for the rule that in the absence of conflicting federal legislation on bankruptcy, the states could continue to provide this type of debtor relief.[69] Turning to the obligation of contract, Trimble took pains to distinguish between contractual rights arising in a state of nature, where they might truly be found in the agreement of the parties, and contractual rights created in the state of society. In the latter case, "the obligation of a contract made within a sovereign State, must be precisely that allowed by the law of the State, and none other.[70] Municipal law was "something which attaches to, and lays hold of the contract . . ." to regulate the conduct of the parties in relation to the terms of the contract.[71] To Trimble the obligation of contracts was based not upon some vague concept of natural rights but firmly established by the "chain of law."[72] His rejection of positivism was based upon practical as well as theoretical reasons, observing that if contracts were construed as arising from universal natural obligations, then the states would lose all rights to legislate concerning contracts.[73]

JOHN MARSHALL'S *OGDEN* DISSENT

Speaking for the minority, in which he was joined by Justices Story and Duvall, Marshall treated the exclusivity issue as if it had been settled.[74] Indeed, the opinion in *Sturges* had been generally seen to authorize state bankruptcy laws, subject only to limitations imposed by the contract clause. Much could have been said concerning the need for a single uniform bankruptcy law. And if even at this relatively late date, the Court had determined that bankruptcy power was exclusive to Congress, it could have achieved two possible goals: (1) Congress would be moved to enact such a uniform law, or (2) no such federal statute would be forthcoming, but the invalidity of all state bankruptcy proceedings would place each state on an equal basis in interstate and foreign trade. In light of the incipient state mercantilism recently negatived in *Gibbons v. Ogden*, Marshall must have recognized the divisiveness and chaos inherent in a multiplicity of divergent state bankruptcy laws. By abandoning an exclusive construction of congressional bankruptcy power, Marshall tacitly agreed with the *Sturges* position—that subject to being preempted by federal legislation, states could enact bankruptcy laws that, under the contract clause, had to be prospective in their operation.

One point formed the focus of Marshall's dissent—that state bankruptcy laws discharging the obligation of private contracts act as an unconstitutional impairment of contractual obligations. Having agreed that bankruptcy powers were concurrent, he would utilize the contract clause to remove the teeth of discharge from the jaws of state bankruptcy proceedings. Challenging the majority's view that state laws enter into contracts when such agreements are made, Marshall held that any law (prospective or retrospective) attempting to alter contractual rights violated the contract clause. This was because the right to contract existed before, and independent of, man's association in society. It was a right based on the law of nature, and no legislative act could impose upon a contract conditions not agreed to by the parties.[75] Removal or modification of a remedy by state action subsequent to the agreement impairs contractual obligations, for it is absurd to say that the obligation remains even if the remedy is destroyed.[76] Hence the contract clause should be held to limit prospective alterations in the law, just as it did retrospective applications.[77]

Marshall held that contractual obligations arise entirely from the consent of the parties. Thus they might agree to a form of discharge analogous to bankruptcy, and it would be binding upon them. But it was hazardous to private property rights if state legislatures could impose conditions upon performance that were not a part of the agreement.[78] While states could alter remedies, the obligation would have to remain intact, and to that degree state power to deal with remedies was also limited. Contractual obligations grew from the acts of the parties and not from the grant of a government. American history in the confederation period demonstrated the destruction of confidence between man and man that results from state legislatures mischievously undermining the sanctity of private faith.[79]

In dealing with contractual obligation, the Chief Justice espoused a positivist, or natural law, view of the subject. He could find no evidence that in moving from a state of nature into political society, man had surrendered more than a governmental power to furnish remedies for breach. Every man retained his right to acquire property, to dispose of it according to his own judgment, and to pledge himself for a future act. And those rights were not conferred by society, but brought into it from the state of nature. Private rights to contract remained unimpaired except as they were restrained by the exercise of necessary governmental regulation. Laws such as the statute of frauds, prohibitions against usury, and required formalities of execution all constituted valid state regulation, as did statutes of limitation. The federal Constitution limited state action as a means of preserving this individual freedom to contract, and also to ensure the sanctity of natural rights derived from private contracts.[80]

Examined in the light of Marshall's opinion in *Marbury v. Madison*, the *Ogden* dissent's view of the relationship of right to remedy becomes even more significant for an understanding of this jurisprudence. In *Marbury* the Chief Justice went to great pains to find that Marbury had a vested property right in his office as a justice of peace in the District of Columbia. Ruling out an action of detinue as a possible remedy, he held mandamus to be the proper mode of obtaining the office and the commission already duly issued. However, it was the nature of the federal government to be a limited sovereignty, where specific statutory grants of judicial power to the United States Supreme Court had to be tested against the constitutional statement of the Court's power. It was in this limitation of the Supreme Court's jurisdiction that Marshall found its inability to provide a remedy. In *Marbury* he permitted the denial of a vested property right because positive law was lacking upon which to fashion a remedy;[81] in *Ogden* he created a right by natural law, a theory of contract that elevated contract rights above limitations by positive law, and which restricted governmental action by abstract theories of natural rights.

MARSHALL'S BANKRUPTCY OPINIONS IN CONTEXT

It is always dangerous to generalize constitutional law trends from the study of a limited number of cases, and quite hazardous to do so from two opinions by a single judge. However, the unique dissenting opinion by Marshall in *Ogden* is certainly worth attention and further efforts to place it in context. Only slightly less notice should be accorded to *Sturges* and what we know of the suppression of dissent in the Court's opinion. The two cases should give us reason to pause in our generalizations about Marshall and his Court in the years after 1815. Historians have long seen a gradual reduction in Marshall's control over the decisions of the Supreme Court, but that decline has been generally viewed as being subsequent to the great constitutional decisions of the 1819, 1821, and 1824 terms—most specifically the period of *McCulloch v. Maryland*, *Dartmouth College v. Woodward*, *Cohens v. Virginia*, and *Gibbons v. Ogden*.[82] However, there is good reason to reconsider that evaluation of Marshall's influence. Haskins and Johnson provide evidence that suggests a weakening of Marshall's control as early as 1810 and certainly during the course of the War of 1812 prize cases.[83] Admittedly that position is taken in the light of statistical analysis and a close look at the overall work of the Supreme Court in the time period 1801 to 1815. At this point in our discussion it is helpful to look at the Marshall bankruptcy decisions in context, and perhaps discover what they mean in terms of the internal workings of the Court, the evolution of constitutional views of the federal union, and the development of Marshall's economic thought.

Internal Business of the Marshall Court

In *Sturges* we find the Chief Justice carefully steering his majority opinion between the rocks of two divergent and dangerous shorelines of jurisprudence. He and his supporting associate justices favored an exclusive interpretation of the bankruptcy provision, and they wished to give a prospective as well as a retrospective construction to the contract clause. Both positions demonstrate a strong commitment to nationalism, particularly as it touches upon the creation of an American trading union that would provide maximum security for property rights as well as a uniform bankruptcy relief. That would diminish the practice of state mercantilism. The compromise reached by the Supreme Court —to condemn bankruptcy legislation that impaired contract obligations retrospectively—was no more than a consensus to permit the generally accepted theory of vested property rights to control this particular case. Neither for Marshall's majority, nor for the minority justices did *Sturges* represent any firm commitment to any given position concerning the contract clause.

On the other hand, the position that the bankruptcy power was exclusive seems to have been weakened by *Sturges*, indicated by Marshall's equivocation over the definition of bankruptcy and insolvency laws, which is less than satisfactory as an explanation of why this issue was not decided in 1819 and left unmentioned in 1827. The array of exclusive federal powers was further diminished in the 1824 decision of *Gibbons v. Ogden* in which the Chief Justice denied that the commerce power was exclusive, sending Justice William Johnson into concurring based upon an exclusive power in Congress that, even when dormant, precluded state legislation.[84] Commenting upon *Gibbons* Felix Frankfurter suggests that Marshall's abandonment of exclusivity reflected his realistic assessment that to hold otherwise would threaten the political character of the individual states.[85] In light of *Sturges* is it too much to suggest that in 1824, as in 1819, it would have been difficult to assemble a Supreme Court majority around the cause of exclusivity?

Marshall's theories of exclusiveness, whether in regard to the commerce or the bankruptcy clause, would seem to have been in eclipse, guarded from public view by the deft presentation of Court opinions that either skirted this issue or resolved cases on less politically inflammatory grounds. The Supreme Court's acceptance of national power began to retreat with the 1812 rejection of Justice Story's pet theory of a federal common law of crime. In 1816 that denial of common law criminal jurisdiction was further eroded by denying to admiralty jurisdiction the right to apply common law principles to offenses committed on the high seas.[86] And it was in 1816 that the Court of Appeals of Virginia defied the Supreme Court's mandate in *Martin v. Hunter's Lessee*;[87] Marshall was disqualified by virtue of self-interest, but is there more than passing significance to the fact that ultranationalist Joseph Story delivered the Court's opinion in *Martin?*

The Evolution of Constitutional Views of the Union

The bankruptcy clause, along with the commerce and contract clauses, was tied into the founding fathers' scheme for a union free of state-oriented mercantilism and marked by federal control of trade with foreign nations and the

Indian tribes. Competition among the states for economic advantage was a major symptom of the terminal illness that afflicted the confederation government. *Gibbons*, as it evolved in New York courts since 1815, illustrated the lengths to which an aggressive and growing commercial state like New York would go in imposing its will upon neighbors.[88] Supported by the able jurisprudence of James Kent, New York's star was in the ascendance and its speed seemed meteoric as the Erie Canal approached completion in 1825. Growing and independent state economic power threatened to upset at the economic level those "good feelings" that seemed to quiet the political scene. New York's liberal bankruptcy relief kept interstate traders from extending credit within the Empire State; and when a New York firm overextended itself the readily available debtor relief laws soon restored it to solvency at the expense of its creditors. As might be anticipated New York merchants refused to overextend themselves in states that did not provide bankruptcy relief, but on the other hand, the easier access to harsh collection procedures educed them to extend credit freely. The New York businessman was a speculative "high-roller" at home and a cautious but prosperous lender in the other American states. New Yorkers benefited from bankruptcy relief at home, while harsh sanctions against out-of-state debtors enriched them in interstate trade.

Although the founding fathers may well have wished to avoid state competition in the area of debtor relief, and hence included a uniform bankruptcy power in the federal Constitution, the circumstances of nineteenth-century America were such that federal-state cooperation was a political necessity. This was particularly true in the absence of a federal bankruptcy act except for the brief time period from 1800 to 1803. The virtual stalemate in federal debtor relief required Marshall to reassess his 1819 position by 1827. Originally all of the above economic arguments would impel him toward an exclusive view of the bankruptcy power. By 1827 he had lost the support of his fellow Virginian, Bushrod Washington, and saw most of the Court arrayed against him. Good political strategist as he was, he seized the opportunity made available in the contract clause, holding that any bankruptcy law that discharged indebtedness unconstitutionally impaired private contracts. Undoubtedly Marshall believed that the last defensive position was to use the instrumentality of the contract clause to limit confiscatory applications of state bankruptcy provisions. Then Congress would have to enact a uniform law, or in the alternative, the invalidity of all state laws would restore equality of competition among the states.

Marshall's View of Law and Economics

Robert Faulkner has provided us with a precise statement of Marshall's economic principles and how they relate to political theory. The Chief Justice considered the security of property to be the foundation for political independence and individual freedom; in fact Faulkner suggests that his concern for property rights was "not much inferior, at least in political importance, to the fundamental right to life itself." Marshall valued property as a reward for labor, and also as a necessity for renewed production and commercial exchange. Faulkner concludes that it was Marshall's overwhelming faith in the value of private property that led him to postulate his theory of an "intrinsic" obligation of contract as set forth in Ogden.[89]

In almost all major respects Faulkner's analysis of Marshall's property views is both accurate and perceptive. But there may be good cause to add another dimension to those conclusions. We must ask how those property views moved Marshall in the direction of an "intrinsic," natural law, basis for contractual obligation, and also how that change in jurisprudential focus was tied to his new views of the federal union? In Fletcher v. Peck the contract clause is applied to public transactions, and this is also true of Dartmouth College v. Woodward. However, in Fletcher Marshall had reason to refer to "rules of property which are common to all the citizens of the United States, and . . . those principles of equality which are acknowledged in all our courts."[90] Why are property rules common to citizens? Do not they inhere in state law? Or are they natural rights that men reserve to themselves even when they enter political society? If such a general, natural right could be successfully interposed against state public action, how much more could it apply to private contractual obligations? These considerations tie the theme of common constitutional limitations present in Fletcher to the "intrinsic" or natural law basis of contractual obligation in Ogden. Marshall's problem in Ogden was to define what the constitutional limits were upon state regulation of contracts, just as in Fletcher he had to decide the limits that should be placed upon state legislative power. He did not live long enough to demonstrate how his "higher law" limitations could be utilized as restraints on rapidly growing legislative power in Jacksonian America. That would be left to later judges who struggled with the same problem in terms of substantive and procedural due process.[91]

Since constitutional law does not develop in a vacuum, but rather reflects the broader evolution of contemporary jurisprudence, Marshall's movement toward a natural law view of the contract clause should be assessed against the background of changing concepts of contractual rights in the nineteenth century. Morton Horwitz, mentioning in passing Marshall's Ogden dissent, traced such a jurisprudential trend among judges, lawyers, and treatise writers. Characterized by a rejection of earlier equitable modification of the strict terms of contracts, the new emphasis was upon strict enforcement of the parties' agreement, regardless of its conscionability or moral rectitude. Among the treatise writers Nathan Dane and Gulian Verplanck published their views before Marshall wrote his 1827 opinion in Ogden. It would be left to Joseph Story in 1836 and his son, William W. Story, in 1844, to set forth a definitive statement of the new view of contracts.[92] Very likely Marshall's *Ogden* dissent, although framed in higher law terms, reflected the early stages of this development.

Beyond the fields of law and jurisprudence, John Marshall's espousal of natural law views of contract may also have been generated by his awareness of the changing political and constitutional situation. After 1815 the American states began to experience the press of reform elements demanding a democratization of the institutions of government and an expansion of the elective franchise. In the Massachusetts constitutional convention of 1820–21 a small articulate conservative minority succeeded in retaining a diluted property basis for the franchise, but conservative delegates to the 1821 New York constitutional convention were swept aside and a new form of government granted the vote to virtually all adult white male inhabitants. In his home state of Virginia, Marshall saw delaying tactics in 1817 postpone the calling of a constitutional convention, but by 1827–28 the General Assembly bowed to popular pressure and authorized a referendum of the voters concerning a constitutional convention. The convention was finally held in 1829–30 but a proposed expansion of the franchise was defeated.[93] Given the erosion of property-based representation in a growing number of state legislatures, the situation of private property seemed precarious. With economic prosperity threatened, Marshall sought a last line of defense in natural law, which ultimately would prove a weak barricade against the power of mass-elected legislatures.

Searching for a new defense for property rights Marshall resorted to a natural law gloss upon the contract clause. Given his background and the pragmatic thrust of so much of his jurisprudence, it seems ill suited to the great expositor of the Constitution. Undoubtedly he was influenced by the political and legal conditions of 1827, and particularly by the developing attitude that contracts should be enforced according to the precise terms of agreement between the parties. His nationalist colleague and companion in the *Ogden* dissent, Justice Joseph Story, may well have shaped his thinking in this regard. But the Chief Justice found it necessary to establish a new basis for economic individualism and free enterprise—a legal position that would prevail against the growing legislative supremacy of the individual states in Jacksonian America. Striving to defend the founding fathers' ideal of an economic common market among the American states, he refused to accept the inevitable—that the very existence of a union of states creates situations in which competition must exist between them.

NOTES

1. U.S. CONST. art. I, § 10.
2. 6 Cranch 87–148 (1810); 4 Wheat. 518–715 (1819); 7 Cranch 164–67 (1812); and 4 Wheat. 122–208. A companion case to *Sturges*, decided on the same day, M'Millan v. M'Neill, 4 Wheat. 209–18 (1819) should be read in conjunction with Sturges.

3. 12 Wheat. 213–69 (1827).

4. P. Jackson, Dissent in the Supreme Court: A Chronology 24 (1969); B. Siegan, Economic Liberties and the Constitution 64 (1980).

5. On the close relationship between the jurisprudence of Marshall and Washington *see* D. Morgan, Justice William Johnson: The First Dissenter, The Career and Constitutional Philosophy of a Jeffersonian Judge (1954) 182; and G. Haskins & H. Johnson, Foundations of Power; John Marshall, 1801–15 (The Oliver Wendell Holmes Devise History of the Supreme Court of the United States vol. 2, 1988).

6. 2 The Papers of John Marshall 333–34 (H. Johnson et al. eds. 5 vols. to date 1974–) [hereinafter cited as Papers of Marshall]; 4 Papers of Marshall liv, 5–6, 93–227; on British debt cases see 5 Papers of Marshall 261–406; Hobson, *The Recovery of British Debts in the Federal Circuit Court of Virginia from 1790 to 1797*, 42 Virginia Magazine of History and Biography 176–200 (1984).

7. 3 Papers of Marshall 5; *see* Marshall's correspondence with Edmund Randolph 2 Papers of Marshall 293–94. The tenuous position of British creditors in Virginia courts is further detailed in 5 Papers of Marshall 260–62.

8. 1 Papers of Marshall 252–55, 272–85; *see* U.S. Const. art. VI.

9. 5 Papers of Marshall 259–68, 280–86.

10. 3 Papers of Marshall 4–14; the circuit court proceedings, including a newly discovered transcript of Marshall's argument, are at 5 Papers of Marshall 295–329. Ware v. Hylton is reported at 3 Dallas 199 (1796).

11. 1 Papers of Marshall 100–4; 2 Papers of Marshall 140–56.

12. 3 Papers of Marshall 109–10.

13. *Id.* at 9; reported at Dallas 199.

14. *Id.* at 94, 102; 5 Papers of Marshall 93.

15. L. Baker, John Marshall: A Life in Law 323 (1974).

16. *Id.* at 323–24; 4 Papers of Marshall 34, 52.

17. P. Coleman, Debtors and Creditors in America: Insolvency, Imprisonment for Debt and Bankruptcy, 1607–1900, 3–15 (1974).

18. *Id.* at 39–51.

19. *Id.* at 91–92. Rhode Island's efforts to make its paper money negotiable in 1786 resulted in a sharp decline in that state's credit reputation, and the widespread belief that debtors controlled the legislature. M. Jensen, The New Nation: A History of the United States During the Confederation; 1781–1789 323–25 (1950); A. McLaughlin, The Confederation and the Constitution, 1783–1798 107–9 (1903).

20. Coleman, *supra* note 17, at 108, 109, 116, 123.

21. *Id.* at 182–83, 200–3.

22. 5 George 2, c. 7 (1732); *see* discussion of Herbert Johnson, *The Prerogative Court of New York, 1686–1776*, 17 Am. J. Leg. Hist. 135 (1974).

23. *See* Benfield v. Solomons, 9 Vessey, Jr. Reports, 77–87, at 85–88; 32 English Reports 530-4, at 33 (Chancery, 1803).

24. A summary of the debate appears in Johnson, *John Jay: Lawyer in a Time of Transition, 1764–1775*, 74 U. Pa. L. Rev. 1260–92, at 1283–84 (1976).

25. Coleman, *supra* note 17, at 16–17. Coleman suggests that New York's bankruptcy law of 1813 discouraged New Jersey and Pennsylvania merchants from extending credit

to New York customers. On the other hand, New York merchants hesitated before conducting business in New Jersey and Pennsylvania where bankruptcy relief was unavailable. *Id.* at 157–58.

26. *Id.* at 17. Coleman notes that little information is available concerning the decision of the Philadelphia Convention to include a provision for a uniform bankruptcy act in its draft constitution.

27. The act of April 4, 1800, 2 Stat. 19–36, was repealed by the act of Dec. 19, 1803, 2 Stat. 248. The act of Aug. 19, 1841, 5 Stat. 440–49, was repealed on Mar. 3, 1843, 5 Stat. 614.

28. Golden v. Prince, 10 F. Cas. 542–47 (No. 5509) (Circuit Court of Pennsylvania, 1814); COLEMAN, *supra* note 17, at 32.

29. COLEMAN, *supra* 17, at 32, 188; Adams Story, 1 F. Cas. 141–52 (No. 66) (Circuit Court of New York, 1817).

30. COLEMAN, *supra* note 17, at 32; Alexander v. Gibson, 1 Nott & McCord 480–501 (January 1819).

31. COLEMAN, *supra* note 17, at vii, 125.

32. Sturges v. Crowninshield, 4 Wheat. 122–208, at 122–208.

33. 4 Wheat. 122, at 123.

34. Appellant's argument are at *id.*, 123–35, 180–91, appellee's arguments are at *id* at 135–80.

35. *Id.* at 131, 190.

36. *Id.* at 144.

37. *Id.* at 172.

38. Ogden v. Saunders, 12 Wheaton 213, at 272–73 (1827).

39. See discussion *supra* notes 27–29.

40. 12 Wheat. 213, 264 (1827).

41. *Id.*

42. 4 Wheat. iii (1819).

43. 12 Wheat. 332 (1827).

44. 4 Wheat. 122, 193 (1819).

45. *Id.* at 195–96.

46. *Id.* at 196.

47. *Id.* at 194–95.

48. *Id.* at 197.

49. *Id.* at 205.

50. *Id.* at 205–7.

51. *Id.* at 207.

52. 4 Wheat. 209–13 (1819).

53. *Id.* at 212–13.

54. 12 Wheat. 213, at 213–14 (1827).

55. Wheaton's arguments are set forth in detail; the presentations of other counsel as reported are a conflation of their arguments in 1824 and 1827. As a reporter Wheaton understandably was performing double duty as counsel for appellant, and thus could not be certain he obtained a full transcript of the arguments of opposing counsel.

56. *Id.* at 218.

57. *Id.* at 222, citing from Grotius, Burlamaqui, Vattle, and Pothier.

58. *Id.* at 228.

59. *Id.* at 233. Actually both sides cited Marshall's biography of George Washington in support of their positions. *Id.* and *Id.* at 247.

60. *Id.* at 234.

61. *Id.* at 235.

62. *Id.* at 239.

63. *Id.* at 241, 253.

64. *See* discussion *supra* notes 37–40.

65. 12 Wheat. 213, at 256–60 (1827).

66. Johnson's careful and well-reasoned opinion is *id.* at 271–92.

67. *Id.* at 283.

68. *Id.* at 308, 313.

69. *Id.* at 314.

70. *Id.* at 320.

71. *Id.* at 317.

72. *Id.*

73. *Id.* at 332.

74. *Id.*

75. *Id.* at 343–44.

76. *Id.* at 352–53.

77. *Id.* at 354. George Mason's notes concerning the Philadelphia Convention's adoption of the contract clause suggest that there may have been an intention to give the contract clause both a retrospective and prospective application, as Marshall suggested. *See* Siegan *supra* note 4, at 66.

78. *Id.* at 350–51.

79. *Id.* at 354–55.

80. *Id.* at 346–51.

81. The specific discussion of rights and remedies is at Marbury v. Madison, 1 Cranch 137, at 162–63; on detinue *see id.* at 73; for the comment on limited government *see id.* at 176.

82. 4 Wheat. 316–437 (1819); 4 Wheat. 518–715 (1819); 6 Wheat. 264–448 (1821); 9 Wheat. 1–240 (1824).

83. *See* HASKINS & JOHNSON *supra* note 5, at 386–89.

84. R. NEWMYER, THE COMMERCE CLAUSE UNDER MARSHALL, TANEY AND WAITE 16–27 (1937; reprinted 1964).

85. *Id.* at 25–27.

86. HASKINS & JOHNSON *supra* note 5, at 633–44; U.S. v. Hudson and Goodwin, 7 Cranch 32–34 (1812); U.S. v. Coolidge, 1 Wheat. 415–17 (1816).

87. 1 Wheat. 304–82 (1816).

88. Johnson, *Gibbons v. Ogden before Marshall*, in COURTS AND LAW IN EARLY NEW YORK (L. Hershkowitz and M. Klein eds. 1978), at 105–13, 147–48.

89. R. FAULKNER, THE JURISPRUDENCE OF JOHN MARSHALL 3–26 (1968).

90. 6 Cranch 135–39 (1810).

91. *See* Corwin, *The Doctrine of Due Process of Law Before the Civil War*, 24 HARV. L. REV. 366–85, 460–79 (1911). For Marshall's view of contracts *see* Isaacs, *John Marshall on Contracts. A Study in Early American Juristic Theory*, 7 VA. L. REV 413–28 (1921).

92. M. HORWITZ, THE TRANSFORMATION OF AMERICAN LAW, 1780–1860 (1977) 180–85.

93. *See* DEMOCRACY, LIBERTY AND PROPERTY: THE STATE CONSTITUTIONAL CONVENTIONS OF THE 1820s (M. Peterson ed. 1966), xv, 6–7, 11–12, 129, 135, 274, 279–81; D. FOX, THE DECLINE OF ARISTOCRACY IN THE POLITICS OF NEW YORK, 1801–1840, 229–69 (1919).

3

John Marshall and His Court: Applied Behavioral Jurisprudence

John Stookey and George Watson

More than on any other Chief Justice, scholars have lavished attention on John Marshall and his Supreme Court.[1] Much of that work has attempted to specify John Marshall's jurisprudence. By jurisprudence is meant his attitudes and values concerning the nature and application of law in our government.[2] The accepted methodology for such studies is a case-based approach, involving textual and logical analysis of opinions and other statements of the individual being analyzed. Our goal is to suggest and demonstrate alternative approaches to discerning the jurisprudence of historical figures, in this case Marshall. Whereas the standard approach is essentially qualitative in nature, we suggest the application of a more quantitative-based analysis of Marshall's opinion and decision behavior.

Traditional jurisprudence research typically proceeds in an inductive fashion. Analysis of decisions and other writings of justices are scrutinized in the political and social context of the times. Descriptions of judicial philosophy and behavior are provided and, on occasion, some attention is given to explaining the sources of this jurisprudence.

While such scholarship is meticulous, insightful, and rich in detail, it has weaknesses, as all methodologies do. First, the individualistic nature of the enterprise is susceptible to idiosyncratic results. Different individuals derive different interpretations, in part because of an absence of consensual rules by which to proceed. Second, there is a post hoc aspect to this traditional approach that gives an impression of finding only what one seeks. Third, too much emphasis on the inductive side of the inquiry reduces the development and testing of somewhat more theoretical propositions or hypotheses.

In contrast, standard empirical inquiry methodology is designed to enhance the reliability of studies, reducing the idiosyncratic finding, by establishing a series of systematic, well-defined steps that facilitate checking and replication. Observations and findings can be subjected to reliability and validity assessments. Moreover, a deductive approach is encouraged that promotes theory and hypothesis testing, again in a systematic and well-defined manner. Such an approach is not designed to replace the meticulous, insightful work of a traditional qualitative analysis, but to complement it and improve its reliability.

Since the late 1940s political scientists have studied the contemporary Supreme Court from what has been called a judicial behavior perspective, which utilizes the systematic empirical inquiry approach just outlined. While it is beyond the scope of this chapter to engage in a full-fledged empirical analysis of John Marshall and the Marshall Court, we do wish to demonstrate how such analyses might proceed. This presentation, then, serves as a sampler, as it were, of applying contemporary empirical techniques to a historical context. In so doing, we hope to assess the promise of such techniques for historical court analyses.

APPLIED BEHAVIORAL JURISPRUDENCE

Unlike those who see understanding justices' jurisprudence as a goal in itself, the judicial behavioralist is motivated at the outset by a desire to understand and explain Supreme Court decisions. The behavioral perspective, it seems to us, makes four assumptions about the role of jurisprudence in providing such an explanation.[3]

1. Understanding a justice's jurisprudence is of great practical significance, because a justice's philosophy of law is the primary determinant of his decisions.

2. While jurisprudence is the primary determinant of judicial behavior, we must consider that a justice's decisions and opinions are also shaped by role perceptions and group dynamics.

3. A justice's jurisprudence, role perceptions, and approach to group dynamics are at least partially a function of that justice's social background and resulting psychological makeup.

4. We can discern a justice's jurisprudence by quantitative analysis and comparison of justices' votes and opinions. A justice reveals his jurisprudence in his decision, and this is most clearly seen by comparing the behaviors of justices. Those with different jurisprudence will vote differently.

These assumptions lead to a research approach different from those normally used to study Marshall's jurisprudence. We can see that research strategy more clearly by outlining the model of justice decision making that underlies the approach. Assumption one tells us that at the most basic level the model simply posits a relationship between the jurisprudence of a justice and his decisional and opinion behavior. In other words, a justice's behavior is primarily a function of his attitudes and views of law and its place in society. Specifically rejected is the notion that decisions are the mechanical result of the interaction of law, precedent, and facts.

Assumption two, however, tells us that the relationship between jurisprudence and behavior is not only direct, but also mediated by role perceptions and group interaction. Role perception refers to a justice's view of the appropriate function of a Supreme Court justice. Role perceptions concern a variety of issues, but at heart relate to whether the justice believes that it is or it is not legitimate for him to allow his jurisprudence to affect his decision. A restraintist is a justice who believes that he should keep his personal jurisprudence out of decisions and defer as much as possible to precedent or elected branches of government. On the other hand, an activist judge is one who believes that it is legitimate for him to express his own jurisprudence in his decisions. In a sense the role variable is a type of gate, through which a justice's jurisprudence may or may not pass on the way to a decision.

The judicial behavioralist also reminds us that the Supreme Court is a collegial body. A justice's decision necessarily must take into account the jurisprudence and role perceptions of other justices. This means that the justice's ultimate decision may sometimes result as much from group pressure or effective leadership as it does from his own jurisprudence.

Assumption three addresses the sources of a justice's jurisprudence. A justice's personality and psychological makeup influence all of the other explanatory factors in the model. One's philosophy of law, role perception, ability and willingness to lead or be led in a group are all at least partially a function of psychological makeup.

These first three assumptions imply the following model of judicial decision making.[4] (See Figure 1.) At the heart of this model is jurisprudence. It is the only factor involved in all paths to judicial decision making. However, jurisprudence by itself is inadequate to understand judicial decision making. Therefore, our approach is what might be called "applied jurisprudence." We are interested in how a justice's jurisprudence interacts with other factors and is applied by that justice to a particular decision.

The fourth assumption of the behavioral perspective is that the paths in the judicial decision-making model can be studied by various quantitative techniques, foremost of which are comparisons of the behaviors of justices. What follows is a brief description of those methods, along with an overview of substantive conclusions that have been reached by using them. Their potential or exploratory application to John Marshall and his court is also addressed.

PATH A: JURISPRUDENCE TO DECISION

The judicial behavioralists see a justice's jurisprudence in terms of attitudes about law, governmental institutions, and social groups. The model asserts that

FIGURE 1. AN APPLIED JURISPRUDENTIAL MODEL
OF JUDICIAL DECISION MAKING

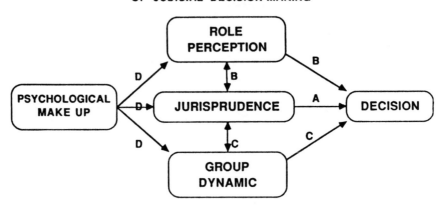

these attitudes will significantly affect his judicial behavior, that is, his decisions. Consequently, an assessment of this path involves the measurement of the justice's behavior and his jurisprudence.

Behavior is most easily and commonly measured as a justice's vote. However, even in the contemporary Court, such a tally is not aways unambiguous. The researcher must be alert to and be able to interpret situations in which a justice concurs in part and dissents in part. In the Marshall Court, this relatively simple procedure of vote counting is often frustrated by the absence of any accounting about who participated in a decision and how they may have voted.

The measurement of jurisprudence is even more problematic. Because of the desire to engage in statistical analysis to test models and hypotheses of judicial behavior, traditional determinations of jurisprudence that do not permit quantification must be rejected. At least two basic methodologies have been applied in contemporary judicial behavior research to measure jurisprudence.

Based on the assumption that a justice's jurisprudence is reflected in his decisions, the first approach performs a statistical analysis of voting behavior to search for patterns and commonalities among groups of cases. An analysis of the common elements of those cases identifies key issues that seem to define key elements of justices' attitudes and values. Two of the more common statistical techniques applied in this initial effort are factor analysis and Guttman scaling.[5]

To take Harold Spaeth's work as an example, we see that he identified freedom, equality, and New Dealism as three dimensions that define the major work of the contemporary Court. The freedom dimension concerns attitudes toward individual rights and liberties, such as speech, press, and criminal defendant rights. Equality deals with attitudes about the rights of various groups, particularly minority groups in society. New Dealism measures attitudes toward government regulation.

Once these basic components of jurisprudence are identified, there are a variety of techniques for deriving a quantitative measure of a justice for each component. The factor analysis approach can produce a factor score, based on a justice's vote in each of the cases included in the factor and on the weight assigned to each case that contributes to the factor. The Guttman scale technique also produces a scale score, dependent upon the justice's placement among the set of cases that make up the scale.[6]

A simpler procedure than factor analysis or scaling for scoring justices uses the basic factors identified through the statistical analyses. Cases are then identified that fall within the definitions of these factors. Each justice in turn is placed along the continuum defined by those cases, based on his vote and on the interpretation by the researcher of what issues are involved in those cases. For Spaeth's categories, a liberal position is defined as (1) pro individual rights on the freedom dimension, (2) pro minority rights on the equality dimension, and (3) pro government regulation of business on the New Deal dimension. A conservative is defined by the opposite views.[7]

A simple percentage analysis is calculated to measure a justice's position on these dimensions. For example, in the 1981–85 terms (inclusive) Justice Brennan voted the liberal position in civil liberties cases eighty percent of the time. In the same set of cases, now Chief Justice Rehnquist voted the liberal position only seventeen percent of the time.[8] Regardless of the scoring technique, the consistent and persistent differences among justices over time seem inescapably to suggest that justices do possess different attitudes and values concerning these dimensions and that those differences are reflected in their voting behavior.

A major methodological problem with this approach is the dependence of the measurement upon the theory. The model asserts the connection between jurisprudence and decision but then proceeds to measure both with reference to voting behavior. Jurisprudence infers behavior, but the behavior is used to measure the jurisprudence. Then, the correlation between the two is touted as support for the model. There are techniques to reduce the circularity of these approaches, but a measure of jurisprudence, independent from vote, is preferred.[9]

David Danelski offers such an independent measurement in a second approach to identifying justices' attitudes and values.[10] He conducted a type of content analysis using the pre-Court speeches of justices to identify major components of their jurisprudence. Danelski found that Justice Brandeis's pre-Court speeches revealed strong opposition to laissez-faire government policies. Conversely, Butler's speeches revealed strong support for laissez-faire policies. Danelski then examined Brandeis and Butler's judicial voting behavior and found significant evidence that each justice tended to vote his attitudes and values. For example, Brandeis never cast a sole dissent in favor of laissez-faire policies, while Butler never cast a sole dissent against laissez-faire policies.

There are two components of Danelski's work that distinguish it from the previous approach. First, it employs a content analysis of written or spoken materials rather than a statistical analysis of voting behavior. This overcomes part of the problem in measuring both jurisprudence and behavior by means of the decisional vote. Second, it moves a step further in establishing independence between the two factors by measuring jurisprudence without any reference to the individual cases considered by the justices.

Of the two approaches, the latter has greater applicability to the Marshall era. A statistical analysis of voting behavior in the Marshall Court encounters two major problems. First, individual voting records must often be inferred, because they are not regularly reported. In general, this is not too critical a problem, since scholars seem to have deduced the voting patterns for most cases. Second, the statistical applications rely on variation in voting patterns and a sufficient number of cases to produce statistically reliable results. Statistical analysis of the Marshall Court may be impeded by the greater unanimity among the total number of cases, as well as by the smaller number of cases considered by the Court in the first place. During the Marshall era, the mean number of cases per year was only about forty, with dissents in an average of about three cases per year.[11]

To the extent that off-Court writings of the Marshall-era justices exist, however, content analysis of these documents might yield decent measures of jurisprudence. For example, Thomas Shevory's use of Marshall's biography of Washington to infer elements of Marshall's jurisprudence makes use of this potential.[12] On the other hand, pre-Court or off-Court writings are less likely to deal directly with judicially relevant topics. Thus, Danelski admits that his content analysis of Brandeis and Butler was affected by the fact that the speeches were given during the World War I era and at least one of the speeches was given on the Fourth of July. As a result, patriotism was a very high value for both justices.[13]

A viable alternative to off-Court writings is the content analysis of justices' opinion writings. These are directly relevant to the judicial issues and yet still maintain a certain independence from the actual vote behavior. Justices who vote the same way for different reasons will presumably register differently in a content analysis.

There is a distinction, to be sure, between the more traditional textual analysis of historians, political philosophers, or nonquantitative judicial scholars and the content analysis of an empirical behavioralist, as noted at the beginning of this chapter. Content analysis has the advantage of systematizing the analysis to increase its reliability, that is, to ensure its replicability. In addition, the resulting quantification of content permits statistical analysis in conjunction with other variables, such as justice voting behavior. On the other hand, content analysis, as a basic positivist methodology, is somewhat subject to the critique of the so-called interpretive mode of analysis that emphasizes the need for perceiving the intentions and true meanings that lie beyond the surface assessed by content analysis and voting behavior.[14]

In deciding what values to look for in the content analysis, the judicial behavioralist should work hand in hand with the traditional scholar. The behavioralist should ask the traditional scholar what attitudinal dimensions seem most important for a particular era. As we have seen for the contemporary Court, dimensions of freedom, equality, and New Dealism seem most relevant. They would be logical categories for a content analysis of the Rehnquist Court. However, they appear clearly inappropriate for the Marshall Court.

Scholars of the Marshall Court appear to agree that at least two attitudinal dimensions were of great concern during that era: (1) nationalism versus states' rights; and (2) government power of regulation versus property rights.[15] Using the second of these for illustrative purpose, we first need to develop a coding system for determining support for government regulation of property rights. We decided to look for supportive or negative comments about government power, on the one hand, and property rights or other rights derived from property, on the other.

As an example, we decided to use the opinions of John Marshall and William Johnson in *Ogden v. Saunders*.[16] *Ogden* is a very well-known example of the divergence of Marshall's Federalist jurisprudence and Johnson's Jeffersonian jurisprudence. If our technique works, this difference should be revealed. For Justice Johnson, we found that seventy-three percent of his mentions of either rights or government power were favorable comments about power. Conversely, fifty-four percent of such comments made by Chief Justice Marshall were favorable toward the concept of rights. As expected, Marshall is clearly supporting the concept of property rights, while Johnson is defending a position in favor of state governmental power to regulate such rights in the name of the common good.

While very tentative, this example suggests that a content analytic technique does have potential for isolating underlying jurisprudence motives in court decisions. Further application of this technique to other less obvious situations may provide a means of analyzing the linkage between jurisprudence and judicial behavior.

While the content analysis of actual opinions may offer some potential as a measure of jurisprudence, it may well be limited by considerations of authorship. The practice of incorporating the language of colleagues, clerks, other opinions, and boiler-plate legal phrases can combine to diminish the utility of content analyzing opinions. This suggests a strategy of using single-authored opinions, but in the final analysis, we encourage experimentation with it, along with suitable validity and reliability checks, as an effort to provide a multimethod, multitrait approach to the analysis of jurisprudence.

PATH B: JURISPRUDENCE TO ROLE
PERCEPTION TO DECISION

Role perception is one of those terms discussed frequently, but not often studied in a systematic way. Commonly this term is conceptualized as dealing with the notion of an activist or restraintist view of a Court's role in the political system. Perhaps the most detailed examination of this concept is that of Bradley Canon, whose delineation of various components concerning the activist/restraintist concept has important measurement consequences.[17] Canon first notes that activism and restraint are overly broad terms and proceeds to distinguish a half dozen different aspects of the basic dimension.

1. Majoritarianism—a measure of the extent to which democratically adopted policies are nullified.

2. Interpretive stability—a measure of the extent to which a court's decisions, doctrines, or interpretations are modified or overruled.

3. Interpretive fidelity—a measure of the extent to which provisions of the Constitution are given strained interpretation or interpretations that violate the intention of framers.

4. Substantive-democratic process distinction—a measure of the extent to which the Supreme Court makes substantive policies without appreciable effect on the maintenance of the democratic process.

5. Specificity of policy—a measure of the extent to which the Supreme Court makes detailed policies in contrast to general policies with the discretion to fill in the details left to other governmental branches or agencies.

6. Availability of alternative policy maker—a measure of the extent to which Supreme Court decisions seriously deprive other governmental policy makers of the opportunity to consider the problems to which the policies are addressed.

While Canon applies the concepts to the entire Court, they could be applied equally to particular justices to determine which justices most often favor activist or restraintist positions on each of these dimensions. Equally possible is the application and specification of similar activist/restraintist issues relevant for the Marshall Court or other Court eras.

Champagne and Nagel studied the role perceptions of Justices Holmes, Brandeis, Stone, and Frankfurter by isolating any dissenting votes of these justices in cases in which the Court declared unconstitutional a municipal, state, or federal statute.[18] In terms of Canon's dimensions, this is a measure of activism and restraint in terms of the majoritarianism dimension. A justice was considered more restraintist when he objected to such interference by casting a dissenting vote. The authors found that whether a justice was activist or restraintist tended to vary considerably by issue area. To Spaeth and Teger, this leads to the conclusion that maybe activism and restraint are just "a cloak for the justices' policy preferences."[19] It certainly seems to support the notion of path B1 in our model, that jurisprudence has some impact on role perceptions. Whether path B2 exists may be questioned, but most scholars agree with Ulmer when he says that restraint and activism may vary according to situation, but role perception still has significance. "For though the so-called restraintists are not always restrained when interpreting the Constitution and state and federal law, they are clearly more restrained than the activists."[20]

Conventional wisdom has seemed to place Marshall as an activist. His role in establishing a strong position for the Court vis-à-vis the other two branches of government and his apparent support for a strong national government are taken as evidence of his activism. Wallace Mendelson, among others, however, builds a persuasive argument that Marshall "is not, as charged, an activist."[21] Regardless, there seems to be some basis for assuming the existence of path B in the applied jurisprudence model, as well as some operationalization that will permit measurement, even if only at some dichotomous or simple ordinal level.

PATH C: JURISPRUDENCE TO GROUP DYNAMIC TO DECISION

Group dynamics concern the patterns of influence on the Court. In other words, to what extent is a justice's decision influenced by the positions or needs of his colleagues rather than his own jurisprudence in isolation? Perhaps the most famous example is Earl Warren securing a unanimous Court in *Brown v. Board of Education*, although other examples are available.[22] In the Marshall Court itself, Marshall's antagonist, Justice Johnson, wrote that "I must either submit to circumstances or become such a cypher in our consultations as to effect no good at all."[23]

One area of focus within this group dynamic area is that of leadership. A common distinction made in this area is between social leadership and task leadership.[24] Social leadership is concerned more with group harmony and collegiality as a goal for group interactions, whereas task leadership is focused more on the group's achievement of instrumental goals or tasks.

Danelski's comparison of Chief Justices Hughes and Stone, using their personal papers, found Hughes able to maximize his influence on the Court by being both the social and task leader. On the other hand, Chief Justice Stone was unable to perform either leadership role.[25] Robert Seddig's analysis finds John Marshall, like Hughes, both a social and task leader.[26] His analysis was based on letters and comments from a variety of colleagues and other historical evidence.

To the extent that anyone attributes to Marshall leadership capabilities based on his ability to control or manage vote outcomes, however, a more careful analysis of the Marshall Court voting record suggests alternative possibilities.

It seems plausible to suggest that the nature of the cases and the nature of the judicial process were as much responsible for the frequent unanimity of vote. As Sheldon Goldman notes, the Marshall Court considered relatively few constitutional law cases (sixty-two cases).[27] Dissents were registered in sixty-three percent of them, compared to an average dissent rate on the Court of sixty-four percent between 1981 and 1985, when constitutional law cases constituted more than half of the cases heard.[28] Alternatively, cases that routinely were heard by the Marshall Court no longer find their way into the modern Court's docket. This occurs in part because of the nature of the times and also because of the modern certiorari process to gain access to the Court. Thus, the Marshall Court accepted virtually all cases coming before it, most of which were easily disposed of by a unanimous Court.

While the studies noted above are confirmatory of the C link in our model, they do not promote the type of quantitative analysis to which this chapter has attempted to point. One of the earliest and still common statistical methods of analyzing Court voting behavior is the bloc analysis. Pioneered by C. Herman Pritchett in his 1941 article, the bloc analysis essentially tallies who votes with whom.[29] It has remained a staple of Supreme Court analysis, even with the emergence of other statistical techniques.

Such an analysis can be applied to any of the Court eras, Marshall's included. Limitations of vote counting in the Marshall era already have been discussed. Nevertheless, the bloc analysis presented in Table 1 is interesting. Read like a mileage map, a particular cell pairs the row and column justices and represents the percentage of cases in which they voted together from among split decision cases in which both participated. Blank cells indicate joint participation in fewer than 10 split decision cases. Of course, it must be remembered, for example, that Cushing never even served on the same Court as most of the other justices during the Marshall era. Do not confuse the number of blank cells as indicating inferior or missing data.

The value of the bloc analysis lies in its systematic tracking of the justices' voting behavior. It helps to confirm what otherwise may be noted by careful observers of the Court. It may reveal some less obvious group dynamics that deserve attention. Most importantly, it helps to quantify another component of our basic model and thus maintains the model's heuristic value for theory and hypothesis testing.

For the Marshall Court, we might first note some considerable agreement between Marshall on the one hand, and Washington, Todd, Duvall, Story, Thompson, and McLean on the other. In addition, the opposition status of the two major figures on the Court, Marshall and Johnson, is suggested by their fifty-two percent agreement in split decision cases. Livingston shows considerable lack of agreement with Johnson (twenty-eight percent) but also less with Marshall than other Court members. Justice Baldwin's late arrival for the Marshall era seems marked by what must be some solo dissents.

TABLE 1.   BLOC ANALYSIS
AGREEMENT RATES IN SPLIT DECISION CASES

	MAR	CUS	PAT	WAS	CHA	JOH	LIV	TOD	DUV	STO	THO	TRI	MCL	BAL
MARSHALL														
CUSHING	• •													
PATERSON	• •	• •												
WASHINGTON	79	80	• •											
CHASE	• •	• •	• •	• •										
JOHNSON	52	• •	• •	54	• •									
LIVINGSTON	60	• •	• •	71	• •	28								
TODD	85	• •	• •	99	• •	45	67							
DUVALL	88	• •	• •	84	• •	48	67	94						
STORY	86	• •	• •	95	• •	50	82	88	90					
THOMPSON	83	• •	• •	• •	• •	62	• •	• •	85	82				
TRIMBLE	• •	• •	• •	• •	• •	50	• •	• •	83	• •	• •			
MCLEAN	90	• •	• •	• •	• •	62	• •	• •	87	87	84	• •		
BALDWIN	29	• •	• •	• •	• •	21	• •	• •	25	22	26	• •	55	

Other efforts to get at the group dynamics of the Court exist, such as small group analysis or the power analysis of Shapely and Schubik.[30] Just as in the other areas of our model, we suggest that content analysis has some potential for assessing group dynamics. For example, Margaret Hermann's use of content analysis to infer personality characteristics of foreign policy decision makers includes a trait labeled "task orientation." Unfortunately, the trait is operationalized in a unidimensional fashion, "a relative emphasis in interactions with others on getting the task done as opposed to focusing on the feelings and needs of others."[31] Distinguishing between a series of task words on the one hand, and affect words on the other, the number of task words as a percentage of both task and affect words is computed.

While Hermann's measure produces a ratio, as it were, of the predominance of task or affect orientation, it seems clear that these may represent two dimensions on which individuals score independently high or low. Indeed a great leader may be one who successfully exhibits both dimensions, as Marshall reportedly did. Whether written opinions of justices can serve as a vehicle for assessing leadership or whether it may take off-Court statements to apply this content analysis is undetermined at the moment. Nevertheless, such an analysis promises insight into Court leadership, whether it be Marshall or the current Chief Justice.

PATH D: PSYCHOLOGICAL MAKEUP TO JURISPRUDENCE, ROLE PERCEPTIONS, AND GROUP DYNAMICS

At the heart of the judicial behavior approach is the assumption that justices vote based upon their attitudes, values, and perceptions. Emulating the social psychologists and others who study political values and attitudes, judicial scholars trace the sources of jurisprudence back through personality, environment, and other socialization experiences. John Schmidhauser's characterization of justices as a "group of like-minded men" was based on the strong similarities in their social backgrounds.[32] Perhaps the most proximate, but least studied, component of these attitudinal sources is personality, or the psychological processes that form the functional bases of attitudes.[33] That this component is little explored is not too surprising given the difficulty of collecting relevant information. Biographers have attempted psychological insights into their subjects.[34] Bolder efforts, albeit among state court judges, are the analyses of directly administered psychological questionnaires by Burton Atkins and his colleagues and the interviews by James Gibson.[35]

As the reader may now suspect, we are prepared to suggest that content analysis is a method that may hold promise for the study of justices' psychological characteristics. It has met with some utility in its application to foreign policy decision makers.[36] More to the point, Philip Tetlock has tested the technique with Court opinions.[37] While Tetlock's particular focus has been with the notion of cognitive complexity, Margaret Hermann has explored assessments of a range of personality characteristics, including self-confidence, need for affiliation, distrust of others, need for power, nationalism, and belief in one's own ability to control events.[38]

Some of these may not easily transfer to the judicial setting. The measurement of self-confidence, for example, focuses on the pronouns "I," "me," "my," "mine," and "myself." Opinion writing is not conventionally conducive to the personal pronoun, even among the self-confident when writing solo opinions. Of course, off-Court writings are a different matter. To the extent that there are writings, letters, speeches, or other statements of justices, whether present or past, a content analysis concerning these personality traits may offer potential.

Tetlock's focus on cognitive or integrative complexity seems to have the greatest potential for taking advantage of analyzing justices' opinions. As Tetlock explains,

Integrative complexity is defined in terms of two cognitive structural variables: differentiation and integration. Individuals at the simple end of the complexity continuum tend to rely on rigid, one-dimensional, evaluative rules in interpreting events, and to make decisions on the basis of only a few salient items of information. Individuals at the complex end of the continuum tend to interpret events in multidimensional terms and to integrate a variety of evidence in arriving at decisions.[39]

His sampling of Supreme Court justices' opinions between 1946 and 1978 produced a connection between integrative complexity and liberal or moderate as opposed to conservative voting records in cases involving economic conflicts of interest. A difference of lesser magnitude, though still statistically significant, was noted between liberals and conservatives on civil liberties and rights cases.

While the civil liberties and civil rights dimensions seem inapplicable to the Marshall Court, it would be interesting to see if Marshall era justices' cognitive complexity may also have a relationship to attitudinal dimensions that are relevant to that Court. For example, we identified nationalism versus states' rights and government power of regulation versus property rights as two important attitudinal dimensions of the Marshall Court. Do these positions, like the liberalism or conservatism of the contemporary Court, relate to a justice's underlying psychological makeup, namely, his cognitive complexity?

CONCLUSION

We have argued that techniques used by judicial behavioralists have utility for the analysis of historical courts, such as that of John Marshall. This begins with the underlying assumption of the judicial behavior scholar that behavior, particularly as measured by vote outcome, is the most important factor in studying the Supreme Court and Supreme Court justices. It proceeds to the basic model of applied jurisprudence, which emphasizes the importance of jurisprudence as a determinant of that behavior, albeit sometimes mediated through role perceptions and the group dynamics of the justices. In addition, the model asserts the significance of factors that affect the development of jurisprudence and these other attitudes and values that affect judicial behavior. Most proximate of these factors is the psychological makeup of a justice.

The application of quantitative techniques to historical settings, in particular U.S. Supreme Courts, is limited in part by the need for variation in the properties being measured. The judicial behavior emphasis on the justices' vote decisions works less well in Courts like the Marshall Court because of the smaller number of cases considered and by the lower level of variation in voting among the justices than is found in the modern Court. Thus, while certain analyses can be applied, like a bloc analysis or simple vote counts over a fairly extensive period of time, such techniques seem to have greater limitations for nineteenth-century Courts.

As a positivist methodology, the judicial behavior approach is also subject to certain criticisms of interpretive and critical philosophies of science.[40] Of course, this applies to modern as well as historical applications. Yet, neither of these approaches offers a suitable solution to follow up its criticisms. Indeed, the purpose of this chapter is to argue in favor of multiple methodologies in the study of the Supreme Court and Supreme Court justices, whether current or historical.

While we have suggested the application of various techniques, it is clear that we feel greater attention to content analysis has value for the study of the Marshall and other historical Courts. It allows the research to take advantage of written opinions, perhaps the richest and most significant source of insight into the justices' thinking. It permits distinction among justices whose vote decision may be the same, thus overcoming a major interpretive critique and establishing a certain independence of measurement between voting behavior on the one hand, and values and attitudes on the other. It is an approach that permits application of the same methodology to off-Court writings and statements of the justices as well. It permits a more rigorous and systematic analysis of content than is typically the case with a more informal textual or linguistic analysis engaged in by traditional historical or philosophical scholars. Yet it provides a quantitative output that permits it to link with the theory development and testing of the quantitatively oriented judicial behavior scholars.

We have suggested, and in some cases demonstrated, potential applications of quantitative techniques to studying the Marshall Court. As a complement to that broad body of traditional research that already has been conducted, we think there is still much to learn and clarify about our earlier Courts. The serious application of some of these approaches can enhance our understanding of these earlier Courts and build toward the development of theory that will provide insight into the modern Court as well.

NOTES

1. *See* for example two classic analyses of Marshall: A. BEVERIDGE, THE LIFE OF JOHN MARSHALL (1916) and R. FAULKNER, THE JURISPRUDENCE OF JOHN MARSHALL (1968).

2. Two of the best known discussions of American jurisprudence are: K. LLEWELLYN, JURISPRUDENCE: REALISM IN THEORY AND PRACTICE (1962) and R. POUND, JURISPRUDENCE (1959).

3. These assumptions are drawn primarily from the pioneering works of Glendon Schubert and C. Herman Pritchett. *See* G. SCHUBERT, JUDICIAL BEHAVIOR: A READER IN THEORY AND RESEARCH (1964) [hereinafter cited as SCHUBERT, JUDICIAL BEHAVIOR]; Schubert, *Academic Ideologies and the Study of Adjudication* 61 AM. POL. SCI. REV. 106 (1967); and C. H. PRITCHETT, THE ROOSEVELT COURT (1948).

4. This model has been described in numerous scholarly works. One of the most complete and readable descriptions is C. SHELDON, THE AMERICAN JUDICIAL PROCESS: MODELS AND APPROACHES 27 (1974).

5. G. SCHUBERT, THE JUDICIAL MIND 97–146 (1965); H. SPAETH, SUPREME COURT POLICY MAKING 119–37 (1979).

6. SCHUBERT, JUDICIAL BEHAVIOR 306–14.

7. These dimensions are discussed and applied in L. BAUM, THE SUPREME COURT 134–42 (1981).

8. S. GOLDMAN, CONSTITUTIONAL LAW 160 (1987).

9. Stookey and Baer, *A Critique of Guttman Scaling: With Special Attention to its Application to the Study of Collegial Bodies,* 10 J. QUANTITY AND QUALITY 251 (1976).

10. Danelski, *Values as Variables in Judicial Decision-Making,* 18 VAND. L. REV. 722 (1966).

11. For a discussion of the low dissent rate on the Marshall Court in comparison to Courts of other Chief Justices, see Johnson, *Some Comparative Statistics on U.S. Chief Justice Courts*, 9 ROCKY MTN. SOC. SCI. J. 90–91 (1972).

12. T. Shevory, *John Marshall as Republican: Order and Conflict in American Political History* [*infra* Chapter 4].

13. D. DANELSKI, *supra* note 10, at 726–27.

14. B. FAY, SOCIAL THEORY AND POLITICAL PRACTICE 70–91 (1976).

15. A. T. MASON AND D. G. STEPHENSON, JR., AMERICAN CONSTITUTIONAL LAW 126–30, 270–75 (1987).

16. Ogden v. Saunders, 12 Wheat. 213 (1827).

17. CANON, *A Framework for the Analysis of Judicial Activism*, SUPREME COURT ACTIVISM AND RESTRAINT 385 (S. Halpern and C. Lamb eds. 1982).

18. Champagne and Nagel, *The Advocates of Restraint: Holmes, Brandeis, Stone, and Frankfurter, id.* at 303.

19. Spaeth and Teger, *Activism and Restraint: A Cloak for the Justices' Policy Preferences, id.* at 277.

20. S. ULMER, SUPREME COURT POLICYMAKING AND CONSTITUTIONAL LAW 34 (1986).

21. Mendelson, *Was Chief Justice Marshall an Activist? supra* note 17, at 57–76.

22. Brown v. Board of Education, 349 U.S. 294. *See also* Danelski, *The Influence of the Chief Justice in the Decision Process of the Supreme Court*, AMERICAN COURT SYSTEMS 506 (S. Goldman and A. Serat eds. 1978), and Howard, *On the Fluidity of Judicial Choice*, 62 AM. POL. SCI. REV. 43 (1968).

23. Letter from William Johnson to Thomas Jefferson (Dec. 10, 1822), in D. MORGAN, JUSTICE WILLIAM JOHNSON: THE FIRST DISSENTER at 181–82 (1954).

24. Bales, *Task Roles and Social Roles in Problem Solving Groups*, READINGS IN SOCIAL PSYCHOLOGY 437–47 (E. Maccoby ed. 1958).

25. Danelski, *supra* note 22, at 506–19.

26. Seddig, *John Marshall and the Origins of Supreme Court Leadership*, U. PITT. L. REV. 785 (1975).

27. GOLDMAN, *supra* note 8, at 160.

28. *Id.* at 157; *The Supreme Court: 1986*, 101 HARV. L. REV. 370 (1987).

29. Pritchett, *Divisions of Opinion among Justices of the U.S. Supreme Court, 1939–1941*, 35 AM. POL. SCI. REV. 890 (1941).

30. Snyder, *The Supreme Court as a Small Group*, 36 SOCIAL FORCES 232 (1958). *See also* Danelski, *supra* note 22, at 525; Shapley and Shubik, *A Method for Evaluating the Distribution of Power in Committee System*, 48 AM. POL. SCI. REV. 787 (1954) as utilized by Krislov, *Power and Coalition in a Nine-Man Body*, 6 AM. BEHAV. SCI. 24–26 (1963).

31. M. HERMANN, HANDBOOK FOR ASSESSING PERSONAL CHARACTERISTICS AND FOREIGN POLICY ORIENTATIONS OF POLITICAL LEADERS 17 (1983).

32. Schmidhauser, *The Justices of the Supreme Court: A Collective Portrait*, 3 MIDWEST J. POL. SCI. 1 (1959). *See also* Ulmer, *Social Background as an Indicator to the Votes of Supreme Court Justices in Criminal Cases: 1947–1956 Terms*, 17 AM. J. POL. SCI. 622 (1973).

33. H. GLICK, COURTS, POLITICS, AND JUSTICE 268 (1988). For a psychological model that presages the applied jurisprudence model presented here, *see* Smith, *A Map for the Analysis of Personality and Politics*, 24 J. SOC. ISS. 15 (1968).

34. J. W. Howard, Mister Justice Murphy: A Political Biography (1968); A. T. Mason, Harlan Fiske Stone: Pillar of the Law (1956); E. S. Corwin, John Marshall and the Constitution (1919).

35. Atkins, Alpert, and Ziller, *Personality Theory and Judging; A Proposed Theory of Self-Esteem and Judicial Policy-Making*, 2 Law and Pol. Q. 189 (1980). *See also* Gibson, *Personality and Elite Political Behavior: The Influence of Self-Esteem on Judicial Decision Making*. 43 J. Pol. 104 (1981).

36. Tetlock, *Personality and Isolationism: Content Analysis of Senatorial Speeches*, 41 J. Pers. and Soc. Psy. 737 (1981).

37. Tetlock, Bernzweig, and Gallant, *Supreme Court Decision Making: Cognitive Style as a Predictor of Ideological Consistency of Voting*, 48 J. Pers. and Soc. Psy. 1227 (1985) [hereinafter cited as Tetlock].

38. Hermann, *supra* note 31, *passim*.

39. Tetlock, *supra* note 37, at 1228.

40. In addition to Fay, *supra* note 14, a presentation of these philosophies of science may be found in R. Bernstein, The Restructuring of Social and Political Theory (1978).

PART II POLITICAL THEORY

4

John Marshall as Republican: Order and Conflict in American Political History

Thomas C. Shevory

JOHN MARSHALL AND THE REPUBLICAN TRADITION

The relationship of John Marshall to Thomas Jefferson, from the standpoint of political theory, is of undeniable significance to arguments regarding the character of the founding period. The ideas and commitments of these two men essentially capture and crystallize the ideological and party conflicts of the late eighteenth and early nineteenth centuries. If the two had political convictions that were essentially similar, then we would be inclined to doubt whether there was anything other than a fairly broad consensus of political values, at least at the level of political leadership, in the nation during the founding period. If, moreover, as has often been argued, the broad consensus that existed was fundamentally liberal and Lockean, we would be justified in considering the "American experiment" as rooted firmly in a particular version of liberal individualism. Credence would be given to Louis Hartz's assertion that, "There has never been a 'liberal movement' or a real 'liberal party' in America; we have only had the American Way of Life, a nationalist articulation of Locke which usually does not know that Locke himself was involved."[1]

Arguments regarding political consensus at the founding period are of more than purely antiquarian interest. They have strong implications for constitutional discourse. For if, as the consensus historians would contend, America was founded upon decipherable and reasonably consistent patterns of political thinking, then constitutional analysis based upon notions of "original intent" would be at least conceivable. If, on the other hand, constitutional government in America was the product of and solution to deep social, economic, and political conflicts, then constitutional interpretation grounded in an original consensus would be more difficult, and perhaps even impossible.[2]

Marshall has been characterized by Albert Beveridge as "the supreme conservative," by William Crosskey as a consummate and determined nationalist, and by Robert Faulkner as a natural rights liberal whose individualist orientations were tempered by certain republican values.[3] While there is much agreement among these authors (each of whom must be recognized as a primary reference for arguments regarding Marshall's political philosophy) with regard to recognition of the significance of contract protection in the lexicon of Marshall's political values, there is also divergence on the question of whether Marshall was an articulate spokesman for a widespread consensus of political values. Both Beveridge and Crosskey tend to emphasize the conflicts of the period of Marshall's tenure on the Supreme Court, conflicts with Jefferson especially, while Faulkner places Marshall solidly within a liberal political consensus.

According to Faulkner, "Marshall's understanding of human liberty revolved . . . about the natural rights to life, to liberty of movement and of opinion, and to the opportunity to acquire property. . . . [I]n his fundamental orientation the Chief Justice did not differ from the other distinguished Americans of his day."[4] And here Faulkner includes Jefferson, Madison, Hamilton, and Washington. Since the publication of Faulkner's book, there have been a number of exercises in Jeffersonian revisionism that have attempted to place the great republican leader outside of the tradition of Lockean liberalism.[5] These have provided some grounds for challenging the consensus view. The consensus view can also be challenged from the "other side," so to speak, by focusing on Marshall's particular expression of what I would call his "republican mythology," especially as it is represented in *The Life of Washington*.

Faulkner does not ignore Marshall's republicanism. Rather, he considers it as an aspect of the Chief Justice's political outlook compatible with his liberal orientation. "Marshall's republicanism completed and ennobled his individualistic jurisprudence.[6] Thus liberalism and republicanism are presented as compatible aspects within an ideological framework. Such a perspective is credible because there are indeed connections between liberal and republican values. Marshall was certainly a "liberal" in the Lockean sense, and the Chief Justice was a key figure in the establishment of American liberalism, especially with regard to his jurisprudential defenses of the right to contract. But the focus on Marshall's liberal aspects and the tendency to view them as compatible with his republicanism result in an incomplete picture of his view of the Constitution.

Developing a working definition of republicanism is not a simple task. Gordon Wood has characterized the "beautiful but ambiguous ideal" of the republic for the founding generation as consisting of a number of interconnected elements. These are: attention to antiquity, acceptance of the public good as a primary value, recognition of the significance of virtue, and acceptance of political and social equality. Underpinning Wood's analysis is a recognition of the ironic relationship of order and instability in republican thinking. Virtue and political goodness were essential, in the republican view, to prevent the unraveling of public order, but also very difficult to achieve. Thus the framers, while great admirers of past republics, recognized that "it was precisely internal discord and conflict for which republics were most widely known."[7]

There are, in my view, significant republican elements in Marshall's view that combine with his liberalism to make his political philosophy highly complex and contradictory. To gain a full picture of Marshall's political philosophy, we must come to terms with the conflicting values within it. And it is precisely the notion of conflict that Marshall borrows most strongly from the republican tradition. Marshall, it is my contention, saw the political world as importantly divided between the elements of virtue, goodness, and stable political order on the one hand, and those of vice, avarice, and passion on the other. Marshall, in other words, is importantly republican in the sense that Machiavelli was in the *Discourses on Titus Livius*. He viewed the political world as an extraordinarily precarious place, where order and virtue were always threatened by common vice and *fortuna*. Appreciation of these aspects of Marshall's thought in turn allows us to draw somewhat different conclusions about his notions of constitutionalism than are generally appreciated.

Marshall's republicanism, then, as did Aristotle's, admits the significance not only of order and virtue, but the reverse of it, that of disorder, vice, and chaos. "Fortune," according to J. G. A. Pocock, "is, first of all, the circumstantial insecurity of political life." Also, the "political symbol of *fortuna* is thus able to stand for Plato's phenomenal world, the image created by our senses and appetites, in which we see only particular things succeeding one another and are ignorant of the timeless principles which give them reality."[8] Political conflicts are "epiphenomena" that imply, but do not always reflect, a deeper metaphysical order. Republicans celebrate order, but they are keenly aware of its fragility. There is thus a strong sense of the precariousness of political society evident in Marshall's thinking, and this influences his evaluation of American historical development and the possibilities for and necessities of common political life. Marshall desires political order and perhaps virtue, but he also sees the political world as easily corruptible if not always corrupted.

Two political forces are available, in Marshall's view, to prevent the subversion of republican order. First and foremost is great leadership; second is a constitution. The great statesman, General Washington being the primary exemplar, epitomized for Marshall the ideals of noble conduct and public spirit. But Marshall understood such magnitude of wisdom and leadership to be a tremendous rarity in the historical development of any political community. Thus, there was a kind of "second best" alternative to the wise ruler; it involved the establishment of a constitution that, while it could not perfectly reflect the ruler's wisdom, could at least stall the tendency toward dissolution away from virtuous conduct in the community after the ruler's death.

This arrangement is "second best" in the sense that Plato's Laws provided a "second best" alternative to the rulership of the philosopher king in the Republic.[9] As Eric Voegelin has written, "The plan of the second-best polis [in The Laws] seems to imply a transition from the 'ideal' of dictatorship by the philosopher-king to the 'ideal' of a government by law, with the constitutional consent of the people."[10] According to this interpretation, the laws are not "just any laws" that are consented to by the people. They are "still the laws of the philosopher-king." And, to transpose this to Marshall, the Constitution comes to represent the "higher part" of the people's character, in a sense, their "true intentions." Such intentions are expressed only with "great exertion" and on rare occasion.[11] Only occasionally will the wise ruler be able to infuse virtue into the people to the extent that the laws that are promulgated and consented to will be an authentic reflection of political virtue. But "the people" will *not* be capable of direct rulership on a day-to-day basis, except in so far as it is filtered through the governing institutions generated from and protected by the Constitution. (An alternative to this would be Jefferson's more fervent commitment to the values promulgated by the popular will.) There are kinds or degrees of popular sovereignty in Marshall's thinking. Marshall's notion of popular sovereignty is thus more complex than Jefferson's fairly straightforward one in which decentralized political control is considered the highest political achievement.

If we examine Marshall's political thinking from the rather dualistic perspective that is being suggested, it helps us to think about his celebrated statement in McCulloch v. Maryland, that constitutions are "intended to endure for ages to come," somewhat differently than is usual.[12] Generally, interpreters are inclined to place the emphasis after the first word of the phrase, so that Marshall is depicted as a strong exponent of the indefinite stability of constitutional government. But, as we recognize and properly consider the tension of *virtu* and *fortuna* in Marshall's thinking, it seems reasonable and appropriate to emphasize the first word in the phrase. Such a reading would underscore the intense temporality of a constitution. Indeed, a constitution would be *intended* to endure, but noble intentions notwithstanding, political forces of dissolution—which are engendered in the chaotic, appetitive aspects of human nature—would permanently endanger it and eventually, no doubt, overwhelm it, especially as it moves away from its grounding in a "moment" of public virtue (that of its founding) that is inspired by crisis, and led by a great statesman (Washington). The Constitution, then, differentiates the stable polity from the world of what Pocock calls "unlegitimated particulars," which is that of "individual wills, passions, and personalities, no longer joined in the moral union of citizenship."[13]

Three components of Marshall's republicanism will now be considered in some detail. First, it is necessary to examine Marshall's view of the relationship of the great character or heroic figure to the many ordinary democratic citizens. Second, attention will be given to Marshall's analysis of paper money and public debt, which he viewed as highly destructive to republican principles. Third, Marshall's views on popular sovereignty and its relationship to the founding and preservation of constitutional government will be analyzed. The aim is to demonstrate that Marshall was, in fact, a kind of conflict historian (as was recognized by Charles Beard), and that he created a political mythology drawn heavily from republican traditions to account for these conflicts and to make sense of them.

Central to Marshall's mythology is the Constitution. As James Oliver Robertson has written, "[M]yths . . . provide available images by which we, perhaps unconsciously but nevertheless consistently and continuously, attempt to resolve the contradictions and paradoxes in our lives, measure the world we live in, judge it, explain it to ourselves and others, define our reality and act upon it."[14] Marshall's *Life of Washington* is laden with contradiction and paradox. The mythology of an enduring Constitution represents his attempt to resolve the immense uncertainties of political life. He thus calls the consensus view into question on two counts. First, his recounting of the American historical experience is saturated with ideological and economic conflicts. He sees neither the founding period nor any other as one of broad consensus. Second, his particular brand of republicanism departs significantly from the liberalism of James Madison and the "radicalism" of Thomas Jefferson, and thus his own thinking is evidence of the inadequacy of the consensus view.

THE GREAT MAN IN THE LIFE OF A REPUBLIC

Marshall's affinity for the biography of the great man is in itself indicative of a political outlook. Marshall engages in what Friedrich Nietzsche called "monumental history."[15] It is the celebration of political character and the exposition of political morality. Faulkner has summarized the essential features of this character. Washington was "generous without being extravagant. He was courageous, restrained, and dignified." He had "practical wisdom . . . especially perspicacity" in political matters. He had, in other words, the kind of aristocratic character defined by Aristotle in the *Nichomachean Ethics* tempered by a "democratic character" that steered him away from pretension, haughty magnificence, and general arrogance.[16]

Yet the celebration of greatness implies the necessity of greatness, and we thus have an alternate image against which to compare the attractive figure of the great man preserving the virtue and dignity of a fledgling republic. True, Marshall recognized a lesser but still laudable virtuousness of the ordinary republican citizen. "The common citizen," according to Faulkner's interpretation, "at best exhibits a kind of stout independence—a willingness to be called 'from the plough' to fight for his personal and especially political prerogatives.

. . . [H]e possesses such virtue as courage and endurance, as well as moderation, 'discipline,' and justice. . . . Industrious and ambitious in peace, the freeman was to be patriotic, self-reliant, and courageous in war."[17] But Marshall's portrait of the ordinary freeholder was not purely affirmative.

In *The Life of Washington* Marshall consistently counterposes great character, whether Washington's, John Smith's, or Marquis de Lafayette's, against the enthusiastic temperament of the nonvirtuous many. The theme is developed early in the biography in the discussion of John Smith, the first representative heroic figure. Marshall's Smith exhibits a variety of laudable characteristics. He was, in fact, "one of the most extraordinary men of his age." Yet his very greatness aroused the resentments of the undifferentiated many, who suspected him and plotted against him, ultimately imprisoning him on the Atlantic voyage "on the extravagant charge of intending to murder the council, usurp the government, and make himself king of Virginia."[18]

It was only as conditions deteriorated upon arrival in the new colony, as supplies diminished and Indians attacked and as the colonists lost health and became miserable, that they came to appreciate Smith's fine qualities. "A sense of imminent and common danger called forth those talents which were fitted to the exigency, and compelled submission to them." Only as the people faced catastrophe did their moral vision sharpen to the point that they could perceive, with some clarity, the nobility of their estranged captain. The great man, unimpaired by the people's wickedness, awaited with magnanimity, prepared to intercede on their behalf. "On captain Smith, who had preserved his health unimpaired, his spirits unbroken, and his judgement unclouded, amidst this general misery and dejection, all eyes were turned, and in him all actual authority was placed by common consent. His example soon gave energy to others."[19]

Marshall sketched a paradigm of political development with his telling of the history of the Jamestown colony. The story of Jamestown is the story of the American republic. The presence of virtue in the community, Marshall suggested, is highly dependent upon sound political leadership, and for this very reason virtue is always endangered. In Jamestown the political order established by Smith was extremely precarious. "The influence of Smith disappeared with the danger which had produced it, and was succeeded by an improvident relaxation of discipline, productive of the most pernicious consequences."[20] The colonists discovered gold, and in its pursuit neglected the demands of sustenance. During Smith's exploration of the Chesapeake Bay, gold fever spread and resulted in famine, and the people initiated insurrection against the colony's leadership. Yet with Smith's return "their fury was sustained." "Encouraged by his example, and coerced by his authority, a spirit of industry and subordination was created among them, which was the parent of plenty and of peace."[21] Virtuous leadership was, in Marshall's version of events, the essential presence behind continued order, stability, and prosperity.[22]

Jamestown's experience would not be unique. It would embody a pattern. The cycle would repeat. "Fortune," as the Renaissance philosophers surmised, "was doomed to repeat her effects."[23] Marshall's history related a constant tension between the wantonness of the many, and reasoned and reasonable demands for order by the great and few. In Jamestown, the superior Smith would be followed by the aristocratic Delaware. Each would find it necessary to impose discipline.

The first volume of *The Life of Washington* compresses the entire history of the thirteen colonies, from the founding of Jamestown to the initial fulminations toward independence. Little is said of Washington. As Beveridge has noted, "In volume one the name of Washington was mentioned on only two occasions described toward the end. The reader had to make his way through more than one hundred thousand words without arriving even at the cradle of the hero."[24] It was thus not a comprehensive history, and important events were sometimes treated inadequately. Marshall did, as Beveridge points out, defend the long introduction as necessary to understanding Washington's life. It was in fact necessary to set the stage for understanding Washington's essential place in the founding of the American political community. Each heroic figure who entered the early story was a kind of George Washington. "The people," as it were, are incapable of governing themselves without a great leader to guide them in moderation and rectitude. Without him they succumb to barbarism.

The biography is reminiscent of Machiavelli's *Discourses*. The Machiavellian counterposition of *virtu* and *fortuna* is expressed as follows:

All writers on politics have pointed out, and throughout history there are plenty of examples which indicate, that in constituting and legislating for a commonwealth it must needs be taken for granted that all men are wicked and that they will always give vent to the malignity that is in their minds when opportunity offers. That their evil dispositions often do not show themselves for a time is due to a hidden cause which those fail to perceive who have had no experience of such contrariness; but in time—which is said to be the father of all truth—it reveals itself.[25]

Machiavelli, the great exponent of modern republicanism, perceived evil and disorder as perpetually threatening the borders of civilization, to be checked only by the great political founder, like Romulus or Lycurgus, and only temporarily. *Fortuna*, because of its essential fickleness, constantly imperils civil society. The greatest leaders, however, do more than simply lead, they instill a sense of public virtue through the activity of constituting or founding a state. "[T]he virtue of the builder is discernible in the fortune of what was built for the city is more or less remarkable according as he is more or less virtuous who is responsible for the start."[26] The citizenry must actively participate in maintaining the order of and faith in the political community.

Pocock draws upon the image of a river to illustrate this Machiavellian conception of the relationship of virtue to public order.

> [W]hile it runs its proper channel, bringing richness and fertility, the themes of order and descending grace are still being invoked; but once we hear that the balance is necessary to prevent 'deluge and inundation,' the river has become that of fortune, against which princes and republics erect dykes by the aid of virtue.[27]

The Jamestown colony, as depicted in the biography, is constantly endangered by such a deluge. While the Indian leader Powhatan maintained peaceful relationships with the settlers at Jamestown, his death ushered the reign of Opechancanough, a "bold and cunning chief," who, presenting the appearance of civility, wooed the colonists into complacency. "Engaged entirely in the pursuits of agriculture, they neglected their military exercises, and every useful precaution." The price of the neglect was inundation. "[I]n one hour, and almost in the same instant, fell three hundred and forty-seven men, women and children; most of them by their own plantation tools."[28] The massacre's effects were profound. "[M]any public works were abandoned; the college institution was deserted; the settlements were reduced from eighty to about eight; and famine superadded its afflicting scourge to the accumulated distress of the colony."[29] Following the Machiavellian model, Marshall depicts the relaxed community as that which courts disaster.

The strongly cyclical character of the movement is also reminiscent of Machiavelli and the classical writers from whom he drew. Machiavelli borrowed from the classical formulation of political types in which each virtuous form had its correspondence in one laden with vice. Principality was counterpoised with tyranny, aristocracy with oligarchy, and democracy with anarchy. As in Plato and Aristotle's schemata, each virtuous form contained the elements of its undoing as a polity moved along a path from principality to anarchy and back. "Either at the suggestion of some good man or because this anarchy had to be got rid of somehow, principality was once again restored. And from this there was, stage by stage, a return to anarchy, by way of the transitions and for the reasons assigned.[30] The mythology of political forms harkens to Hesiod and Homer. It manifests the tension, central to Platonic philosophy, between the ideal form and its phenomenal representation.

While the presence of such a complex model is not apparent in Marshall's writings in *The Life of Washington*, his history conjuring more of an unadorned dualism, it displays a continuous wobble between a state of virtue and one of vice as one of its most striking features. The history of the revolutionary war is a chronicle of the triumph of the virtuous hero, the great general, who by his tremendous example, by an act of political will of awesome proportions, was able to win a war while never having achieved adequate economic, political, or even moral support. Thus, while Marshall did perceive the possibilities for and value of a virtuous citizenry, he was skeptical about its dependability over the long term after the exhaustion of its initial enthusiasm. He lacked high regard, for example, for its undisciplined representation in the form of the state militia.[31]

DEBT AND DEMOCRATIC DECLINE

Money is the second key symbol in Marshall's republican mythology. A coherent political perspective requires attention to the economic world. In Marshall's case, money is an aspect of political morality and psychology. He associated decline and the vice that causes it to the rise of paper money. This important aspect of Marshall's thought found an appropriate representation in the Constitution itself. It is the theme that is established early in the biography and carries throughout. It is this theme that helps to draw myth and narrative together to illustrate the political psychology extant in Marshall's theorizing.

"The connection," says Norman O. Brown, "between money thinking and rational thinking is so deeply ingrained in our practical lives that it seems impossible to question it."[32] Yet it is obvious that there are irrationalist aspects of the "money complex" that represent deep symbolisms about culture and the individuals who comprise it and, of course, those who analyze and write about it, as Marshall did. Psychological theories in general, and Brown's analysis of money in particular, can yield useful insights into Marshall's economic ideas, only the beginnings of which can be outlined here.

Brown can point to the authority of no less a rationalist than J. M. Keynes that "the special attraction of gold and silver is due not to any of the rationalistic considerations generally offered in explanation but to their symbolic identification with the Sun and Moon."[33] Thus, gold's symbolic significance has found powerful expressions at key junctures in American history, often during times of political and economic turmoil, as during the governing crisis of the 1780s, the farm revolt of the 1890s, the Great Depression of the 1930s, and even the "cultural revolutions" of the 1970s. Marshall was a strong advocate of gold and silver as specie and maintained a deep suspicion about paper money "schemes."

That paper money represented depravity for Marshall is expressed at many points in The Life of Washington. One example is provided by the case of Massachusetts, which incurred substantial debts early on in the French and Indian Wars and contended with them via "large emissions of paper money [so] that a considerable depreciation took place, and specie disappeared." The governing authorities unwisely attributed the inflation that ensued not to increased circulation of currency, "its true cause," but to the "decay of trade."[34] Predictably, the immediate result was social conflict. Three factions sprang forward, each with a plan to contain the problem. The first, which we might label the "Party of Virtue," was "actuated by the principle 'honesty is the best policy.'" It was, Marshall assures the reader, quite minuscule, reflecting the quantity of virtue in any given political community. A second faction, which me might call the "Easy Money Party," proposed a private bank to issue bills of credit based upon a pledge of real estates. A third, which we can christen the "Responsible Investment Party," proposed a loan of bills from the government to mortgage real estate, the interest being used to pay off the colony's debt. The first faction, as it was small and perhaps politically astute, merged with the third, resulting in a simple division between those who wanted a policy of responsibility and those who wanted to find "the easy way out." Marshall's analysis slips comfortably into a dualism that pits those with virtue against those without it.

In Marshall's version, the public finance group immediately made a series of loans that were to be repaid with five percent interest per annum, which tended toward increased depreciation of the currency, resulting in more loans, further depreciation, hence, an accelerating downward spiral. As a result, the colony's governor, Mr. Shute, felt what we would now call a real decline in salary and thus demanded an increase, which the legislature refused to supply. The executive-legislative conflict that resulted from this salary dispute lasted, according to Marshall, over a decade, and eventually found its way into the English parliament. The King's pronouncement that Shute should receive a fixed salary sufficient to meet his demands led to friction between the colonial legislature and the King. It was, in other words, a first indication of conflicts that would augur an eventual political revolution.

The colonial legislature simply refused to follow the King's instructions, "Because it is the undoubted right of all Englishmen, by *magna carta*, to raise and dispose of money for the public service, of their own free accord, without compulsion."[35] Various compromises were attempted to allow both the governor and the King to save face, but the representative assembly of Massachusetts declined each. Not until Shute's retirement did the King concede the right of the assembly to decide on salary on a yearly basis. Yet this final settlement allowed the colonists essentially to win.

Marshall spent a good deal of effort chronicling this episode, because he "regarded [it] as an early and an honourable display of the same persevering temper in defence of principle, of the same unconquerable spirit of liberty, which at a later day, and on a more important question, tore the British colonies from a country to which they had been strongly attached."[36] As its causes could be attributed to paper currency, Marshall suggests the profound and highly destabilizing consequences of the simple and shortsighted introduction of such. Not only did it stir legislative defiance in Massachusetts, but once initiated the depreciation's effects never entirely dissipated and eventually provoked "discontents" in a number of colonies.

From attention to Marshall's account of these events, we can again distill a pattern of temporal development. The introduction of a form of paper currency was itself the result of political conflicts that arose from war with barbaric forces (literally—the Indians). Its introduction indicated the presence of unseen moral and political corruptions, which, once promoted, unleashed dormant internal disputes. The first presence of American party strife is discernable. Evident conflict with authority of the crown is manifest for the first time. The stability of the colony has been essentially undermined; its foundation, once disturbed, can never be entirely repaired.

There is more at stake, in other words, in Marshall's reportage, than a simple description of economic history. Marshall's vision is not a liberal one in which order is restored to a threatening "state of nature" by a rationalistic reimplementation of the social contract. Marshall teaches that the introduction of paper currency augers the collapse of political order; it indicates nothing less than a radical deficiency in the existent structure of the political form. While its implications and consequences can be temporarily masked or deflected, its historical imperatives will inevitably prevail.

Marshall's recounting of other actions taken with respect to the currency problem during a later period of the same set of wars reveals his thinking on the connection between political leadership and the economic order of the community. New England incurred larger and larger debts during the many years the wars lasted, which they handled by generating more currency. "Instead of availing themselves of peace, to discharge the debts contracted during the war, they eagerly desired to satisfy every demand on the public treasury, by farther emissions of bills of credit, redeemable at future and distant periods." All problems faced by the colony were blamed on the scarcity of money "and this scarcity was to be removed, not by increased industry, but by putting an additional sum in circulation."[37] The result was accordingly increased depreciation of the value of the currency.

The mass of people were, of course, unable to perceive the destructiveness of the system as they held out "the hope of discharging contracts with less real value than that for which they were made; and to substitute cunning and speculation, for honest and regular industry" (a harbinger of future state actions under the Articles of Confederation). The colony was saved only by the intervention of a farsighted and virtuous republican leader, Mr. Hutchinson, speaker of the Massachusetts assembly. He proposed the idea of redeeming the paper for its real value in specie. This scheme was, however, considered "Utopian" by "many well meaning men" who felt that such a quick depreciation would too greatly shock the colony's economy. But "with great difficulty" the plan was instituted. The results were almost magical as virtue was reinstilled into the populace as "[t]he evils which had been apprehended were soon found to be imaginary."[38]

A community's sustenance depends not on the virtue of a citizenry, which is prone to corruption, but on leaders who can "with great difficulty" prevail against them. Whatever the merits of Federalist economic theory, it is difficult to attribute Marshall's historical recounting of these events to a strictly economic analysis. The immediacy of the transformation in the Massachusetts colony, as depicted by Marshall, was so dramatic (and seems so unlikely, considering our present knowledge of the great difficulties of economic management, even in small communities) that it must be taken for political allegory. The underlying allegorical significance appeals to the mythology of republicanism in which virtue is political and derived from the authority of the statesman.

It is not surprising, then, that Marshall considered the notion that "aggregate value cannot be arbitrarily increased" by augmenting currency as a "political" truth.[39] Concerned, as he was, with the infusion of virtue into the community, he saw prosperity or the lack of it as an indicator of republican virtue (or lack of it). He was not, in other words, so much interested in the economics of prosperity, an essentially liberal concern, as with the distribution of public goodness. Political economy, for Marshall, is political allegory. Economic history is a morality play.

The authors of the classic text on American elite ideology, *The American Business Creed*, once attempted to account for the psychology that lies behind the resistance to nonspecie currencies. "Throughout the advocacy of the gold standard," they argued, "runs the feeling that only metallic money is of real, honest value. Other kinds of money are, in contrast, just pieces of paper. . . . Money is suspect when it can be created at will, without the hard work of mining it."[40] Hard work is an essential virtue in the liberal lexicon of values. What makes Marshall's economics republican is his emphasis on the "will," rather than on the work. Paper money for Marshall is pure will. It is ungrounded in a commitment to public goodness. Paper money represents will undisciplined by demands of civil conduct and public sacrifice. Paper money is temporal, as are republics without the guidance of proper political leadership. Gold lasts. It outlives the vagaries of political rise and decline. For Plato, those who perceived the order behind phenomenal flux would have souls of gold. For Marshall, republican principles are founded upon heroes with golden souls who protect economies with gold specie. For Plato, the psychology of the golden-souled was a clear harmony. For Marshall, a society disconnected from gold would represent a psychology of irrationality and disorder.

The introduction of currency is a significant moment in the story of a community. It foretells the inevitability of future decline. In essence, it is Pocock's "Machiavellion moment." "It is a name for the moment in conceptualized time in which the republic was seen as confronting its own temporal finitude, as attempting to remain morally and politically stable in a stream of irrational events conceived as essentially destructive of all systems of secular stability."[41]

Paper currency symbolized the irrationalist elements that threaten political life that arise from within the human soul. Like the great leader, the gold standard is, for Marshall, another precarious and often unsuccessful dike with which we dam the forces of civilizational decay.

The symbolism of money was highly important in the political outlooks of all Federalists. The large debt that remained after the revolutionary war was a source of deep concern. Not only did it echo the debt crisis that had existed so long in Britain, but it symbolized the promiscuity of the mass of common farmers, and hence provoked fear of democratic nimiety. "Perhaps most frightening," writes Reisman, "was the growing awareness among gentlemen of pockets of deep alienation. Popular conventions, which met with increasing frequency to set prices at pre-Revolutionary levels, declined to invite gentlemen to their proceedings."[42] While it is true that the gold standard "seems unaccountably to have been omitted from the Constitution," it is also true that the concern with debt and the circulation of paper money as a means to depreciate it for the debtors was reflected in the legal tender and contract clauses of the Constitution.

The Constitution, in other words, fulfilled the symbolic mission of suppressing irrationalistic drives for self-dissolution. It became the dam to hold back the forces of popular will as they would become disconnected from the virtuous order imposed by the great republican statesman. And thus as Justice Marshall became the chief judicial exponent of the liberal notion of right in contracts in the *Dartmouth College* case, *Fletcher v. Peck* and *Ogden v. Saunders*, he was extending the republican tradition as well. He carried its mythology into the nineteenth century attached to liberal legality. Moreover, if the Constitution was conceived as a dike, and Marshall stood with his finger in it, holding back the deluge, it is clear that the endurance of the document through time and history would by no means be assured. Thus Marshall's liberalism is infused with a sense of radical insecurity, as are the first significant expressions of commanding constitutional authority. Ironically, the Constitution, conceived in the name of the people, finds its definitive early interpretive transformations in the hands of a republican whose historical sense indicates that "the people," without disciplined leadership, constantly imperil the order of virtuous political life.

THE CONSTITUTION AND THE PEOPLE

Unsurprisingly, the opposition of discipline, virtue, and wise leadership to the slackness of the many is a theme developed with much enthusiasm and in greater detail during Marshall's discussion of the events leading up to the writing and ratification of the Constitution. "The great exertions which had been made by those states in the course of the war, had accumulated a mass of debt, the taxes for the payment of which were the more burdensome, because their fisheries had become unproductive." The outcome was "lax notions concerning public and private faith," which prompted many to see the need for stronger government "sufficiently ample for the protection of the rights of the peaceable and quiet, from the invasions of the licentious and turbulent part of the community."[43]

The "disorderly spirit" that Marshall condemned unleashed itself in "unlicensed conventions." The character of these assemblies was illegitimate; they "vot[ed] their own constitutionality." The groups were motivated by "hostility" and "resentment." They were "tumultuous," "against taxes," and "against the administration of justice," "against lawyers and courts," and, perhaps most atrociously, they demanded "the circulation of a depreciated currency . . . as a relief from the pressure of public and private burdens." Marshall quotes Colonel Humphries's correspondence to Washington approvingly, that "'there was a licentious spirit prevailing among many of the people; a leveling principle . . . and a desire to annihilate all debts, public and private.'"[44]

The imagery of chaos and apocalypse is pervasive. Against this stands the necessity for a "firm constitution." Marshall quotes General Knox that "'Our government must be braced, changed, or altered to secure our lives and our property.'" The Constitution in essence became a barrier erected not, in the optimistic language of the framers, to secure a "more perfect union" and "the blessings of liberty," but to buttress the aspiration for order, discipline, and virtue against the impulses of barbarity, passion, and license.

The Constitution, which became for Marshall the institutional representation of Washington's character, would act to galvanize and cement republican order into the community and work, at least temporarily, to stem a destructive tide. The "party denominated the federal" prevailed in the first elections and it became their charge "to organize a government, to retrieve the national character, to establish a system of revenue, and to create public credit." Such a set of tasks would be "arduous duties," which were "imposed on them by the political situation of their country."[45] Such accomplishments would likely have been impossible without Washington's leadership. He alone was able to stand above the unfolding mythic struggle. "His character was held sacred, and the purity of his motives was admitted by all." And, in spite of conflict that reached all the way to his cabinet (between the secretaries of state and treasury), the "great majority of people" felt "devoted affection" for the President. Yet, as always, there was underlying conflict "in several of the state assemblies, especially in the southern division of the continent, serious evidence of dissatisfaction were exhibited."[46]

Marshall's interpretation of the conflict between Jefferson and Hamilton conceives it as indicating a larger conflict emerging within the society that was a threat to the temporary order and stability that had been imposed by the example of

Washington's character. At first at least, it was not so much that Hamilton was right and Jefferson wrong, but that the presence of the conflict between these two characters, both of whom Marshall represents as having sincerely held political beliefs, each with a degree of merit, foretells the awakening of a truly national conflict. The mere presence of conflict at the highest levels casts doubt upon Washington's ability to command the citizenry. Thus, "the schism in the cabinet was a subject of extreme mortification to the President."[47] And Washington, at this point in his life and career, seemed almost unable to suppress it. "[His] earnest endeavors to sooth the angry passions and to conciliate the jarring discords of the cabinet were unsuccessful. The hostility which was so much and so sincerely lamented sustained no diminution, and its consequences became every day more diffusive."[48]

Marshall viewed this cabinet conflict as one of the chief causes of the Whiskey Rebellion. One of its "immediate effects," so he tells us, "was the encouragement they afforded to a daring and criminal resistance which was made to the execution of the laws imposing a duty on spirits distilled within the United States." Marshall's hierarchical understanding of the distribution of virtues within the society is evident. A flaw at the top of the structure weakens and cracks, and the forces of entropy begin to seep and eventually gush outward. Invariably there are those lurking on the borders of civilization determined to subvert it at the least expression of political weakness. Marshall was clearly not inclined to celebrate rebellion and revolutionary enthusiasm as Jefferson the future President, who, ironically, seemed to enjoy considering the possibilities of a "little rebellion now and then."

The intense ongoing struggle infected the question of what ought to be the American position in English-French hostilities. Marshall had no sympathy with the French revolutionists. They "formed the mad and wicked project of spreading their doctrine of equality among persons, between whom distinctions and prejudices exist to be subdued only by the grave."[49] But it is their effect upon the directions of American party struggles that Marshall finds most baneful. The "fervour of democracy" was beginning to overtake the nation and might soon affect even the President. The party divisions "which are inherent in the nature of popular government, by which the chief magistrate, however unexceptional his conduct, and however exalted his character, must, sooner or later, be more or less affected, were beginning to be essentially influenced by the great events of Europe."[50] The struggle between England and France, and the tendency of the "democratic societies" of America to identify with the French Revolution, each represented the perils of popular sovereignty in Marshall's eyes. Many Americans, including Jefferson, saw the French Revolution as the manifestation of an essentially democratic impulse. When the monarchy was overthrown "the people of the United States seemed electrified by the measure, and its influence was felt by the whole society."[51] "The constitution of France, therefore, was generally received with unqualified plaudits."[52] The French "constitution" in Marshall's view was not democratic, in spite of its denomination as such by the Jacobins and the American Republicans.

The revolution did not, to Marshall's thinking, actually represent the will of the French people. "The course of the revolution," he states, "had been attended with circumstances which militate against a full conviction of its having been brought to its present stage, by such a free, regular, and deliberate act of the nation, as ought to silence all scruples about the validity of what had been done."[53] We know, from Marshall's statements in *McCulloch* and other opinions, that he, sometimes at least, saw such a calm and deliberate action as exactly what transpired during the writing and ratification of the American Constitution. Popular will, for Marshall, had two aspects, which correspond to classical and republican notions of the divisions within the human soul, and which can achieve two very different political outcomes. Given the proper grounding in virtue, strong leadership, and perhaps a fair amount of good fortune, the people are capable of achieving their best aspects and representing them in the form of "balanced government."[54] In this atmosphere, Marshall suggests, authentic popular sovereignty is expressed. A constitution, conceived under such circumstances, does not "settle" the problem of class interest and political passion, but it does create dikes, which prevent conflict from overwhelming stable order, at least for a time.

The French Revolution, on the other hand, in spite of its nominally democratic character, did not represent the people's genuine aspirations. The people of France were acting irrationally and thus were not capable of bona fide consent. Incapable of deliberate choices, they were swept, unknowingly, into a despotism of violence. Marshall thus expressed sympathy with those who "doubt whether the present possessors of power ought to be considered as having acquired it with the real consent of France, or as having seized it by violence." France, thus, essentially had no constitution and Marshall doubted "whether the existing system could be considered permanent, or merely temporary."[55] Permanence connotes stability, a victory of deliberation over passion. In this country the fever rose as well. Marshall characterized as "extraordinary" the "sentiment" that "the people alone were the basis of government. All powers being derived from them, might, by them, be withdrawn at pleasure."[56] Marshall's view of the democratic elements is harsh. He states that the "friends of the administration" (of which Jefferson is clearly one) "were so blinded by their passion for France as to confound crime with meritorious deeds, and to abolish the natural distinction between virtue and vice." They "were not the friends of real and rational liberty."[57]

The effects upon America were extremely unsettling to Marshall, as they posed a potential threat to "authentic" democratic government at home. The proclamation of neutrality provided the opportunity for democratic elements even to challenge the exalted place of Washington. "[I]t presented the first occasion . . . for assaulting a character, around which the affections of the people had thrown an armour theretofore deemed sacred."[58] Washington, however, remained unaffected. And the "zeal and enthusiasm" that seemed to greet Citizen Genet in support of the French revolutionaries against the British, "found no advocate in either branch of the legislature." The "people's body" was ultimately checked only by the vitality of Washington's residual authority. "That this circumstance is, in great measure, to be ascribed to the temperate conduct of the executive, and to the convincing arguments with which its decision were supported, ought not to be doubted." The executive stood its ground of neutrality in spite of the fact that the "odium" that the decision produced "sustained no diminution."[59]

CONCLUSION

It is important finally, to consider that whatever the actual history of the early American period, Marshall's perception of it is worth our attention. What may have transpired at Jamestown, in the colonial New England legislatures, or between Hamilton and Jefferson, will continue to be the subject of historical disputation, and that is entirely as it should be. Apprehension of Marshall's historical sensibilities, while it will not resolve historical disputes, does illuminate the political thinking of this most influential Chief Justice and thus contributes to our understanding of the interpreted Constitution. In Marshall's fractious history, dangerous conflicts stained the American political tapestry. Preexisting Washington, they also led him toward office. They threatened his administration, reflecting antagonisms between regions and classes.

Marshall, while admirably attempting an "objective" recounting of events, conceived a historical perspective that was ideologically republican in terms of its depiction of the relationship of the forces of what he considered as virtue and vice. Thus Charles Beard was correct to characterize Marshall as a conflict historian. The conflicts that Marshall perceived as basic to American history ultimately correspond to two forms of popular rule, one deliberate, rational, and constitutional, the other impassioned, irrational, and illegitimate. These also correspond to the republican distinctions between a world governed by *virtu* and one overwhelmed by *fortuna*. The conflict historian and the republican revisionist are thus members of the same community of historical interpretation. John Diggins is therefore probably wrong to assert that, "With Jefferson America left the world of classical republicanism behind."[60]

The death of Washington would place new demands on the developing nation. No longer would the conflicts of the few and the many be subject to the wise ordering of America's greatest general and statesman. And, of course, fundamental conflict was not long suppressed as Jefferson's election and his disputes with the Court put Marshall in the position of, in effect, taking Washington's place. In this sense Marshall's *Life* is autobiography. While he never claimed for himself the virtues of the country's "first father," his authoritative proclamations of the Constitution's virtues in the face of Republican attacks effectively made Marshall, like Washington, an indispensible protector of the young republic. He would interpret the Constitution to channel what he saw as dangerous democratic energy toward constructive ends in a perhaps ultimately futile attempt to forestall the fulfillment of the "Machiavellian moment."

NOTES

1. L. HARTZ, THE LIBERAL TRADITION IN AMERICA: AN INTERPRETATION OF AMERICAN THOUGHT SINCE THE REVOLUTION 11 (1964).

2. *See* C. BEARD, AN ECONOMIC INTERPRETATION OF THE CONSTITUTION OF THE UNITED STATES (1960).

3. 4 A. BEVERIDGE, THE LIFE OF JOHN MARSHALL 461–517; 2 W. CROSSKEY, POLITICS AND THE CONSTITUTION IN THE HISTORY OF THE UNITED STATES (1953); and R. FAULKNER, THE JURISPRUDENCE OF JOHN MARSHALL (1968).

4. FAULKNER, *supra* note 3, at 4.

5. *See* R. MATTHEWS, THE RADICAL POLITICS OF THOMAS JEFFERSON: A REVISIONIST VIEW (1984); G. WILLS, INVENTING AMERICA: JEFFERSON'S DECLARATION OF INDEPENDENCE (1978). *But see* J. P. DIGGINS, THE LOST SOUL OF AMERICAN POLITICS (1984).

6. FAULKNER, *supra* note 3, at 46.

7. G. WOOD, THE CREATION OF THE AMERICAN REPUBLIC: 1776–1787, at 59 (1969).

8. J.G.A. POCOCK, THE MACHIAVELLIAN MOMENT: FLORENTINE POLITICAL THOUGHT AND THE ATLANTIC REPUBLICAN TRADITION (1975).

9. THE LAWS OF PLATO (T. Pangle trans. 1980); THE REPUBLIC OF PLATO (F. M. Cornford trans. 1961).

10. 3 E. VOEGELIN, ORDER AND HISTORY: PLATO AND ARISTOTLE 218 (1957).

11. McCulloch v. Maryland, 4 Wheat. 316 (1819).

12. *Id.*

13. POCOCK, *supra* note 8, at 95.

14. J. ROBERTSON, AMERICAN MYTH: AMERICAN REALITY 21 (1980).

15. *See* F. NIETZSCHE, THE USE AND ABUSE OF HISTORY 12–13 (A. Collins trans. 1957).

16. FAULKNER, *supra* note 3, at 124–33.

17. *Id.* at 125.

18. 1 J. MARSHALL, THE LIFE OF WASHINGTON 24 (Citizen's Guild ed. 1926).

19. *Id.* at 26.

20. *Id.* at 29.

21. *Id.* at 33.

22. Marshall's was an oversimplified understanding of early Virginia history. For a more complete view, which places much responsibility for these internal conflicts on harsh leadership, *see* T. WERTENBERG, VIRGINIA UNDER THE STUARTS (1914).

23. POCOCK, *supra* note 8, at 78.

24. 4 BEVERIDGE, *supra* note 3, at 242.

25. N. MACHIAVELLI, THE DISCOURSES OF NICCOLO MACHIAVELLI 216–17 (1950).

26. *Id.* at 208.

27. POCOCK, *supra* note 8, at 363.

28. 1 MARSHALL, *supra* note 18, at 53–54.

29. *Id.* at 54–55.

30. MACHIAVELLI, *supra* note 25, at 214.

31. *See* 1 MARSHALL, *supra* note 18, at 474.

32. N. BROWN, LIFE AGAINST DEATH: THE PSYCHOANALYTIC MEANING OF HISTORY 234 (1959).

33. 1 MARSHALL, *supra* note 18, at 247.

34. *Id.* at 218.

35. *Id.* at 230.

36. *Id.* at 236.

37. *Id.* at 280.

38. *Id.* at 281.

39. *Id.* at 280.

40. F. SUTTON, S. HARRIS, C. KARPIN, and J. TOBIN, THE AMERICAN BUSINESS CREED 243 (1956).

41. POCOCK, *supra* note 8, at viii.

42. Reisman, *Money, Credit, and Federalist Political Economy* in BEYOND CONFEDERATION: ORIGINS OF THE CONSTITUTION AND AMERICAN NATIONAL IDENTITY 128–42 (R. Beeman, S. Botein, and E. Carter eds. 1987).

43. 4 MARSHALL, *supra* note 18, at 221.

44. *Id.* at 221, 222, 223.

45. *Id.* at 401.

46. *Id.* at 403.

47. *Id.* at 452.

48. *Id.*

49. *Id.* at 460.

50. *Id.* at 480.

51. *Id.* at 482.

52. *Id.*.

53. 5 *Id.* at 12.

54. 4 *Id.* at 482.

55. 5 *Id.* at 12.

56. *Id.* at 56.

57. *Id.* at 151.

58. *Id.* at 14.

59. *Id.* at 82.

60. J. DIGGINS, THE LOST SOUL OF AMERICAN POLITICS: VIRTUE, SELF-INTEREST, AND THE FOUNDATIONS OF LIBERALISM 40 (1984).

5

John Marshall on History, Virtue, and Legality

RICHARD A. BRISBIN, JR.

Historians often recount the politics of the early American republics as an adversarial contest between two political party ideologies, Federalist and Jeffersonian. Their discussion posits the existence of two parties that proposed different social and economic theories or that behaved like twentieth-century liberals and conservatives.[1] Yet the discussion of conflicts between the two party ideologies often ignores how the liberal democratic state emerged from hierarchical and republican forms of political association.

Between the Stamp Act crisis of 1765 and the ratification of the Constitution a paradigm of liberal democratic political organization emerged in America; however, the new political paradigm lacked a firm cultural and institutional basis. During the decades of the early nineteenth century John Marshall contributed to the legitimation of the liberal political reconstruction of the revolutionary era. This chapter is a study of the political values of the Chief Justice and his contribution to the transition of American politics into the liberal democracy of the nineteenth century.

MARSHALL AND THE POLITICAL IDEAS OF HIS ERA

Marshall expressed his political beliefs during a period of a major change in the paradigms of political discourse in the West.[2] The predominant paradigm of political practice in the eighteenth-century world was hierarchical or patron-client.[3] Although the American colonies avoided the extremes of European patron-client politics, there was control of all significant economic and security decisions by the Privy Council in London and the colonies had patterns of hierarchical politics.[4]

When the American revolutionaries criticized the "corruption" caused by hierarchical politics in the American colonies, they employed legal arguments and the political ideas of the classical republican paradigm of politics. The legal arguments used against royal authority during the English revolution of the seventeenth century and in defense of customary legal privileges and liberties reappeared in the American attack on the imperial reassertion of hierarchical control by parliamentary agents in the colonies.[5]

The other critique of hierarchical politics, classical republicanism, emphasized the value of the organic solidarity of the community as a defense against the threat of despotism by British leaders.[6] Republican theorists assumed that people realize their complete moral and rational nature only in the political community. According to their reading of history, republics fail if the reason of the community and the harmony of traditional principles of right reason found in natural law and the common law give way to private passions. Since political change in time might lead to the abandonment of reason, the degeneration or "corruption" of civic virtue (defined as a passion for the public good), and the rise of a monopoly on power or "despotism," republicans viewed change warily.

Because they feared that a politics of large-scale institutions caused the corruption of human nature and the decline of civic virtue, they favored decentralized rule and small republics. They believed that the political space of the small republic permitted direct popular action to resolve problems by means of the community meeting, the jury, the militia muster, and popular conventions. Through such activities the community would rationally discuss and develop a consensus on the best course of action. The community also would select the virtuous leaders or statesmen who would dispassionately promote the good life for the community by enforcing the consensus of community sentiment. Justice and the good life were achieved when rational actions produced a peaceful society filled with autonomous individuals who could share in the pursuit of the common good.[7]

The success of the American Revolution created the need for a stable political order of large scale to bind the states into a nation. A new paradigm of liberal democracy offered potential for a governance of the large polity not afforded by republicanism.[8] By combining the ideas of John Locke on human nature and government with the ideas of the Scottish Enlightenment scholars on economics and interest, and the constitutional ideas of Baron de Montesquieu and the English legal tradition, American politicians crafted a unique liberal democracy.[9]

American liberal democracy emphasized the conflict of human interests. Liberal democracy transferred political debate from the search for the common good to the organization of the best means of controlling interests in the more complex social and political world of postrevolutionary America. In a liberal political world the public reserved the capacity to alter political institutions over time to improve the exercise of their interests. Through the exercise of this liberty, democratic citizens would realize infinite possibilities in their lives and political communities.

Liberal democracy also narrowed the space of political activity. Politics became a science confined to the technique of governing. The liberal polity banned ranks and paid little attention to moral order, virtuous leadership, and the control of passion.[10] Liberalism reduced the public role in politics from debates about the common good to discussions of the technique of controlling interests. Liberalism thus freed human interests from community concerns and allowed individuals the space to choose to participate in politics or to enjoy a peaceful life free of community definitions of the good life. In the liberal state justice became the preservation of personal liberty from the community by rules or laws. To develop and enforce the rules and laws necessary to preserve liberty, the government became a secular and soulless set of institutions. Government was not to seek great ends or to educate people for the service to the common good. It was to maintain the rules and laws protecting the liberties of interests and servicing the needs of interests.[11]

Although the drafting of the Constitution was the preeminent event in the creation of a liberal democratic politics in America, liberal politics did not achieve legitimacy and functional richness until Jacksonian times.[12] During the early republic two institutions emerged to educate the citizenry in the legitimacy of liberal politics and to enforce the liberal ideology: the mass political party and the courts.[13]

The Jeffersonian movement supported the transition to a liberal democracy in the United States through its conviction that parties could help people organize to govern themselves.[14] Through the party the people would mobilize to control legislative policy making. Although Jeffersonians did not fully realize the governing potential of mass parties, their commitment to collective efforts to control politics pointed the way to the mass political party representing selected interests devised by the Jacksonians.[15]

American courts, constitutionally separated from the other institutions of government, became an independent force in policy making in the early republic. No longer an arm of royal administration and an instrument of gentry control of the laboring classes, they began to create a body of rules favoring economic development through the efforts of private interests. They "released the creative energy" of the people to pursue personal interests.[16]

Most scholarship on John Marshall, with a few exceptions, has not examined the place of his thought in relation to the construction of the liberal democratic state of parties and courts. Robert Faulkner illustrated how Marshall constructed his political positions on a foundation of ideas drawn from liberal political discourse.[17] In contrast, William Nelson argued Marshall's ideas came more from eighteenth-century sources.[18] George Haskins and Herbert Johnson portrayed Marshall as an instrumental figure in the transformation of

American politics to a "rule of law" guided by the institutional authority of the Supreme Court but designed for democratic ends.[19] G. Edward White placed Marshall within the classical republican tradition, and he saw Marshall as a member of a Court resisting the elimination of the classical republican paradigm of politics. The Marshall Court, from his perspective, attempted to "recast" republicanism "to conceal cultural tensions and divisions" at a time of "cultural change." But White's interpretation failed to examine or explain the inclusion of liberal elements in the decisions of the Marshall Court.[20] Thus, little has been written that explores directly how Marshall's political beliefs fit into the transition between the eighteenth-century classical republican ideology and the legal and institutional structures of nineteenth-century American politics. Because this chapter seeks to associate the fundamental political values of John Marshall with the transition of political thought and the development of the institutions of the American state, it will explicate two aspects of the beliefs that define his paradigm of politics: "history" or his understanding of the ability of society to resolve its problems through time; and "virtue" and "legality," his beliefs in the value of certain patterns of human activity in public space.[21]

JOHN MARSHALL'S PERCEPTION OF HISTORY

For the classical republicans of eighteenth-century Britain, history was a means of contemplating the wisdom and goodness of God's plan or the wisdom of the laws of nature. During the first half of the century, the educated class used history to teach deference, to educate youth in the concept of virtue, to urge the replication of the past, and to reinforce customs. History taught that the world was not subject to human invention.[22] It held that any change in politics or law had to occur through natural or divine processes.[23] This perspective defined liberty only as the freedom to act within the bounds of received tradition. The static quality of the classical and traditional vision of political time taught men to cast their fate to fortune and accept the inevitable natural decline of all human institutions. Through time the corrupting forces of ambition, interest, and luxury would expand and, like a disease, cause the death of republican institutions. For Americans like John Adams, this philosophy of history suggested that constitutional institutions were but a temporary barrier against the resurgence of despotism.[24]

Countering this interpretation of history, British historians like David Hume and Edward Gibbon adopted a more unilinear historical perspective. They believed that history could teach lessons about political action that could obviate the natural tendency to political corruption. Indeed, Hume sought to turn politics into a science, freeing it from fortune and human error.[25] They drew a view of a liberal world freed from the blinders of religion and aware of the possibilities of human existence. Americans like Benjamin Franklin and Thomas Jefferson adopted and extended these ideas. They combined faith in the liberating effect of science, conditions in America that permitted people the opportunity to use natural faculties, and the lessons of the national founding to provide a philosophy of history that suggested that man had unlimited potential in political time.[26]

John Marshall retained a fear of political corruption throughout his life. Much of his reflection on the past was an effort to stave off corruption and loss of civic virtue that could cause the erosion of American liberty. Also, in his use of historical materials he was anxious to teach the lesson that the Constitution was the critical event in American political time, an exceptional achievement that could retard the historical trend toward the corruption of politics. Yet at times he expressed confidence that the people could preserve and improve on the achievement of 1787, a theme running throughout his historical writings, his views on commerce, his nationalist statements, and his applications of international law.

Marshall often used history to teach the merits of civic virtue. His biography of George Washington is very much a lesson in the value of civic virtue for the protection of liberty and the good life. Throughout the biography he portrayed Washington in the most flattering terms. He showed every aspect of Washington's character to be worthy of emulation. Also, he attempted to illustrate that the critics and opponents of Washington willingly or unwillingly used a politics of passion and emotion that threatened the security of American liberty. For example, the supporters of France during his Presidential administrations were labeled "a powerful and secret combination against liberty." Marshall identified them as a party and faction that multiplied evil and that tended "to abolish all distinction between virtue and vice."[27] The result was a history of the United States and especially of the Revolution that had a conspiratorial cast. Everywhere were the secret combinations against liberty, the demagogues who through the mechanisms of party and faction appealed to the passions of the people to insure only their own interests. Against this powerful combination, endeavoring to protect liberty against decline, stood Washington the defender of civic virtue.

In his opinions Marshall rarely used historical knowledge. He cited the *Federalist Papers* at a few critical junctures to associate his ideas with the intent of the framers, but there was little use of historical materials on the national founding.[28] Marshall alluded to what he considered to be the general objectives of the framers, and he tried to teach the values of order and virtue upon which their objectives rest.[29]

Only three of his opinions contained extended use of historical materials. In *Craig v. Missouri*, a case on the authority of state governments to issue notes to circulate as currency, he provided a history of money in the colonies and the United States. The historical lesson was that paper money is "evil" and pernicious. Thus, he found the law of Missouri allowing the issuance of paper notes to be not only a violation of the constitutional authority of the national government, but bad policy signaling a lack of civic virtue in light of history.[30]

In *Johnson and Graham's Lessee v. M'Intosh* Marshall voided sales of lands by Indian tribes to settlers after a lengthy discourse on the history of Indian-settler legal relations. The history, drawing on materials from his first edition of the Washington biography, illustrated the lands belonged to the United States by the succession to a title gained by right of conquest. The Indians were deemed to be only "occupants" of the land. The opinion also implied that conquest was a virtuous action, turning wilderness into productive land, and that national control of the land by conquest was based on the "soundest principles of wisdom and national policy."[31]

In *Worcester v. Georgia*, considering the claim of the Cherokee Indian nation to exemption from state law, Marshall examined again the history of Indian-settler relations to prove that the Cherokee nation was a "distinct community, occupying its own territory," in a contractual legal relationship with the national government. The opinion's use of history confirmed national control over Indians by right of conquest, and it implied the virtues of the paternal protection afforded by national control of Indian property rights.[32] The state thus had no legal authority over the Cherokees.

Marshall also made it clear that the virtue of the national government was superior to that of the Cherokees. In *Cherokee Nation v. Georgia* Marshall noted that the framers excluded the Indian tribes for initiating suits in federal courts because "the idea of appealing to an American court of justice for an assertion of right or a redress of wrong had, perhaps, never entered the mind of an Indian or of his tribe. Their appeal was to the tomahawk, or to the government."[33] Thus, the history of Indian behavior taught a lesson about the superior virtue of the national system of law to the remedies for grievances employed by the Indians.[34]

Although most classical republicans feared that commerce would cause the corruption of civic virtue, Marshall conceived of commerce as a civilizing force in society, as the source of national power to defend liberty, and as a source of broadly distributed economic power in society.[35] Unlike John Adams and John Taylor of Caroline, he did not see the private interest in commerce and the growth of manufacturing as a threat to civic virtue. Like many in the mainstream of Jeffersonian thought, he viewed commerce as virtuous industry and as the development of private virtues with public ramifications. His only major differences with the Jeffersonians were over the role of the national government in commercial development and, less importantly, the place of commercial agriculture.[36]

Marshall wanted a national commercial system because it would promote national greatness. In turn, national greatness would protect the legacy of the Revolution.[37] In *Gibbons v. Ogden* he broadly defined the authority of the national government over a liberally defined conception of commerce. He also wrote that a "narrow construction" of the commerce clause "would cripple the government and render it unequal to the objects for which it is declared to be instituted, and to which the powers given, as fairly understood, render it competent. . . ."[38] The grant of commercial regulatory power in the Constitution was to be read as "an investment of power for the general advantage, in the hands of agents selected for that purpose. . . ."[39] The Congress, with this power "complete in itself" might use its "wisdom" and "discretion" to exercise the power to its "utmost extent" within constitutional limitations.[40] Thus, as in *Brown v. Maryland*, Congress was free to make commercial regulations that restricted state authority, that enhanced life in the community, and that prevented the return of "[t]he oppressed and degraded state of commerce previous to the adoption of the constitution."[41]

Marshall was himself active in commerce. He supported the establishment of a branch of the Bank of the United States in Richmond,[42] and he worked for a system of internal improvements in Virginia.[43] He and his brother invested heavily in the Fairfax lands, and he subsequently became concerned about the protection of land titles by Western land speculators.[44] He took advantage of the greatness of the nation to enrich himself and at the same time to improve his community through time, actions that intermingle civic virtue and the liberal pursuit of self-interest and a liberal progressive vision of history.

John Marshall was a nationalist, but he was not a consolidationist. His desire for a strong national government was rooted more in a fear of historical decline of the security for private interests provided by the nation-state than in a desire to extend its political hegemony. From his perspective the Constitution offered the possibility of an institutional protection against the decay caused by localized interests or uncontrolled factionalism and protection against the danger posed by foreign intervention.[45] For example, in *Cohens v. Virginia* he contended that the constitutional state was to be a bulwark against threats to liberties and "perils it may be destined to encounter" through history. Its supremacy was essential if the choice of the people to use a national scheme of government was "essential to their liberty and to their happiness."[46] The interests of the states and the powers of state governments had to be subordinate because they could be hostile to the choice of the people for the national "Union" created by the Constitution.[47]

Marshall's nationalism and his use of federal judicial power in support of national interests led him into a conflict with critics in Virginia like John Taylor of Caroline. The Virginians believed in the classical republican concept of the small republic. This belief caused them to advance the proposition that the national government resulted from a compact among the states, a compact that restricted federal legislative and judicial authority over state governments. The danger they saw facing American liberty was not the corruption caused by factionalism and the pursuit of self-interest. Instead, they feared the creation of a wealthy aristocracy by the national government. Taylor reasoned that the use of implied powers by the Congress would foster this class and produce the oppression "universally caused by pecuniary fanaticism." Taylor and other Virginians like Spencer Roane thus sought to curb national power largely because they feared it as a threat to the virtue of the agrarian world in which they lived.[48] Ironically, while Marshall used a classical republican theory of history to defend the value of liberal political institutions, his Virginia opponents used a classical republican conception of the virtue of small republics to attack his decisions.

Despite his hostility to the compact theory of the Union, Marshall's nationalism did not insure the hegemony of national power because he respected the concurrent powers of state governments. States could resolve conflicts in their courts if they did not impede federal laws, states could regulate commerce if they did not threaten the flow of interstate trade, and states could restrict personal rights.[49] Consequently, Marshall's Union was one in which the national government and its judiciary were to act to curtail the factional conflicts among and within the states. Its powers were to be used to prevent the historical decay of the constitutional principles that established liberal political institutions.

Through his interpretations of international law, Marshall sought to fend off threats to the historical achievement of the Revolution through the encouragement of peace. To insure peace and prevent national decline he supported American neutrality during the Washington administration.[50] But his experience in France at the hands of Talleyrand and his agents X, Y, and Z in 1797 and 1798 convinced him that the United States had to be recognized as an equal on the international scene for the nation to survive in peace.[51] Especially he came to believe that peace had to be secured by law and not simply by bribes offered to other nations or by commercial or military leadership.

Marshall pursued his desire to shield the nation from a decline caused by external forces through his decisions on the law of nations and related cases with an international dimension. Marshall's use of international law drew on standard European sources and pragmatically avoided allegiance to any specific school of international jurisprudence.[52] The United States was to "receive the law of nations in its modern state of Purity and refinement,"[53] as "founded on the great and immutable principles of equity and natural justice" as applied by the courts of various nations.[54] "A nation would justly be considered as violating its faith . . . which should suddenly and without previous notice, exercise its territorial powers in a manner not consistent to the usages and received obligations of the civilized world."[55]

From this standard he derived several related principles to insure peace. American law was to be construed when possible to avoid conflicts with the law of nations.[56] Treaties were to be strictly construed.[57] American courts were to respect the laws and judicial decisions of other nations recognized by the United States.[58] Federal courts could not provide relief when the incident occurred within the jurisdiction of another nation.[59] American law did not extend to foreign warships in American waters, in part because "[t]he world being composed of distinct sovereignties, . . . mutual benefit is promoted by intercourse with each other and by an interchange of those good offices which humanity dictates and its wants required. . . ."[60]

Besides applying the law of nations, Marshall supported executive and legislative branch foreign policy decisions that protected the nation from external threats. The courts, according to Marshall, should read treaties arranged by the executive as the law of the land and as intended by the executive or Congress.[61] The only caveat was his decision that the discretion of a president to deal with an international crisis was limited by the situation and any statutory procedures established by the Congress.[62]

To promote peaceful contacts among nations and their peoples, Marshall's opinions on the law of nations protected private interests. He held that Americans had to respect the property of foreign nationals; damage to their interests by American officials was improper and deserved compensation, for "[t]he honor and character of the nation are concerned with suppressing such irregularities."[63] He left undisturbed the property rights of individuals in regions acquired by the United States.[64] He protected the rights in property of neutrals during wartime by restricting American control over friendly sovereigns.[65] He attempted to protect the economic interests of American merchants whose goods were caught in the vicissitudes of war.[66] He protected the property rights granted under a treaty even after the treaty was repealed.[67] He recognized the international legality of foreign law allowing the slave trade even though the slave trade violated domestic American law.[68] The only restrictions he placed on property interests involved the seizure of assets of foreign nationals in wartime or as arranged by treaty.[69]

In a letter to Justice Joseph Story, Marshall confessed a fear that the Constitution was "not to be so long lived as its friends have hoped."[70] Southern threats and nullification especially troubled him.[71] He reaffirmed the value of the nation's founding principles, but he offered little comfort for its future. He evidenced limited faith that the political institutions of the nation could ultimately escape the wheel of fortune. Thus, Marshall's version of history has a classical republican content. But his concern for commerce, his desire to fend off threats to the Constitution through the use of law, and his respect for private property interests indicate the influence of liberal ideas on his actions. In these concerns he displayed an appreciation of the use of political institutions and law as a restraint on interest and as a palliative against the threat of national decline.

JOHN MARSHALL AND THE NATURE OF POLITICAL ACTIVITY

At the Virginia Convention that ratified the Constitution, Marshall said, "What are the favorite maxims of Democracy? A strict observance of justice and public faith, and a steady adherence to virtue."[72] For Marshall public opinion was not to be the sole desideratum of proper public policy.[73] Marshall placed power in the hands of national leaders to insure that political activity served the community good. Decisions in "political space," in institutions at a point in time, had only to secure the broadly defined goals offered by community sentiments. He conceived of political leaders acting not just as delegates but also as virtual representatives. In considering whether the residents of the District of Columbia could be taxed without representation, he wrote, "Although in theory it might be more congenial to the spirit of our institutions to admit a representative from the district, it may be doubted whether, in fact, its interests thereby would be rendered more secure. . . ."[74]

Marshall's concern with the public virtue of political leaders rested on the assumption that men possessed "factious" tempers and interests that had to be controlled by the virtuous in the public arena.[75] Yet despite the strength of his conviction on the necessity of virtuous leadership, Marshall broke from it in one significant respect: his liberal theory of law.

Marshall's concern with the virtue of leaders appears in his views on partisanship, his biography of Washington, his definition of the role of the judiciary at the Virginia Constitution Convention of 1829-30, and his support of the doctrine of implied powers. He thought that party and interest conflicts caused the neglect of the greater community good and encouraged leadership that lacked civic virtue.[76] He especially associated this sort of interested and "corrupt" politics with the person of Thomas Jefferson.[77] Marshall saw only the decline of the nation in the Jeffersonian emphasis on party and local democracy. In contrast, he always saw himself as free of partisanship.[78] During the dispute over the Alien and Sedition Acts in 1798 he criticized his Federalist allies for creating "useless" party strife by enacting these laws.[79] He feared partisanship. In a letter written in his last years, he summarized his fears, writing, "Vast masses, united closely, move in opposite directions, animated with the most hostile feelings toward one another—What is to be the effect of all this? . . . I now dread the consequences which I once thought imaginary."[80]

In his biography of Washington, Marshall made a case for leadership by the patriot statesman.[81] Using an argument similar to the classical republican glorification of virtuous leadership, and especially Lord Bolingbroke's idea of the patriot king, he made Washington the exemplar of the traits necessary among leaders of free people. Washington was a "real republican, devoted to the constitution of his country, and to the system of equal political rights on which it is founded," who possessed the traits of republican greatness.[82] The traits included Washington's direction of his ambition to the service of the public good, his innate respect for others, and his civic morality. Washington also was praised for a humanism grounded in religious morality, his caution, his "systematic" conduct, his ability to understand human motives, and his "practical good sense" and "sound judgment" in public affairs. Marshall used the example of Washington to praise leaders who do not seek greatness and personal honor. For Marshall, Washington was unconcerned with personal aggrandizement, lacked a penchant for wiliness and intrigue, and never engaged in duplicity. He had "incorruptible" integrity.[83] Washington had a classic virtue, a "firmness" rather than a desire for "popular favour";[84] his was not the cunning virtue of a Machiavellian prince.

Marshall voiced attachment to the classical conception of virtuous leadership during his service at the Virginia Constitutional Convention of 1829–30.[85] The major issues confronting the convention were suffrage and apportionment. Although he presented a petition from his constituents calling for expanded suffrage, Marshall expressed a reluctance to make significant alterations in the method of selecting legislators. He sought a compromise between the virtual and the delegate approaches to representation defended at the convention by the different regions of the state.[86] He also spoke in favor of judicial independence in addressing the questions of life tenure and judicial removal for judges. For Marshall the "whole good" of the convention was threatened by "the evil of changing the tenure of the judicial office."[87] "The independence of all those who try cause between man and man, and between a man and his Government, can be maintained only by the tenure of office."[88] Life tenure, he believed, would cause men of "capacity, and of legal knowledge" to seek judicial office and prevent the "greatest scourge" on a people, a "corrupt, or a dependent judiciary."[89]

Marshall also defended the Virginia system of county courts at the convention. These courts had legislative and petty judicial functions much like the English justices of the peace in quarter sessions. An elite of lawyer-planters controlled these courts because of the self-perpetuating method of membership selection. The judges nominated replacements to the court, the governor appointed the nominee, and the new judge went on to serve a term for life.[90] Thus, a body of social betters tied to the traditions of the community, the class with civic virtue, controlled local public policy. Marshall stated that the members of the court were the best judge of "who are fit persons to fill them."[91] He was against further legislative control or professionalism in the county court.[92]

His argument for implied congressional powers shows Marshall defending the exercise of legislative authority in an effort to improve the public happiness and public liberty. Marshall displayed a confidence in the capacity of the people to select legislators to enhance their interests.[93] He then assumed that the legislators had to be entrusted with ample powers to secure the happiness and prosperity of the nation.[94] Within the "dictates of reason" they could select the means to execute its constitutional powers, and, "[i]t would be unwise to attempt to provide, by immutable rules, for exigencies which, if foreseen at all, must have been seen dimly, and which can best be provided for as they occur."[95] "Congress must possess the choice of means, and must be empowered to use any means which are in fact conducive to the exercise of a power granted by the constitution."[96] To restrain the powers of the legislators unreasonably would render "the Government incompetent to its great objects. . ." of benefit to the community.[97] Therefore, "the powers of a state cannot rightfully be so exercised as to impede and obstruct the free course of those measures which the government of the states united may rightfully adopt."[98]

Despite his attention to the virtue of leaders as a means of control over the politics of interest, Marshall's application of law to conflicts is characterized by a liberal approach to social control. Like James Madison in *The Federalist* No. 10, Marshall did not presume that the virtue of political leaders could be guaranteed.[99] Madison's response to this problem was the creation of conflicting interests in the large republic, Jefferson's solution was party conflict, but Marshall preferred the supremacy of law. By establishing the supremacy of a national body of law the choices of leaders would be controlled by more than their own virtue. A legal check on leaders would prevent irrational action and insure that they remained loyal to the preferences of the electorate. Because Marshall's use of law equated the achievement of a just society with rule following, it adhered to a basic premise of liberalism that law should be an instrument of political control and not an expression of community morality or a means of educating persons about the common good.

The argument for judicial review employed by Marshall in *Marbury v. Madison* evidences his attachment to the liberal idea of law. In the first part of the opinion he discussed the right of Marbury to a commission as justice of the peace in the city of Washington and compared the right to the discretion of the executive to withhold the commission. He found that the "President is invested with certain important political powers, in the exercise of which he is to use his own discretion, and is accountable only to his country in his political character and to his conscience."[100] This direction extended to subordinate executive officers operating under Presidential authority. Despite the assumption of an executive discretion that could be used in support of civic ends, he recognized legal limits on its use. The vested right of Marbury to his commission restricted the use of executive power; the executive could not "sport away the vested rights of others."[101] Because Marbury had rights protected by legislative act, the executive had violated his legal duty to act in the furtherance of protected liberty.[102]

In the second part of the opinion Marshall considered the availability of judicial relief for the damage to Marbury's right. First, Marshall affirmed the supremacy of the Constitution over ordinary legislative acts.[103] Second, he used the concept of separated powers to determine, "It is emphatically the province and duty of the judicial department to say what the law is."[104] In interpreting the Constitution, Marshall placed great confidence in the capacity of the judiciary to fulfill its constitutional function. His conception of the role of the judiciary assumed that it had the legal authority to interpret the will of the people as contained in the Constitution. Therefore he concluded that the Court could determine if Marbury could constitutionally obtain judicial relief under the provision on mandamus in the Judiciary Act of 1787.[105] Finally, Marshall noted that the judiciary's oath of office compelled it to exercise its judgment and place the Constitution above ordinary law.[106] The decision thus not only established the principle of judicial review, it recognized the Supreme Court as an institution that could use its legal power when other public officials acted in defiance of the constitutionally stated wishes of the people.

Marshall also wrote on the need for courts to provide a rational or "scientific" common law in tune with republican principles, to respect the statutes drawn by legislatures, and to use their power within the scope of constitutional language on jurisdiction and separated powers. Marshall diminished the scope of the common law and removed the Court from the construction of a social consensus through the common law. He often regarded common law as a reference library of solutions to disputes or a compendium of forms of action rather than a device designed to protect natural rights in property.[107] Drawing on this principle, he recognized and accepted that the Judiciary Act of 1789 incorporated many common law forms of action into federal practice, and he applied state common law in federal civil cases. He also relied on English precedents to support his arguments during his law practice.[108] But he avoided considering or refused to vote for the incorporation of a substantive common law of crimes into federal law by the Court.[109] Because the common law of crimes offered the potential for dragging the Court into partisan conflicts, his vote promoted his idea of a Court that could resolve the conflict of interests from a position of neutrality.[110] Second, he promoted a common law that was rational and that, because of its reasonableness, provided workable legal solutions to disputes between interests.[111] To insure reasonableness, the common law usually needed "[e]xact uniformity of decision," and "when principles are departed from, those substituted in their place ought to be so strongly marked, as not to be misunderstood."[112]

Marshall was reluctant to challenge statutes.[113] His treatment of statutes normally respected the intentions of the legislature, for, "The sole duty of the court is to construe . . . [the] statute according to the words and intent of the Legislature."[114] He established the doctrine that federal courts will adopt a state's construction of its own statutes.[115] Although he broadly construed some statutes in his effort to provide nationalizing constitutional interpretations, this was not his general practice. Words were to be taken in their "natural and usual sense." Statutes were to be read so that "every part is to be considered, and the intention of the legislature to be extracted from the whole."[116]

The jurisdiction of courts was always of concern to Marshall.[117] He recognized that federal court jurisdiction was restrained by the legal authority of the other branches. Although defensive of the autonomy of federal courts from the states, he believed that Congress had the authority to restrict, assign, or especially, augment federal judicial jurisdiction in matters beyond the scope of Article III of the Constitution.[118] He created the political questions doctrine to restrain the Court's power over foreign affairs, in recognition of the legal authority of the other branches.[119] He sought to curtail jury activity that, although representative of the community, went against judicial instructions in the law.[120] Marshall's approach to jurisdiction and his creation of the political questions doctrine thus allowed the Court to protect its legal role in a world of interests and factional politics. The concern for court jurisdiction also signaled a modern professional mind, one concerned with institutionalizing the scope and boundaries of the law and the authority of judges.

Consequently, Marshall's conception of law indicates a limitation on his trust in the virtue of leadership. Although he often favored a prominent place for virtue in the politics of the new republic, law was to guard against the follies of leaders. As a check and control, law became one of the liberal institutional restraints that, like parties, would insure the people's Constitution and the liberties it afforded would remain in place.

CONCLUSION

John Marshall stands as a transitional figure in American political thought. In his understanding of history and political time he remained wedded to many of the cyclical ideas of classical republicanism. Yet his understanding of history also recognized the need for commercial development and the security of the nation across a linear time frame. Likewise, the influence of classical republicanism caused him to demand decision making in political space by virtuous leaders. Yet his views on decision making also advanced the ideas of legalistic and liberal organizational politics. Fearing a historical cycle of corruption and tied to the classical concept of civic virtue, Marshall never made a complete transition to the principles of liberal democracy. Yet he could not avoid the influences of a liberalizing constitutional and political culture on his actions.

NOTES

1. This approach appears in 2 A. Beveridge, The Life of John Marshall 44 (1916–19), which states the thesis, vols. 2 and 3 apply it; Holcombe, *John Marshall as Politician and Political Theorist*, in Chief Justice John Marshall 24 (W. M. Jones ed. 1956); Lerner, *John Marshall and the Campaign of History*, 39 Colum. L. Rev. 396 (1939).

2. For detail on these changes, *see* J. G. A. Pocock, The Machiavellian Moment (1975); A. Hirschman, The Passions and the Interests (1977); and S. Wolin, Politics and Vision 286–434 (1960).

3. The elements of patron-client politics are described in Kaufman, *The Patron-Client Concept and Macro-Politics*, 16 Comp. Stud. in Soc. & Hist. 284 (1974); and Lemarchand & Legg, *Political Clientelism and Development*, 4 Comp. Pol. 149 (1972). For descriptions of the hierarchical aspects of eighteenth-century British politics, *see* N. Landau, The Justices of the Peace 1679–1760 (1984); G. Mingay, English Landed Society in the Eighteenth Century (1963); L. Namier, England in the Age of the American Revolution 3–41 (2d ed. 1961); L. Namier, The Structure of Politics at the Accession of George III (1957); Thompson, *Eighteenth-Century English Society*, 3 Soc. Hist. 133 (1978).

4. *See* J. Smith, Appeals to the Privy Council from the American Plantations (1950) on English control. On colonial elites, *see* R. Towns, (1976); Jordan, *Political Stability and the Emergence of a Native Elite in Maryland, 1660–1715*, in The Chesapeake in the Seventeenth Century 243 (T. Tate and D. Ameriman eds. 1979); Murrin, *The Myths of Colonial Democracy and Royal Decline in Eighteenth-Century America*, 5 Cithara 53 (1965); and C. Syndor, Gentlemen Freeholders (1952); Syndor, *The Responsible Gentry of South Carolina*, in Town & Country 174 (B. Daniels ed. 1978).

5. F. McDonald, Novus Ordo Seclorum 9–142 (1985); J. Reid, In a Defiant Stance (1977); and J. Reid, In Defiance of the Law (1981) discuss both the radical and legal sources of American politics. The legal arguments are discussed in C. McIlwain, The American Revolution (1923). Berthoff & Murrin, *Feudalism, Communalism, and the Yeoman Freeholder*, in Essays on the American Revolution 256 (S. Kurtz and S. Hutson eds. 1973) discuss the Revolution as a reaction against hierarchical politics.

6. B. Bailyn, The Ideological Origins of the American Revolution (1967); Hutson, *Court, Country, and Constitution*, 38 Wm. & Mary Q. 3d ser. 337 (1981); Pocock *supra* note 2, at 506–52; C. Robbins, The Eighteenth Century Commonwealthmen (1959); Shalhope, *Toward a Republican Synthesis*, 29 Wm. & Mary Q. 3d ser. 334 (1982); and G. Wood, The Creation of the American Republic, 1776–1787 (1969) discuss the classical republican contribution to the American Revolution and political thought.

7. Aristotle, Politics 1.13; 4.8–16; Cicero, De Officiis, Cicero, Des Republican I. 25–26; III. 3, 7–8, 22; V. 5–7 provide the classical roots of the paradigm. For its effect on

English thought, *see* Z. Fink, The Classical Republicans (1945); J. G. A. Pocock,*Virtues, Rights, and Manners*, in Virtue, Commerce and History 41–43 (1985), and Pocock, *supra* note 2, at 333–505.

8. Wood, *supra* note 6, at 532–36.

9. As suggested by J. G. A. Pocock, *Authority and Property*, in Virtue, Commerce and History, *supra* note 7, at 51–71, the origins and definition of American liberalism are more complex than is suggested in some widely read studies like L. Hartz, The Liberal Tradition in America 3–86 (1955).

10. *See* Appleby, *What is Still American in the Political Philosophy of Thomas Jefferson?*, 39 Wm. & Mary Q. 3d ser. 287–309 (1982); J. Appleby, Capitalism and a New Social Order 79, n. 1 and *passim* (1984); Appleby, *Republicanism in Old and New Contexts*, 43 Wm. & Mary Q. 3d ser. 20–34 (1986).

11. The definition of liberalism here draws on J. Diggins, The Lost Soul of American Politics 60–66 (1984); A. Hirschman, The Passions and the Interests (1977); S. Holmes, Benjamin Constant and the Making of Modern Liberalism (1984); and Wolin, *supra* note 2, at 286–351.

12. As described in Formisano, *Deferential-Participant Politics*, 68 Am. Pol. Sci. Rev. 473–87 (1973).

13. S. Skowronek, Building a New American State 24–31 (1982).

14. *See* Appleby, *What is Still American in the Political Philosophy of Thomas Jefferson?*, 39 Wm. & Mary Q. 3d ser. 287–309 (1982); J. Appleby, Capitalism and a New Social Order 79, n. 1 and *passim* (1984); Appleby, *Republicanism in Old and New Contexts*, 43 Wm. & Mary Q. 3d ser. 20–34 (1986). Much scholarship stresses the classical republican or English Country Party element in Jeffersonian thought: L. Banning, The Jeffersonian Persuasion (1978); Banning, *Jeffersonian Ideology Revisited*, 43 Wm. & Mary Q. 3d ser. 3–19 (1986); Murrin, *The Great Inversion, or Court versus Country*, in Three British Revolutions 404–30 (J. G. A. Pocock ed. 1980); and Pocock, *supra* note 2, at 526–37, but unlike the work of Appleby it fails to emphasize how that tradition eroded during the early republic and was replaced by liberalism among most Jeffersonians, with the exception of the Old Republican wing of the party.

15. *See* L. Banning, Jeffersonian Persuasion, *supra* note 14, at 161–78, 273–302; R. Hanson, The Democratic Imagination in America 106–20 (1985); Wallace, *Changing Concepts of Party in the United States*, 74 Am. Hist. Rev. 453–91 (1968).

16. The transformation to a more specialized judiciary is partially recounted in Brisbin, *Before Bureaucracy*, 10 The Old Northwest 141–74 (1984). Policy objectives of nineteenth-century American law are discussed in, among many works, L. Friedman, A History of American Law 171–201, 273–302 (2d ed. 1985); H. Hartog, Public Property and Private Power (1983); M. Horwitz, The Transformation of American Law, 1780–1860 (1977); and J. Hurst, Law and the Conditions of Freedom in the Nineteenth Century United States (1956).

17. R. Faulkner, The Jurisprudence of John Marshall 4 (1968).

18. Nelson, *The Eighteenth-Century Background of John Marshall's Constitutional Jurisprudence*, Mich. L. Rev. 893–960 (1978).

19. G. Haskins & H. Johnson, Foundations of Power 7, 365, 395–406 (The Oliver Wendell Holmes Devise History of the Supreme Court of the United States vols. 3–4, 1981).

20. G. E. WHITE, THE MARSHALL COURT AND CULTURAL CHANGE, 1815-35, at 48-75 (The Oliver Wendell Holmes Devise History of the Supreme Court of the United States, vols. 3-4, 1988). White defines five values guiding the Marshall Court; however, the predominant paradigms of political action were republicanism and liberalism.

21. This chapter was completed and originally delivered before the publication of White, *id.*, in which great attention was paid to concepts of time and space and republicanism and liberalism at 48-75. The attention to time and space and republicanism and liberalism in this chapter draws on the work of WOLIN, *supra* note 2, and the materials cited in notes 5-11.

22. *See* Davis, *The Augustan Concept of History* in REASON AND IMAGINATION 213-39 (J. Mazzeo ed. 1962); and J. G. A. Pocock, *Modes of Political and Historical Time in Early Eighteenth-Century England*, in VIRTUE, COMMERCE AND HISTORY *supra* note 7, at 91-102.

23. *See* D. BOORSTIN, THE MYSTERIOUS SCIENCE OF THE LAW 53-84, 166 (1941).

24. L. KERBER, FEDERALISTS IN DISSENT 122-29 (1970).

25. *See* D. HUME, *That Politics May be Reduced to a Science, Of the Origin of Justice and Property*, and *Of the Original Contract*, in DAVID HUME'S POLITICAL ESSAYS 12-23, 28-38, 43-61 (C. Hendel ed. 1953). Hume believed that while the danger of corruption could be avoided, progress was not ordained; see J. G. A. Pocock, *Hume and the American Revolution*, in VIRTUE, COMMERCE AND HISTORY *supra* note 7, at 143-56; and Trevor-Roper, *Gibbon and the Publication of the Decline and Fall of the Roman Empire 1776-1976*, 19 J. LAW & ECON. 489-505, esp. 504 (1976).

26. Persons, *The Cyclical Theory of History in Eighteenth Century America*, 6 AM. Q. 147-63 (1954).

27. 2 J. MARSHALL, THE LIFE OF GEORGE WASHINGTON 348-49 (1835 ed.).

28. *See* McCulloch v. Maryland, 4 Wheat. 264, 390, 406, 416-18; Gibbons v. Ogden, 9 Wheat. 186, 198-201 (1824); Brown v. Maryland, 12 Wheat. 419, 438-39, 445-46 (1827).

29. *See* Cohens. v. Virginia, 6 Wheat. 264, 390, 406, 416-18; Gibbons v. Ogden, 9 Wheat. 186, 198-201 (1824); Brown v. Maryland, 12 Wheat. 419, 438-39, 445-46 (1827).

30. Craig v. Missouri, 4 Pet. 410, 432-36 (1830). Compare Faw v. Marsteller, 2 Cranch 10 (1804) for further evidence of his hostility to paper money.

31. Johnson and Graham's Lessee v. M'Intosh, 8 Wheat. 543, 572-604 (1823).

32. Worcester v. Georgia, 6 Pet. 515, 542-62, esp. 561-62 (1832).

33. Cherokee Nation v. Georgia, 5 Pet. 1, 18 (1831). Marshall conceived of Indian treaties as a contract vesting property rights rather than as international agreements, Meigs v. M'Clung's Lessee, 9 Cranch 11, 18 (1815), further restricting the availability of judicial relief for the tribes. See the perspective commentary in Newmyer, *On Assessing the Court in History*, 21 STAN. L. REV. 544-47 (1969).

34. WHITE *supra* note 20, at 703-30 implies that the reliance of Marshall on common law caused a neglect of the natural rights of Indians.

35. For similar interpretation of commerce, *see* Hume, *Of Commerce*, in D. HUME *supra* note 25, at 130-41.

36. On the commercial views of Adams and Taylor, *see* L. WHARTON, POLITY AND THE PUBLIC GOOD (1980). On Jeffersonian commercial concepts, *see* Appleby, *Commercial Farming and the 'Agrarian Myth' in the Early Republic*, 68 J. AM. HIST. 833-49 (1982); APPLEBY, CAPITALISM AND A NEW SOCIAL ORDER, *supra* note 14 at 25-50; and D. McCOY, THE ELUSIVE REPUBLIC 185-259 (1980).

37. *See* FAULKNER, *supra* note 17, at 38–40.

38. Gibbons v. Ogden, 9 Wheat. at 188.

39. *Id.* at 189.

40. *Id.* at 196–97; *see also* The Brig Wilson v. United States, 30 F. Cas. 239, 245; 1 Brock. 423, 431–32 (1820).

41. Brown v. Maryland, 12 Wheat. at 445.

42. Marshall, Petition, 1792, in 2 THE PAPERS OF JOHN MARSHALL, 118–20 (C. Cullen and H. Johnson eds. 1977) [hereinafter PAPERS OF MARSHALL].

43. *See* 4 BEVERIDGE, *supra* note 1, at 42–45.

44. *See* Marshall, *Hite v. Fairfax*, in 1 PAPERS OF MARSHALL 151–164 (H. Johnson, ed. 1974); *Fairfax Lands, Editorial Note*, 2 PAPERS OF MARSHALL 140–49; 1 BEVERIDGE *supra* note 1, at 191–96; 2 *id.* at 203–11; and HASKINS & JOHNSON, *supra* note 19, at 357–65.

45. Marshall, *Speech (Virginia Convention to Ratify the Constitution, 2 June 1788)*, 1 PAPERS OF MARSHALL, *supra* note 42, at 260–61.

46. Cohens v. Virginia, 6 Wheat. at 380.

47. *Id.* at 388–94, 402–4.

48. *See* J. TAYLOR, CONSTRUCTION CONSTRUED AND CONSTITUTIONS VINDICATED (1820) and *Roane's 'Hampden' Essays*, in JOHN MARSHALL'S DEFENSE OF MCCULLOCH V. MARYLAND 106–54, esp. 133–37 (G. Gunther ed. 1969).

49. Cohens v. Virginia, 6 Wheat. at 414–15; Gibbons v. Ogden, 9 Wheat. at 209–11; Brown v. Maryland, 12 Wheat. at 443–48; Willson v. Black Bird Creek Marsh Co., 2 Pet. 250 (1829); Barron v. Baltimore, 7 Pet. 243 (1833).

50. Letter from Marshall to Augustine Davis (Sept. 11, 1793), 2 PAPERS OF MARSHALL, *supra* note 42, at 201–7; letter from Marshall to Augustine Davis (Oct. 16, 1793), 2 PAPERS OF MARSHALL, *supra* note 42, at 221–28; and letter from Marshall to Augustine Davis (Nov. 13, 1793), 2 PAPERS OF MARSHALL, *supra* note 42, at 231–47.

51. *See* Dumbauld, *John Marshall and Treaty Law*, 50 AM. J. INT'L. L. 69–80 (1956); MARSHALL, *Paris Journal*, 3 PAPERS OF MARSHALL, *supra* note 42, at 84, 181; 2 PAPERS OF MARSHALL *supra* note 42, at 231–47.

52. *See* Dumbauld, *John Marshall and the Law of Nations*, 104 U. PA. L. REV. 40 (1955); WHITE, *supra* note 20 at 893; B. ZIEGLER, THE INTERNATIONAL LAW OF JOHN MARSHALL 6–11 (1939).

53. Brown v. United States, 8 Cranch 110 (1814).

54. The Venus, 8 Cranch 253, 297 (1814) (Marshall, C. J., concurring); *see also* Thirty Hogsheads of Sugar v. Boyle, 9 Cranch 131, 198 (1815).

55. Schooner Exchange v. McFadden, 7 Cranch 116, 137 (1812).

56. Murray v. Schooner the Charming Betsey, 2 Cranch 64 (1804).

57. The Nereide, 9 Cranch 388, 419 (1815).

58. Church v. Hubbart, 2 Cranch 187 (1804); Rose v. Himely, 4 Cranch 241, 271–79 (1808); Hudson v. Guestier, 4 Cranch 293 (1808); Williams v. Armyrod, 7 Cranch 423 (1813); Thirty Hogsheads of Sugar v. Boyle, 9 Cranch at 131; Kirkpatrick v. Gibson, 14 F. Cas. 683, 2 Brock. 388 (1828).

59. The Ship Richmond v. United States, 9 Cranch 102 (1815); Beverly v. Brooke, 2 Wheat. 100 (1817).

60. Schooner Exchange v. McFadden, 7 Cranch at 136.

61. Foster and Elam v. Neilson, 2 Pet. 253, 307, 309, 315 (1829).

62. Little v. Barreme, 2 Cranch 170 (1804).

63. The Anna Maria, 2 Wheat. 327, 355 (1817).

64. Henderson v. Poindexter's Lessee, 12 Wheat. 530 (1827); Soulard v. United States, 4 Pet. 511 (1831); United States v. Percheman, 7 Pet. 51, 87 (1833); Delassus v. United States, 9 Pet. 117, 133–34 (1835).

65. The Nereide, 9 Cranch at 410–19; See also The Mary, 9 Cranch 126 (1815); Ship Societe, 9 Cranch 209, 209–12 (1815); The Atlanta, 3 Wheat. 409 (1818).

66. The Venus, 8 Cranch at 297 (1814) (Marshall C. J., concurring); The Merrimack, 8 Cranch 317 (1814); The Frances, 8 Cranch 335 (1814).

67. Chirac v. Lessee of Chirac, 2 Wheat. 259 (1817).

68. Negress Sally Henry v. Ball, 1 Wheat. 1 (1816); The Antelope, 10 Wheat. 66, 115–22 (1825).

69. Higginson v. Mein, 4 Cranch 415 (1808); Kempe's Lessee v. Kennedy, 5 Cranch 173 (1809); Brown v. United States, 8 Cranch at 122–123; Bright's Lessee v. Rochester, 7 Wheat. 535 (1822); Carnel v. Banks, 10 Wheat. 181 (1825). These decisions were influenced by his conception of citizenship; see HASKINS & JOHNSON, supra note 19, at 493–525.

70. Letter from Marshall to Joseph Story (Dec. 30, 1827), in AN AUTOBIOGRAPHICAL SKETCH OF JOHN MARSHALL 37 (J. S. Adams ed. 1937).

71. See Letter from Marshall to Joseph Story (Sept. 22, 1832, Dec. 25, 1832, Nov. 16, 1833, Aug. 2, 1834, Oct. 16, 1834), in THE ECONOMIC AND POLITICAL DOCTRINES OF JOHN MARSHALL 105–6, 140–45, 151–52 (J. Oster ed. 1914).

72. Marshall, Speech, 10 June 1788, 1 PAPERS OF MARSHALL, supra note 42, at 256.

73. Frisch, John Marshall's Philosophy of Constitutional Republicanism, 20 REV. POL. 4405 (1958).

74. Loughborough v. Blake, 5 Wheat. 317, 324–25 (1820).

75. FAULKNER, supra note 17, at 8–10.

76. See id. at 164–73.

77. Letter from Marshall to Joseph Story (June 27, 1821), in Warren, The Marshall-Story Correspondence, 21 WM. & MARY Q. 2d ser. 13 (1941).

78. Letter from Marshall to Joseph Story (May 1, 1828), in Smith, Unpublished Letters of John Marshall, 14 PROC. MA. HIST. SOC. 2d ser. 336 (1900).

79. Marshall to a freeholder (Sept. 20, 1798), 3 PAPERS OF MARSHALL, supra note 42, at 505–6.

80. Marshall to Hillhouse (May 26, 1830), quoted in FAULKNER, supra note 17, at 191.

81. 1 MARSHALL, supra note 27, at iv. See also FAULKNER, supra note 17, at 191.

82. 2 MARSHALL, supra note 27, at 447.

83. 2 Id. at 348–49, 446–47; and Marshall, Speech (in House of Representatives on the Death of Washington), 19 Dec. 1799, 4 PAPERS OF MARSHALL 46–48 (C. Cullen ed. 1984).

84. Letter from Marshall to Timothy Pickering (Mar. 15, 1827), in Smith, supra note 78, at 333.

85. Discussed by FAULKNER, supra note 17, at 122–26.

86. PROCEEDINGS OF THE VIRGINIA STATE CONVENTION OF 1829–1830, 25031, at 561–62 (1830).

87. *Id.* at 616.

88. *Id.* at 619.

89. *Id.* at 619; *see also* at 729.

90. *See* A. ROEBER, FAITHFUL MAGISTRATES AND REPUBLICAN LAWYERS (1981).

91. PROCEEDINGS, *supra* note 86, at 604–5.

92. *Id.* at 524, 531, 533–34.

93. Marshall, *Speech (Virginia Convention Ratifying the Constitution), 10 June 1788*, 1 PAPERS OF MARSHALL, *supra* note 42, at 265; letter from Marshall to Augustine Davis (Oct. 16, 1793), 2 PAPERS OF MARSHALL, *supra* note 42, at 221; McCulloch v. Maryland 4 Wheat. at 404–5.

94. McCulloch v. Maryland, 4 Wheat. at 408–10.

95. *Id.* at 415–16.

96. United States v. Fisher, 2 Cranch 358, 396 (1805).

97. McCulloch v. Maryland, 4 Wheat. at 418; *see also Marshall's 'A Friend of the Constitution' Essays* in MARSHALL'S DEFENSE, *supra* note 48, at 170–71.

98. Weston v. Charleston, 2 Pet. at 466 (1829).

99. THE FEDERALIST No. 10, at 56–65 (J. Madison) (J. Cooke ed. 1961).

100. Marbury v. Madison, 1 Cranch 137, 165–66 (1803).

101. *Id.* at 166.

102. *Id.* at 171.

103. *Id.* at 176–77.

104. *Id.* at 177.

105. *Id.* at 178.

106. *Id.* at 180.

107. 5 PAPERS OF MARSHALL, *supra* note 42, at xxxiii, lix (C. Hobson ed. 1987). For examples of his use of common law see Ex parte Watkins, 3 Pet. 193 (1830); and Scott v. Lloyd, 9 Pet. 418 (1835). The one element of Marshall's legal theory reflecting republican political ideas is his commitment to a natural right of property; *see* Dartmouth College v. Woodward, 4 Wheat. 518 (1819); Ogden v. Saunders, 12 Wheat. 213, 344–57 (1827) (Marshall, C. J., dissenting).

108. Goebel, *The Common Law and the Constitution*, in CHIEF JUSTICE JOHN MARSHALL, *supra* note 1, at 106–8; *Editorial Note*, 5 PAPERS OF MARSHALL, *supra* note 42, at 459–62.

109. United States v. Hudson and Goodwin, 7 Cranch 32 (1812). See also Ex parte Bollman and Ex parte Swartwout, 4 Cranch 75, 94 (1807); United States v. Smith, unreported (1808); *see* HASKINS & JOHNSON, *supra* note 19, at 641.

110. On the politics of the common law of crimes, see HASKINS & JOHNSON, *supra* note 19, at 354–56, 633–46; Jay, *Origins of the Federal Common Law*, 133 U. PA. L. REV. 1003–1116, 1231–1333 (1985); and Preyer, *Jurisdiction to Punish*, 4 LAW & HIST. 223–65 (1986).

111. For an example, *see* Lidderdale v. Robinson, 15 F. Cas. 502, 2 Brock. 159 (1824). Note Marshall's rejection of the technical use of an error in pleading to allow a case's dismissal; Sheehy v. Mandeville, 7 Cranch 208, 217 (1812), an example of his desire for a reasonable common law.

112. Owens v. Adams, 18 F. Cas. 926, 1 Brock. 72 (1803).

113. Ex parte Randolph, 20 F. Cas. 242, 243–45, 2 Brock. 475, 478–80 (1833); FAULKNER, *supra* note 17, at 74–76.

114. United States v. Stansbury, 1 Pet. 573, 575–76 (1828). *See also* Oneale v. Thornton, 6 Cranch 53, 67–68 (1810); Durousseau v. United States, 6 Cranch 307, 314–16 (1810); United States v. Wiltberger, 5 Wheat. 76, 95 (1820); Postmaster General v. Early, 12 Wheat. 136, 148 (1827); The Adventure, 1 F. Cas. 202, 1 Brock. 235 (1812).

115. Polk's Lessee v. Wendal, 9 Cranch 87, 98 (1815).

116. United States v. Fisher, 2 Cranch at 386. *See also* Scott v. Negro Ben, 6 Cranch 3, 7 (1810). For a contrary interpretation, *see* Mendelson, *John Marshall's Short Way with Statutes*, 36 Ky. L. Rev. 284–88 (1948).

117. *Legislative Bill, 25 Dec. 1786*, 1 Papers of Marshall, *supra* note 42, at 193–97; letter from Marshall to Albert Gallatin (1790), 2 Papers of Marshall, *supra* note, 42, at 49–50. Cases on jurisdiction not discussed below that insured federal jurisdiction powers include Marbury v. Madison, 1 Cranch at 137; Hepburn and Dundas v. Ellzey, 2 Cranch 445 (1804); United States v. Nourse, 9 Pet. 8 (1835); Prentiss v. Barton's Executors, 19 F. Cas. 1276, 1 Brock. 389 (1819).

118. United States v. More, 3 Cranch 159 (1805); Ex parte Bollman and Ex parte Swartwout, 4 Cranch at 93–125; Durousseau v. United States, 6 Cranch at 313–14; Bank of the United States v. Deveaux, 5 Cranch 61, 84–87 (1809); Slocum v. Mayberry, 2 Wheat. 1, 9–12 (1817); United States v. Bevans, 3 Wheat. 336, 386–91 (1818); Osborn v. Bank of the United States, 9 Wheat. 738, 816–36 (1824); Wayman v. Southard, 10 Wheat. 1, 42 (1825); Williams v. Norris, 12 Wheat. 117 (1827); Southwick v. Postmaster General, 2 Pet. 442 (1829); Lessor of Fisher v. Cockerell, 5 Pet. 248, 252–59 (1831).

119. Marshall, *Speech (U.S. House of Representatives on Thomas Nash, aka Jonathan Robbins), 7 Mar. 1800*, 4 Papers of Marshall, *supra* note 42, at 95–96; United States v. Palmer, 3 Wheat. 610, 637–38 (1818).

120. Taylor v. Brown, 5 Cranch 234, 238 (1809).

6

Marshall v. Jefferson: Beyond "Sanctimonious Reverence" for a "Sacred" Law

Richard K. Matthews

For it is not *what is* that makes us irascible and resentful, but the fact that it is not as it *ought* to be.

—Hegel

On the two hundredth anniversary celebration of the birth of Chief Justice John Marshall, at a conference at Harvard Law School entitled "Government Under Law," Justice Felix Frankfurter opened the proceedings with a valuative address that contained the following anecdote. The story recounts a single, relatively unimportant encounter between Marshall and his historic adversary, Thomas Jefferson. Upon learning that Alexander Hamilton was urging Marshall to run for Congress, Jefferson wrote to James Madison that "I am told that Marshall has expressed half a mind to come. Hence I conclude that Hamilton has plyed him well with flattery & solicitation, and I think nothing better could be done than make him a judge."[1]

From the start, it appeared as if fate had decided to cast these two giants together. Cousins by birth, it was Jefferson as governor who signed Marshall's license to practice law in the State of Virginia; and it was Marshall who as Chief Justice administered the Presidential oath of office to Jefferson and who presided over the acquittal of Aaron Burr in his conspiracy trial. However, it was their "confrontation" during Marshall's tenure on the Supreme Court that has furnished the weightiest material for examining their relationship.

Frankfurter's address is interesting in that he takes the opportunity to assess Marshall's career as Chief Justice. Marshall's legacy, claims Frankfurter, resides in the fact that he is the nation's only judge who—as judge—is also "a great statesman." Frankfurter appreciates the role that history played in helping create a politically opportune time frame in which Marshall could carve out his unique imprint as statesman and founder. His admiration for Marshall does not hinge on an admiration for spectacular legal theorizing; in fact, the contrary seems to be Frankfurter's position. Marshall's "essential heritage . . . because of the very nature of constitutional law, does not lie in specific precepts, definite rules more or less easy of application in new circumstances." Had Marshall been, observes Frankfurter, what Oliver Wendell Holmes called an "originator of transforming thought" the bench would have been an inappropriate place for him: "Transforming thought implies too much discontinuity, to be imposed upon society by one who is entrusted with enforcing its law."[2]

Neither *Marbury v. Madison* nor *Gibbons v. Ogden* stands as Marshall's single greatest opinion according to Frankfurter.[3] *McCulloch v. Maryland*, undoubtedly one of Marshall's most celebrated opinions, is Frankfurter's candidate for the jewel in Marshall's crown. Here Marshall unabashedly "expressed the core of his constitutional philosophy: 'it is a constitution we are expounding.'"[4] In *McCulloch* Marshall squares off against Jefferson's strict construction of the Constitution and his interpretation of states' rights.

When asked by President Washington to evaluate the constitutionality of the bank bill, Jefferson argued that

the foundation of the Constitution is laid on this ground: That "all power, not delegated to the United States, by the Constitution, nor prohibited by it to the States, are reserved to the states or the people." To take a single step beyond the boundaries thus specially drawn around the powers of Congress, is to take possession of a boundless field of power, no longer susceptible of any definition.

He concluded, therefore, that the bill was unconstitutional. Upon turning his attention to the necessary and proper clause as justification for the bank, Jefferson maintained that mere expediency was no justification: "the Constitution allows only the means which are 'necessary,' not those which are merely 'convenient' for effecting the enumerated powers." Even more narrowly, he claimed that "Nothing but a necessity invincible by any other means" can justify government action under the necessary and proper clause. Given the strength of Jefferson's conviction on this question, it is important to note that he concludes his opinion to Washington by explaining that if the President finds the arguments "pro and con" to "hang so even as to balance his judgement, a just respect for the wisdom of the legislature would naturally decide in favor of their opinion."[5]

As a democrat, Jefferson had to embrace this final point; and, during his own Presidency he never exercised the veto. It may well be that Frankfurter's view of the "core thought" of Marshall's jurisprudence—that is, that Marshall's Court (or any Court) could legitimately "expound" the Constitution—comprises the major portion of the ground for separating Jefferson from Marshall. Jefferson was a radical democrat, offended at the notion that either the Supreme Court or any nonelected body, as opposed to the people, should think that it was empowered to expound the Constitution; Marshall was a classic, eighteenth-century liberal who perceived himself as authoritatively entitled to create the appropriate Leviathan to control the governed since the governed were incapable of controlling themselves.

Jefferson's letter to Madison about Hamilton's solicitation of Marshall's candidacy to Congress cryptically captures the historic irony in the relationship between Jefferson and Marshall: The judicious Marshall consistently outwitted Jefferson in the real world of constitutional politics. And yet, in the universe of political ideas, the story remains a bit more complicated, perhaps even tragic. It is the intention of this chapter—drawing on the valuable work of others, particularly the eloquent and insightful efforts of Robert K. Faulkner—to characterize concisely Marshall's political theory and then to contrast it with Jefferson's radical politics—a clear and present, dangerous alternative to Marshall's liberalism.

JOHN MARSHALL

While most historic accounts of the conflicts during the formative years of the republic of 1787 focus on the political battles between Jefferson and Hamilton, these studies could just have easily, and perhaps more profitably, focused on the less direct, but equally telling, philosophic differences between Marshall and Jefferson.

Thomas Shevory notes four, not necessarily incompatible, views of Marshall: Albert Beveridge sees "the supreme conservative"; William Crosskey a "consummate and determined nationalist"; and Robert Faulkner, "a natural rights liberal whose individualist orientations were tempered by certain republican values." Shevory presents the fourth Marshall, a classic republican.[6] Given the ongoing historiographic debates generated by the illuminating work of Bernard Bailyn, Lance Banning, J.G.A. Pocock, and others it is logical that a republican Marshall should be discovered.[7] Shevory appreciates the intrinsic difficulties associated with this task, not the least of which is the meaning of republicanism itself. Forrest McDonald perceptively notes that the classical definition of republican was abandoned by Madison cum Publius when he redefined republic to be "nothing more and nothing less than 'a government which derives all its powers directly or indirectly from the great body of the people, and is administered by persons holding their offices during pleasure, for a limited period, or during good behavior.'" McDonald argues that it was not only "presumptuous" for Madison to appropriate the word republic to describe the new government created in 1787, but also "prophetic" for "thenceforth *republic* would mean precisely what Madison said it meant."[8] Marshall can indeed be characterized by these four descriptive terms: conservative, nationalist, natural rights liberal, and republican. The tension in Marshall revolves around the last two: it becomes impossible to reconcile classic republican virtues with Marshall's brand of liberalism; and, in the end, his liberalism wins out.

Marshall consistently advocated the necessity of governmental protection of individual rights; the chief right needing protection being property. Like most of the framers, including James Madison, Marshall viewed the protection of property in all its forms as "the first object of government." Property rights are natural rights to Marshall. In *Ogden v. Saunders* he writes that they derive "from the right which every man retains to acquire property, to dispose of that property according to his own judgment and to pledge himself for a future act. These rights are not given by society, but are brought into it."[9] Marshall believed that the community ownership of property in Jamestown and Plymouth plagued and nearly destroyed the early settlers; giving "industry its due reward" through the creation of modern property rights with "exclusive property in the product of its toil," was the foundation of good government.[10] The right to acquire, and exclude others from, property is essential to a healthy commonwealth. The inevitable, historic tensions among individuals equally possessed of this right are not self-evident to Marshall, as they are to Jefferson from his firsthand view of class-divided France. At the Virginia ratifying convention Marshall appears to have argued that an individual's self-interest automatically harmonizes with the community's interest: "the interest of the community is blended and inseparably connected with that of the individual. When he promotes his own, he promotes that of the community. When we consult the common good, we consult our own."[11]

Shays's Rebellion was particularly instructive for Marshall, as it was for most of the framers. It signaled the need for centralized, national protection for the property rights of all individuals, especially creditors, as well as the necessity of a strong government to control the alarming democratic tendencies in the states. Although Marshall believed that a degree of popular participation was fundamental to republican government, a property qualification for voting was also essential for stability. Moreover, once this simple political act of voting was accomplished, the masses were to let their representatives do the governing. Faulkner eloquently captures the essence of Marshall's politics as "less of, by, and for the people than from, on, and for the people."[12] Like Hobbes, Locke, Hamilton, and Madison, Marshall is a nondemocratic liberal; that is to say, he stands in the mainstream of Anglo-American political thinking. While Faulkner's formidable interpretation of Marshall presents a rich portrayal of an acquisitive liberal tempered by Tocquevillian (republican) morality, from the other side of the coin Marshall can be viewed as a quintessential, possessive individualist.[13]

A fundamental premise of all liberal theories that embrace possessive individualism is fear: fear of others—individuals and groups—as well as the uncertainty of the future.[14] A mechanism appropriate to checking such apprehension is a strong, unambiguous Leviathan. Anything less will lead to a political life that is poor, nasty, brutish, and short. Marshall believed that the government constructed in embryo in 1787—which he helped create through a series of rulings designed to strengthen the central government and the courts—could provide the social equilibrium needed to allow its citizens to pursue their own self-interest without fear of invasion of others and secure in the knowledge that the fruits of their industry would be protected. Marshall viewed the Constitution as the keystone to this political system; to him, it was a virtually flawless and "sacred" text. Confronted with the presence of an ambiguous section of the Constitution in *United States v. Maurice*, he wrote: "I feel no diminution of reverence for the framers of this sacred instrument, when I say that some ambiguity of expression has found its way into this clause." Faulkner captures Marshall's attitude toward the Constitution with his observation that "In his own way Marshall too tried to found a 'political Religion.'"[15] Jefferson's political ideas, on the other hand, reject the liberal prejudices concerning individuality, property, and government.

THOMAS JEFFERSON

Because Thomas Jefferson was governor of Virginia, minister to France, secretary of state, vice-president, and President of the United States, it shocks the historic "common sense" of most Americans to conceive of him as a *radical* alternative to Madison, Hamilton, or even Marshall. But there may well be (at least) two Jeffersons: the one who held the aforementioned political offices, and the Jefferson who contemplated and espoused political ideas. The first, sworn to fulfill the functions of his office, was a dutiful servant of his government; the second, liberated from the restraints of office and obligation, was a speculative, occasionally spectacular, political theorist. In Holmes's phrase, Jefferson was an "originator of transforming thought."

To be sure, Jefferson's prolific pen never produced a single, systematic treatise of his political beliefs to which scholars can turn to investigate and debate. Still, there does exist among his thousands of private letters and scores of public documents the clear outlines of a radical political theory. What Benjamin Barber would call "strong democracy."[16] Although the precise details of this alternative politics remain outside the confines of this chapter, some of the fundamental notions to Jefferson's political vision—a vision that rejects many of the liberal prejudices concerning property, government, and humanity—can be glimpsed by a discussion of his conceptions of each of these topics. To that end, a brief look at Jefferson's reaction to the Constitution of 1787 is needed.

THE CONSTITUTION OF 1787: "A DEGENERACY IN THE PRINCIPLES OF LIBERTY"

Behind closed doors and sealed shutters in Philadelphia, the framers caucused over the best practicable plan of government for the new nation while Jefferson impatiently awaited news of the proceedings in France. Deploring the implementation of secrecy during the drafting of the document, Jefferson first learned of the details of the Constitution approximately a month after the convention adjourned.[17] Jefferson's initial reaction was ambiguous: "There are very good articles in it: and very bad. I do not know which preponderate." Yet he concluded his remarks to William Stephens Smith by observing that Shays's Rebellion was not the prelude to anarchy that the framers had perceived it to be, but a blessing since it reminded Americans that "the tree of liberty must be refreshed from time to time with the blood of patriots and tyrants." Jefferson had good reason to believe that the "[c]onvention has been too much impressed by the insurrection of Massachusetts: and in the spur of the moment they are setting up a kite to keep the hen yard in order. I hope in god that this article will be rectified before the new constitution is accepted."[18]

By the time Jefferson wrote to Madison to thank him for the copy of the draft he had sent, Jefferson had several weeks to think about the Constitution and he presented a more detailed, if still equivocal assessment of the plan.

I like the general idea of framing a government which should go on of itself peaceably, without needing continual recurrence to the state legislatures. I like the organization of the government into Legislative, Judiciary and Executive. I like the power given the legislature to levy taxes; and for that reason solely approve the greater house being chosen by the people directly. . . . I am captivated by the compromise of the opposite claims of the great and little states, of the latter to equal, and the former to proportional influence. I am much pleased too with the substitution of the method of voting by persons, instead of that of voting by states: and I like the negative given to the Executive with a third of either house, though I should have liked it better had the Judiciary been associated for that purpose, or invested with a similar and separate power.

Jefferson also offered two fundamental objections to the plan: the omission of a bill of rights and the failure to require rotation in all offices, especially the president. "A bill of rights," he lectured Madison, "is what the people are entitled to against every government of earth . . . and what no just government should refuse, or rest on influence." The failure of legislating rotation in office, Jefferson predicted, will mean that "the first magistrate will always be re-elected." Jefferson concluded his letter by suggesting two options to bring about the desired changes. Adoption, and then immediate amendment; or, convening a second convention after "canvassing" the people to appreciate fully their reaction to the proposed Constitution.[19] Exhausted and not overly optimistic about the prospects of either the ratification of the Constitution or its ability to govern if ratified, Madison could not have been cheered by Jefferson's "hope [that] you will not be discouraged from other trials, if the present one should fail of it's full effect."[20]

In the winter of 1788, Jefferson privately advocated a plan that would realistically force the addition of a bill of rights to the Constitution. "Were I in

America, I would advocate it warmly til nine should have adopted, and then as warmly take the other side to convince the remaining four that they ought not to come into it til the declaration of rights is annexed to it." Jefferson's second concern, the "perpetual re-eligibility of the President," continued to trouble him but he recognized that on that specific issue he stood alone and hence dropped his crusade against it. He closed this letter expressing no small amount of concern over what he perceived to be a significant shift in public opinion in the states on the issue of the appropriate balance between individual liberty and governmental authority.

But I own it astonishes me to find such a change wrought in the opinions of our coun-trymen since I left them, as that threefourths of them should be contented to live under a system which leaves to their governors the power of taking from them the trial by jury in civil cases, freedom of religion, freedom of the press, freedom of commerce, the habeas corpus laws, and the yoking them with a standing army. This is a degeneracy in the prin-ciples of liberty to which I had given four centuries instead of four years.[21]

By the spring, Jefferson had further modified his views: "Indeed I have presumed it would grow on the public mind, as I confess it has on my own," he told Edward Carrington. After recalling that originally he wished nine states would adopt so that the remaining states could hold fast, demanding a bill of rights as the price for their consent, Jefferson confided to Carrington that he had been persuaded of the merits of adoption by all the states and then amendment.[22] Nevertheless, when word of Jefferson's hostage strategy indirectly reached Patrick Henry, no political ally of Jefferson's, the opportunistic Henry urged the Virginia ratification convention to follow Jefferson's advice and withhold consent until appropriately amended. This move forced Madison into the uncomfortable position of arguing against considering the opinions of anyone not in attendance at the convention even though he believed that Jefferson's complete, and more thought-out, posi-tion favored unqualified adoption.

Although Madison correctly understood Jefferson's evolving view in favor of ratification, it is not clear that Madison appreciated Jefferson's unwavering ra-tionale. It was not Jefferson's position that the document, upon further reflec-tion, appeared to protect the liberty that Americans had fought so hard to secure and Jefferson advocated so unequivocally; rather, it was Jefferson's own democratic principles that led him to support the plan as it became increasingly evident to him that public opinion in the states supported adoption: "After all," he wrote Madison, "it is my principle that the will of the Majority should always prevail. If they approve the proposed constitution in all it's parts, I shall concur in it cheerfully, in hopes that they will amend it whenever they shall find it work[s] wrong."[23] Three years before his death, discouraged by the ongo-ing and *un*democratic expansion of the Constitution at the hands of Marshall's

Court as well as the failure of the amendment process to bring about legitimate constitutional change, Jefferson exclaimed that "another general convention can alone relieve us."[24] At most, it can be said that Jefferson warmed up to some of the ideas contained in the Constitution, while remaining adamantly opposed to its failure to include a bill of rights. More importantly, he was alarmed at the recent alterations in public sentiment on political principles: an ongoing diminution in the fear of governmental power and the abandonment of the notion of constant vigilance for the preservation of liberty both signaled danger to him. What is genuinely intriguing with regard to Jefferson and his concept of law is not contained in his reactions from France to the Constitution, but exists in several letters in which he speculates on the legitimate, time-bound authority of *all* laws and constitutions.

PROPERTY: "THE EARTH BELONGS TO THE LIVING"

While the Declaration of Independence will always be considered Jefferson's most significant contribution to political theory, a more appropriate choice could be considered his 6th of September, 1789, letter to James Madison, usually entitled "The Earth Belongs to the Living." In this letter Jefferson firmly reestablishes his credentials as a radical political thinker. Writing from Paris where the dire consequences of class-divided society became permanently etched in his memory, Jefferson raised the crucial question of whether one generation of men has a right to bind another. Jefferson answers negatively: "no such obligation can be so transmitted." He sets out in the remainder of this letter to explain to Madison—who as Publius, author of *The Federalist*, was firmly committed to the new Constitution—the full impact of his "self-evident" truth "'that the earth belongs in usufruct to the living': That the dead have neither powers nor rights over it."

As is well known, Jefferson rejected Locke's trilogy of life, liberty, and estate when penning the Declaration of Independence and substituted the more felicitous, abstract, and potentially radical pursuit of happiness. While scholars disagree over Jefferson's intention, it seems clear from his letter to Madison that one reason for his rejection of property from the list was because he, unlike Marshall, did not consider it to be an individual's natural right. "The portion occupied by any individual," he writes, "ceases to be his when himself ceases to be, and reverts to the society."[25] At the point an individual dies, if society has legislated inheritance laws, then those laws apply; if no such laws have been constructed, first occupant takes control during his or her lifetime. "But the child, the legatee, or the creditor takes it, not by any natural right, but by a law of the society of which they are members, and to which they are subject." What is important to notice is that an individual cannot, "by natural right, oblige the lands he occupied, or the persons who succeed him in that occupation, to the payment of debts contracted by him." The political community must consciously construct the laws of descent for its collective lifetime: The same principle of individual, civil rights ceasing over time applies as well to society as a corporate entity. In fact, Jefferson specifically argued that the termination of one generation's legitimate power and the reconstruction of political power by the succeeding generation is a matter of natural right: generations "derive these rights not from their predecessors, but from nature."[26]

The implications of this notion are staggering. Jefferson understands this, and specifically explains to Madison the economic and political consequences. While society may decide that creditors can demand payment of debts from the property holdings of the deceased (or conversely, society may also appropriately decide against this), society cannot make an analogous decision with regard to either their own corporate debts or control of property.

But a material difference must be noted between the succession of an individual, and that of a whole generation. Individuals are parts only of a society, subject to the laws of the whole. These laws may appropriate the portion of land occupied by a decedent to his creditor rather than to any other, or to his child on condition he satisfies the creditor. But when a whole generation, that is the whole society dies, as in the case we have supposed, and another generation or society succeeds, this forms a whole, and there is no superior who can give their territory to a third society, who may have lent money to their predecessors beyond their faculties of paying.[27]

Jefferson's conclusion is simple: "No generation can contract debts greater than may be paid during the course of its own existence."

Like Hobbes, Locke, and John Rawls, who use variations on the state of nature myth, Jefferson also employs an intellectual fiction, that of the passing of one generation and the establishment of a new generation, to assist him in presenting his case to Madison. From the mortality tables available to him, Jefferson (mis)calculated that a "new" generation enters the world approximately every thirty-four years. Based on further considerations, Jefferson finally established nineteen years as "the term beyond which neither the representatives of a nation, nor even the whole nation itself assembled, can validly extend a debt."[28]

Jefferson realized the unsettling nature of his idea. He proposed that the United States announce that this principle would be the foundation to their political position on all questions of debt in the future. This would put both "the lenders, and the borrowers also, on their guard." The most immediate benefit of this fiscal position would be to harness "the spirit of war, to which too free a course has been procured by the inattention of money-lenders to this law of nature, that succeeding generations are not responsible for the preceding." He concludes this portion of the argument with the assertion that "the question of reimbursement," after the public adoption of this principle, then becomes "a question of generosity and not of right."[29] Jefferson does not rest here. He pushes his position beyond the confines of economic considerations into the realm of politics. What applies to questions of property obtains for *all* laws: Extending the logic of "the earth belongs to the living," he asserts that "no society can make a perpetual constitution, or even a perpetual law. The earth belongs always to the living generation. They may manage it then, and what proceeds from it, as they please, during their usufruct."

GOVERNMENT: BEYOND "SANCTIMONIOUS REVERENCE"

Like the control over property and the passing on of debts, so too "the constitution and the laws of their predecessors extinguished then in their natural course with those who gave them being. . . . Every constitution then, and every law, naturally expires at the end of 19 years. If it be enforced longer, it is an act of force and not of right." The mere political capacity of humans to repeal prior legislation is an insufficient mechanism to Jefferson who correctly understood that "the power of repeal is not an equivalent."[30] Just as individuals must be permitted to create their own economic rules of the game, so too humans must be provided with an opportunity to construct their own politics, to build their own world. To allow laws to exist beyond a society's lifetime of twenty years is a violation of natural law and an insult to humanity. It is imperative not to become bogged down over the notion of a society having a two-decade life: The precise time dimension is not as critical as is Jefferson's point that at some predetermined moment—while the next generation still has the opportunity to create its own world—the present laws and institutions must automatically cease, or violate natural law.

This 1789 letter to the "Father of the Constitution" was not an isolated expression of this idea. In another letter written the 12th of July, 1816, to Samuel Kercheval, Jefferson echoes and amplifies his revolutionary themes. In this private letter intended solely for Kercheval's own information and not for public attribution, Jefferson candidly admits that Virginia's constitution is not republican. And by implication, neither is the federal Constitution. In his letter Jefferson advocates universal, white male suffrage, as he did throughout his life, and also calls for direct election for *all* offices, including the executive and judiciary. Jefferson was keenly aware of, and unlike Madison, embarrassed by the undemocratic nature of political systems that restricted participation to one house of a single governmental branch. Jefferson's own model of a good government was quite different. In a four-tier, pyramid structure Jefferson outlines the provinces of each segment of the government. The top would handle "all concerns foreign and federal"; the state governments, at the next level, would deal with the matters pertinent to their citizens exclusively; the third level, "county

republics," would handle all countywide concerns; finally, and most importantly, would be "the ward republics, for the small, and yet numerous and interesting concerns of the neighborhood." In this governmental model, where
"division and subdivision" is the guiding principle to management, "the whole
is cemented by giving to every citizen, personally, a part in the administration
of public affairs."[31]

Jefferson's view of the ward republics is instructive, demonstrating that he,
like Rousseau, understood the necessity for humans, to be fully human, to participate in politics according to Aristotle's dictum of ruling and being ruled.
The wards provided the political space in which humans could pursue happiness in its public dimension. Any government lacking such a space could not
allow all of its citizens to pursue happiness and must, therefore, in accordance
with the principles of the Declaration of Independence be overthrown. Jefferson fully appreciated the omission of a public space in the Virginia and United
States constitutions. As Hannah Arendt notes,

On the American scene, no one has perceived this seemingly inevitable flaw in the structure of the republic with greater clarity and more passionate preoccupation than Jefferson. His occasional, and sometimes violent, antagonism against the Constitution . . .
was motivated by a feeling of outrage about the injustice that only his generation should
have in their power "to begin the world over again."

Arendt compares Jefferson's ward republics to the Paris communes and the
soviets.[32] Of course, such a dynamic political space is the last thing the framers
of the Constitution wanted: from their perspective of the 1780s, the problem of
the American republic was that it was too democratic. Not so Jefferson. He en-
visioned the wards fulfilling multiple functions: first, to check local, petty
tyrants; second, to maintain the spirit of revolution created in 1776; third, to
provide for the general education of society; and, fourth, to ensure a space
where citizens could practice the art of politics. He writes to Kercheval:

Divide the counties into wards of such size as that every citizen can attend, when called
on, and act in person. Ascribe to them the government of their wards in all things
relating to themselves exclusively. A justice, chosen by themselves, in each, a constable,
a military company, a patrol, a school, the care of their own poor, their own portion of
the public roads, the choice of one or more jurors to serve in some court, and the
delivery, within their own wards, of their own votes for all elective officers of higher
sphere, will relieve the county administration of nearly all its business, will have it better
done, and by making every citizen an acting member of the government, and in the offices nearest and most interesting to him, will attach him by his strongest feelings to the
independence of his country, and its republican Constitution.

Jefferson concludes his letter with an explicit reiteration of "the earth belongs
to the living" theme. At a minimum, every nineteen years each generation has

"a right to choose for itself the form of government it believes most promotive of its own happiness." On this occasion, Jefferson suggested that the ward republics would make an excellent mechanism to collect the voice of the people. "The mayor of every ward . . . would call his ward together, take the simple yea or nay of its members, convey these to the county court, who would hand on those of all its wards to the proper general authority. . . ."[33] In this mode of instructed delegates, a mass participatory democracy could be created to settle political questions pertinent for the entire nation on those rare occasions such national issues arose.

Jefferson believed humans are capable of self-government because he held a fundamentally different view of humanity from that of Marshall, Madison, Hamilton, or even Thomas Paine. Where the latter four begin with a market, liberal concept of man, Jefferson begins with a moral and social concept of humanity.

HUMANITY: "GENEROUS SPASMS OF THE HEART" OR "FRIGID SPECULATIONS"

Rejecting market concept of justice and individuality, Jefferson explains to John Adams his disagreement with Count Destutt de Tracy:

I gather from his other works that he adopts the principle of Hobbes, that justice is founded in contract solely, and does not result from the construction of man. I believe, on the contrary, that it is instinct, and innate, that the moral sense is as much a part of our constitution as that of feeling, seeing, or hearing; as a wise creator must have seen to be necessary in an animal destined to live in society.

Order and harmony comprise Jefferson's universe. An organic conception of society led him to conclude that humans had been created with a sense of justice. Even stronger than Rousseau's position in his "Second Discourse" that humans instinctively do not like to see other creatures suffer, Jefferson's argument is that "Nature hath implanted in our breasts a love of others, a sense of duty to them, a moral instinct" that makes them social creatures. In his celebrated image: "The Creator would indeed have been a bungling artist, had he intended man for a social animal, without planting in him a social disposition." To be a moral creature requires the presence of others: "To ourselves . . . we can owe no duties, obligation requiring also two parties. Self-love, therefore is not part of morality."[34] By reducing self-love and providing both "education, and the instruction of restraint," humans, quite naturally, can lead moral, social lives. Notice that reason plays a minimal role in human morality: Morality is a matter of the heart, of the senses; it is not an intellectual affair. As Jefferson tersely put it: "State a moral case to a ploughman and a professor. The former will decide it as well, and often better than the latter, because he has not been led astray by artificial rules."[35]

The fullest expression of the role of the moral sense contrasted to the intellect occurs in a unique letter to Maria Cosway. While the letter, a dialogue between Jefferson's Head and his Heart, presents itself as an immediate, stream-of-consciousness reaction to the parting of Cosway from Jefferson's company, evidence indicates that it was a well-thought-out exposition, which Jefferson elected to make a copy of for posterity. The Head clutches the painful moment of separation to lecture the Heart on the folly of its nonpragmatic logic. In its place, the Head offers a calculus of pain and pleasure worthy of Hobbes, Bentham, Freud, or any contemporary market economist. The richly expressive passage will be cited at length.

This is not a world to live at random in as you do. To avoid these eternal distresses, to which you are forever exposing us, you must learn to look forward before you take a step which may interest our peace. Everything in this world is a matter of calculation. Advance then with caution, the balance in your hand. Put into one scale the pleasures which any object may offer; but put fairly into the other the pains which are to follow, and see which preponderates. The making an acquaintance is not a matter of indifference. When a new one is proposed to you, view it all round. Consider what advantages it presents, and to what inconveniences it may expose you. Do not bite at the bait of pleasure till you know there is no hook beneath it. The art of life is the art of avoiding pain: and he is the best pilot who steers clearest of the rocks and shoals with which it is beset. Pleasure is always before us; but misfortune is at our side: while running after that, this arrests us. The most effectual means of being secure against pain is to retire within ourselves, and to suffice for our own happiness. Those, which depend on ourselves, are the only pleasures a wise man will count on: for nothing is ours which another may deprive us of. Hence the inestimable value of intellectual pleasures. Ever in our power, always leading us to something new, never cloying, we ride, serene and sublime, above the concerns of this mortal world, contemplating truth and nature, matter and motion, the laws which bind up their existence, and that eternal being who made and bound them up by these laws. Let this be our employ. Leave the bustle and tumult of society to those who have not talents to occupy themselves without them.[36]

The Heart initially responds by rebalancing the Head's scale. But ultimately the Heart rejects the Head's atomistic and utilitarian ethos:

Let the gloomy Monk, sequestered from the world, seek unsocial pleasures in the bottom of his cell! Let the sublimated philosopher grasp visionary happiness while pursuing phantoms dressed in the garb of truth! Their supreme wisdom is supreme folly: and they mistake for happiness the mere absence of pain. Had they ever felt the solid pleasure of one generous spasm of the heart, they would exchange for it all the frigid speculations of their lives, which you have been vaunting in such elevated terms. Believe me then, my friend, that that is a miserable arithmetic which would estimate friendship at nothing, or at less than nothing. Respect for you has induced me to enter into this discussion, and to hear principles uttered which I detest and abjure. Respect for myself now obliges me to recall you into the proper limits of your office.

Lecturing the Head about the appropriate domains in which each is sovereign—the Head, science, the Heart, morality and politics—the Heart exclaims that the Head lacks "feelings of sympathy, of benevolence, of gratitude, of justice, of love, of friendship." The reason for this failure is simple: "Morals were too essential to the happiness of man to be risked on the uncertain combinations of the Head. She laid their foundation therefore in sentiment, not in science. That she gave to all as necessary to all: This to a few only, as suffering with a few."[37] Jefferson does not claim that all individuals are fully rational creatures. In fact, he believes the contrary. Nevertheless, all humans have a moral sense, which permits and obligates them to participate in politics. He concludes the letter with the Heart chastising and silencing the Head that "as far as my recollection serves me, I do not know that I ever did a good thing on your suggestion, or a dirty one without it."[38]

Given Jefferson's position on human sociability and an innate moral capacity, that he held anarchism as a sort of Platonic ideal toward which legislators ought to aspire—even though its achievement, because of the rise in population, was unattainable—should be no surprise. Writing to James Madison sometime after news of Shays's Rebellion reached Jefferson, Jefferson attempted to calm the fearful Madison:

Those characters wherein fear predominates over hope may apprehend too much from these instances of irregularity. They may conclude too hastily that nature has formed man insusceptible of any other government but that of force, a conclusion not founded in truth, nor experience. Societies exist under three forms sufficiently distinguishable. 1. Without government, as among our Indians. 2. Under government wherein the will of every one has a just influence, as in the case in England in a slight degree, and in our states in a great one. 3. Under governments of force: as is the case in all other monarchies and in most of the other republics.

Although he acknowledges that it "is a problem, not clear in my mind, that the first condition is not the best," his perspective on the Indians as stateless communities to be envied and emulated repeatedly appears throughout Jefferson's life. To Jefferson, the only thing the Indian community needed to be more ideal was increased technology and science, to help free them from the domination of nature. And this he tried to provide for them, failing to realize that it would simultaneously destroy their simple tribal existence. What is politically significant is that these primitive communities function for Jefferson, as for some contemporary left-wing theorists such as Herbert Marcuse, as alternative models of society, based not on competitive self-interest but on shared values, norms, and experiences that are distinctly nonliberal in their essence. Gad Horowitz calls these tribal communities "love cultures," and contrasts them to the "warlike hate cultures" of modern liberal societies.[39] Social as well as moral creatures, humans are environmentally determined beings who must knowingly participate in creating their own environment; who, if surrounded by the appropriate social and political culture, could continually evolve to a near stateless society. Like Rousseau, Jefferson embraced the concept of human perfectibility; he too understood that humans were equally capable of self-destructive and dominating measures. Nevertheless, here may be the ultimate point in Jefferson's radicalism—his recognition of the necessity of providing citizens with the opportunity for failure in order for them to achieve freedom. No society could be considered democratic if it did not allow its citizens, on a daily basis, to govern themselves. Wise Platonic philosopher-kings or Rousseauean legislators could not sit in final judgment permitting only those actions of which they approved. As Jefferson explained to Du Pont de Nemours: "We both consider the people as our children and love them with parental affection. But you love them as infants whom you are afraid to trust without nurses; and I as adults whom I freely leave to self-government."[40]

CONCLUSIONS: JEFFERSONIAN POLITICS

Jeffersonian politics consisted of a noble and ennobling activity in which all must be permitted to engage. This comprised part of the self-evident truths that Jefferson espoused. In addition, property rights, both civil (individual) and natural (social), were intended to maintain economic and political freedom. Property rights must be politically altered in accordance with the progress of humanity; as Jefferson maintained, "legislators cannot invent too many devices" to keep property laws in harmony with human development. Following his own logic, Jefferson advocated that all male Virginians who did not already possess twenty-five acres of land be given up to that amount of land by the state; this grant simultaneously gave individuals the vote.[41] No one has appreciated this dimension to Jefferson more tellingly than C. B. Macpherson, who notes:

This justification of property rests, in the last analysis, on the right to life at a more than animal level: freedom from coerced labour and arbitrary government are held to be part of what is meant by a fully human life. At the same time this justification is an assertion of the right to the means of labour: the whole point is that by working on his own land or other productive resources a man can be independent and uncoerced.[42]

Jefferson's politics, then, contains natural rights not to be denied access—not merely to the means of production, but more importantly—to a certain democratic style of life. A style by which humans define themselves as political and moral creatures, who express their humanity through their labor and their personal relationships, and who pursue happiness as both a social and individual *telos*.

Jefferson in 1816 gave this advice to Kercheval concerning constitutions:

> Some men look at constitutions with sanctimonious reverence, and deem them like the ark of the covenant, too sacred to be touched. They ascribe to the men of the preceding age a wisdom more than human, and suppose what they did to be beyond amendment. I knew that age well; I belonged to it, and labored with it. It deserved well of its country. It was very like the present, but without the experience of the present; and forty years of experience in government is worth a century of book-reading; and this they would say themselves, were they to rise from the dead. I am certainly not an advocate for frequent and untried changes in laws and constitutions. I think moderate imperfections had better be borne with; because, when once known, we accommodate ourselves to them, and find practical means of correcting their ill effects. But I know also, that laws and institutions must go hand in hand with the progress of the human mind. As that becomes more developed, more enlightened, as new discoveries are made, new truths disclosed, and manners and opinions change with the change of circumstances, institutions must advance also, and keep pace with the times. We might as well require a man to wear still the coat which fitted him when a boy, as a civilized society to remain ever under the regimen of their barbarous ancestors.[43]

If "the earth belongs to the living," then we have been ruled from the grave for far too long. By Jefferson's logic, the "sacred," second United States Constitution has ruled as a matter of force, not of right, during the past 180 years. At the beginning of this chapter I suggested that Marshall was the victor in his political conflicts with Jefferson. I also implied that in terms of their ideological confrontation the story was not as simple: if Marshall is the victor, Americans are the losers. To be sure, Marshall's ideas have become America's. Nevertheless, as we turn to the next century, perhaps America can find the heroic will needed to return to its more democratic roots in Jefferson, who can serve as a guide to lead us beyond the possessive individualism and self-interest narrowly understood that currently threatens to suffocate the republic in a sea of vulgar materialism.

NOTES

This chapter draws on my Radical Politics of Thomas Jefferson (1984). I would like to acknowledge a research grant from Lehigh University which helped to make the writing of this article possible.

1. Address by F. Frankfurter, Harvard Law School, 2–3 (Sept. 1955).
2. *Id.* at 5. While Jefferson's political ideas certainly make him a creator of "transforming thought," Jefferson would agree with Frankfurter's position on the inappropriateness

of such a person sitting on the Court; however, he would also maintain that Marshall's actions as Chief Justice attempted to transform not only the Court but also the entire scheme of constitutional government created in 1787.

3. Just as Jefferson criticized Marshall concerning *Gibbons*, Frankfurter believed that in his delineation of the commerce clause Marshall "indulged in observations not only beyond the necessities of the cases but outside the demands of his own analysis." *See id.* at 6; and Thomas Jefferson: Writings, 1469–77 (M. Peterson ed. 1984) [hereinafter cited as WRITINGS].

4. Frankfurter, *supra* note 1, at 3.

5. WRITINGS, *supra* note 3, at 416–19. *See* N. CUNNINGHAM, JR., IN PURSUIT OF REASON: THE LIFE OF THOMAS JEFFERSON, 164–67 (1987).

6. Shevory, *John Marshall as Republican* [*infra* Chapter 4].

7. B. BAILYN, THE IDEOLOGICAL ORIGINS OF THE AMERICAN REVOLUTION (1967); L. BANNING, THE JEFFERSONIAN PERSUASION (1978); J. G. A. POCOCK, THE MACHIAVELLIAN MOMENT (1975); *See* Matthews, *Liberalism, Civic Humanism, and the American Political Tradition: Understanding Genesis*, 49 J. POL. 1127–53 (Nov. 1987).

8. F. McDONALD, NOVUS ORDO SECLORUM, 287 (1985). Of course, it should be pointed out that by this minimalist definition, the Soviet Union also qualifies as a republic.

9. Ogden v. Saunders, 12 Wheat. 346 (1827). Jefferson believed only societies, not individuals, possessed natural property rights.

10. Quoted in Faulkner, *John Marshall*, in AMERICAN POLITICAL THOUGHT, 76 (Frisch ed. 1971). This section of the chapter follows—but draws different conclusions from—Faulkner's article, and his splendid THE JURISPRUDENCE OF JOHN MARSHALL (1968) [hereinafter cited as JURISPRUDENCE].

11. 3 THE DEBATES IN THE SEVERAL STATE CONVENTIONS ON THE ADOPTION OF THE FEDERAL CONSTITUTION 232 (Elliot ed. 1836).

12. Faulkner, *John Marshall*, *supra* note 10, at 88.

13. C. MACPHERSON, POSSESSIVE INDIVIDUALISM 46–61 (1962).

14. Faulkner, *John Marshall*, *supra* note 10, at 70, perceptively argues that "at the basis of acquisitive society is apprehension, the fear of future dangers."

15. FAULKNER, JURISPRUDENCE, *supra* note 10, at 219.

16. B. BARBER, STRONG DEMOCRACY (1984). Jefferson's political theory fits Barber's model better than Barber realizes.

17. 12 THE PAPERS OF THOMAS JEFFERSON 355–56 (Boyd ed. 1950–) [hereinafter cited as PAPERS]. In anticipation of the conclusion of the convention, Madison, on September 6, had already sent Jefferson a copy of the document. But it did not reach him until December. For a concise account of this time in Jefferson's life *See* CUNNINGHAM, *supra* note 5.

18. 12 PAPERS, *supra* note 17, at 356. It is not clear which article Jefferson is referring to in this passage. The most likely sections appear to be either Article I, Section 9, Paragraph 2, or Article IV, Section 4.

19. It takes considerable imagination to believe that Madison, or most of the framers, would welcome the idea of "canvassing" the people prior to a constitutional convention.

20. 12 PAPERS, *supra* note 17, at 439–41. Lacking a national veto over all state legislation, Madison told Jefferson that he doubted that the new government had sufficient power to control the democratic tendencies in the states. Characteristically, Jefferson did not share Madison's concern.

21. *Id.* at 558.

22. 13 PAPERS, *supra* note 17, at 208.

23. *Id.* at 442.

24. M. Peterson, JEFFERSON AND MADISON AND THE MAKING OF CONSTITUTIONS, 16 (1987).

25. 15 PAPERS, *supra* note 17, at 392.

26. *Id.* at 393–94.

27. *Id.*

28. This tenure of nineteen years assumes that the debt is being incurred during the first year of the new community; if the generation has been in power for a decade, they can obligate themselves only for the remainder of their control, i.e., nine years.

29. 15 PAPERS, *supra* note 17, at 595–96.

30. *Id.* at 596.

31. THE PORTABLE JEFFERSON, 557 (Peterson ed. 1975) [hereinafter cited as PORTABLE].

32. H. ARENDT, ON REVOLUTION, 235–38 (1963).

33. PORTABLE, *supra* note 31, at 561.

34. *Id.* at 542.

35. 12 PAPERS, *supra* note 17, at 15.

36. 10 *Id.* at 448–49.

37. *Id.* at 450.

38. *Id.* at 451.

39. Horowitz, *The Faucaultian Impasse*, POL. THEORY 73–75 (Feb. 1987).

40. 11 THE WORKS OF THOMAS JEFFERSON, 522 (Ford ed. 1904).

41. 1 PAPERS, *supra* note 17, at 329–86.

42. C. MACPHERSON, DEMOCRATIC THEORY, 135 (1973).

43. PORTABLE, *supra* note 31, at 558–59.

PART III INTERPRETIVE PRACTICE

7

McCulloch and "The Dilemmas of Liberal Constitutionalism"

Ira L. Strauber

The status of *McCulloch v. Maryland*[1] as a classic of (Marshall's)[2] jurisprudence may make a defense of it appear anachronistic, if not superfluous. But assaults on liberal legal reasoning out of Critical Legal Studies (hereafter, CLS), specifically Mark Tushnet's critique of federalism in "The Dilemmas of Liberal Constitutionalism,"[3] justify (perhaps require) another look at Marshall's reasoning.

Tushnet's basic complaint is that liberal-legalism (as CLS refers to it) is intrinsically inconsistent and incoherent. It is inconsistent because case-law is arbitrary: despite appeals to the rule of law, case-law reasoning actually does not evidence principled criteria for reconciling competing interests. Instead, legal reasoning depends on premises, characterizations, and conclusions about political situations undersubstantiated, if not unsubstantiated, by actual political conditions. This evidentiary arbitrariness undermines the rule of law, but does not mean that just any policy may prevail. Rather, it bespeaks the political incoherence of liberal ideology, which despite its professed democratic aims and values, is dominated by the idea and practices of private property, and associated political and social values,[4] making it a systematically antidemocratic handservant for elites who control the unequal distribution of political and economic power in America. This CLS attack falls on *McCulloch* as the first in a long line of attempts to formulate a conception of federalism by integrating liberalism (as the theory and practices of the political will: aggregating conflicting individual interests, through the political process, to determine the public good) and constitutionalism (as the theory and practices of political reasoning: applying legal rules to control potential abuses of the political process). Federalism, as we know, is designed to preserve the integrity of republican government by ensuring constant political competition (between the Union and the states). The idea is to enumerate powers of governments, thereby multiplying and dividing arenas of aggregation, and have the judiciary identify usurpations of powers. Tushnet characterizes these goals as doomed, in theory and practice, because the two dominant conventions of federalism, liberalism and constitutionalism, are ultimately irreconcilable.

Liberalism and constitutionalism cannot be brought together without contradiction because of the arbitrariness of liberalism, which, he asserts, has "gone essentially unchallenged in the dominant institutions of this country since the framing of the Constitution."[5] As I understand it, arbitrariness infects McCulloch (and its progeny) both rhetorically and metaphysically. Rhetorically, federalism reveals itself to be a sham because lines drawn ostensibly to control for abuses of political power are so indeterminate (ambiguous and contradictory) that it is impossible to say why the limits are drawn where they are. This indeterminacy is fatal for federalism because it means it is impossible to say whether the will of the people ought to control or whether the rule of law is required to intervene. Nevertheless, it is rhetorically functional because arguments about liberalism and constitutionalism mask the use of the law to privilege and defend nondemocratic interests and policies. The so-called rule of law varies according to judges' predilections about political exigencies of the moment, so it is actually political will, not judicial reason, that controls the distribution of power. The ultimate cause of this criterial arbitrariness is liberal metaphysics: specifically, what CLS contends is an antinomy between the will and reason. Liberalism depends on the belief in the autonomy of individual desires and interests, the metaphysical foundation of the principle of the will of "the people" as sovereign. However, since Hobbes, Tushnet points out, liberalism also acknowledges that the autonomy of the will, and the conflict that attends competing wills, entails "accept[ing] the infliction of harm on everyone else as we pursue our own ends."[6]

Consequently, liberalism, recognizing the necessity of avoiding a war of all against all, or the many against the few, introduces reason into the picture. Through the rule of law, or constitutionalism, rules and principles are imposed to protect the politics of aggregation from itself. But, CLS contends, this check cannot be metaphysically consistent or coherent with the will because reason denies what the will confirms: the idea that the expression of desires and interests (the vox populi) is both necessary and sufficient to constitute the good. Hence, whenever reason intervenes to impose restrictions on the will (salus populi) it violates the liberal foundation of the good (the vox populi).

Moreover, the indictment protests, in politics, the will (or sovereignty) resists interventions that challenge its ultimate authority. Conflicts between the Union and states, and the Court between them both, necessarily undermine one political process or the other. Federalism cannot balance liberal politics and the rule of law, because the centrality of the metaphysics and politics of the will necessarily fosters beliefs and social structures that emphasize freedom from interference in the satisfaction of acquisitive desires. These liberal beliefs are reinforced by capitalism, which gives primary content to acquisitiveness and, in so doing, reinforces the liberal momentum toward the aggregation of power in a strong central government to foster its own growth and transformations. In short, liberalism and capitalism undermine constitutionalism and its efforts to constrain political power, because they require that constitutionalism be abandoned for a "doctrine that says there are limits to governmental power . . . without having broader implications for the exercise of power generally."[7] In a liberal society, power can be understood in no other way.

The purpose of this chapter is to test, within the context of this indictment, *McCulloch*'s defense of the power of Congress to incorporate the Bank of the United States (BUS) and its immunity to the Maryland tax. This test will focus on the ideology behind *McCulloch*, by which I mean the liberal conventions that control what governments may do in politics. It will confirm many CLS particulars, specifically regarding the rhetorical ambiguities and inconsistencies in *McCulloch*. But it will also provide evidence that CLS overstates its case, for whereas CLS takes these particulars as part of a pattern of liberalism's incoherence, it is possible to argue that they are actually strengths. CLS's mistake is in underestimating the rhetorical function of ambiguity and inconsistency as expressions of pragmatism and consequentialist considerations about the uses and abuses of political power. Such pragmatism and consequentialism are central to liberalism, and Tushnet's critique fails to credit their role in integrating liberalism and constitutionalism. Thus, perversely from a CLS perspective, its indictment of inconsistencies and ambiguities gives us an opportunity to deepen our appreciation of *McCulloch* as a classic of liberal jurisprudence.

CONSTITUTIONALISM AND LIBERALISM IN McCULLOCH: AN INTRODUCTION

To set the stage, I want to emphasize some of the familiar economic and political dimensions of *McCulloch*. The Bank was rechartered to meet the financial crises that followed the War of 1812. The Maryland tax was on all banks not chartered by the state, but was aimed directly at the BUS. The primary economic cause of the tax was that the BUS had achieved an intolerable competitive financial edge over state institutions. Politically, the tax on BUS was another effort by a state to counter what was perceived to be the odious growth of national power.

Independent of CLS, there is reason enough to conclude a close, if not intimate, association between the politics of federalism in *McCulloch* and capitalism. It has been said that "with few exceptions Marshall's great opinions in which the Constitution was construed in favor of nationalism had their origins in economic conflicts, a fact which gave Marshall the opportunity to promote a nationally supported capitalism."[8] And many read *McCulloch* as teaching the lesson that when national politics and capitalism coalesce, the states must recede politically, regardless of what federalism might seem to require. This granted, the salient issue then becomes whether *McCulloch* is so replete with transparently arbitrary distinctions about sovereignty as to actually subvert the rule of law.[9]

One way to get at this issue is to analyze the way in which legal and political language works in the opinion. The rhetorical test that follows depends on close scrutiny of the structure of the opinion: specifically, how political and legal language about sovereignty actually works to thread liberalism and constitutionalism together to form the fabric of Marshall's doctrine of federalism.

Much of what I say about *McCulloch* is familiar, and this analysis depends on that familiarity. Beginning with the first sentences of the opinion, this test attempts to show how *McCulloch*'s treatment of liberalism and constitutionalism depends as much on plain politics and ordinary political pragmatism as it does on formal legal reasoning.

In the case now to be determined, the defendant, a sovereign state, denies the obligation of a law enacted by the legislature of the Union; the plaintiff . . . contests the validity of an act which has been passed by the legislature of that State. The constitution of our country, in its most interesting and vital parts, is to be considered; the conflicting powers of the government of the Union and its members, as marked in that constitution, are to be discussed. . . . No tribunal can approach such a question without a deep sense of its importance and of the awful responsibility involved in its decision. But it must be decided peacefully, or remain a source of hostile legislation; perhaps of hostility of a still more serious nature.[10]

The first point about these sentences is the explicit designation of Maryland as a "sovereign state," a term juxtaposed to the "legislature of the Union." This designation and juxtaposition are straightforward and yet ambiguous, if not ultimately dissembling. What makes this possible is the political and legal place of sovereignty in American politics, an ambiguity that, along with consequentialist reasoning, constitutes the basic structure of the opinion. Thus, to understand how *McCulloch* deploys the ambiguity of sovereignty, we need to separate its political from its constitutional implications.

It goes without saying that while sovereignty is a commonplace eighteenth- and nineteenth-century political term, it does not appear in the Constitution and takes on rule of law properties only by implication from construction of the document as a whole. In *McCulloch*, "sovereignty" carries two implications about state power, one political and the other legal. The political one is not contentious: it conveys Maryland's positive law authority, which resides in a state's exclusive and indivisible legislative independence, or monopoly of power within territorial limits. It follows from this that a state has ultimate discretion (that is, last say or authority) regarding the proper use of that power.

However, the structure of American politics provides for a Union that represents national legislative independence and discretion within a context of state legislative independence and discretion. Theoretically, this is problematic because sovereignty is indivisible, and for the Union and states to both be sovereign would appear to be a political contradiction. Nonetheless, *The Federalist* argued that such a "division of . . . sovereign power" is a theoretical consequence of states having divested power to the Union, and therefore is implicit in the tenor of the Constitution.[11] As they saw it, federalism resolves this contradiction, and creates a more perfect Union in the bargain, by drawing lines that augment the Union's authority without destroying state sovereignty.

But, of course, advocates for the states denied that the politics of federalism requires a rule of law conception of sovereignty as popular. They agreed that the Constitution, as the fundamental rule of law, represents the "constitution" of a political community (the nation); but their view was closer to a "compact" between states that delegate power (within limits) to "constitute" a Union and a nation. In this context, then, the rhetorical effect of Marshall's "sovereign state" resonates with the uncertainty of one of the root legal problems of nineteenth- (and twentieth-) century American political theory: To what extent does the Union's authority leave the states distinct and independent entities, but nonetheless superintended by the Union?

While ambiguity about sovereignty is inevitable, Marshall does not succumb to it; rather he uses it to confirm Maryland's positive-law authority (and to that extent its sovereignty) while denying the appropriateness of state sovereignty theory for describing constitutional politics. To transform sovereignty from its ambiguous connotations about the constitution of the nation, and what governments may do in the structure of American politics, into (seemingly) unequivocal rule of law talk about what the Constitution requires of them, Marshall links (often contestable) general and abstract political and legal formulations to context-specific practical considerations. The effect of this is not so much to defend rule of law implications drawn from the premises of popular sovereignty as to attack the political consequences of the theory and politics of state sovereignty.

The second point about these first sentences is that they provide a subtle example of this consequentialist maneuver. Marshall makes explicit the threat of the war of all against all if this conflict is not resolved judicially. In the last line of this first paragraph, Marshall asserts that "[o]n the supreme court of the United States has the constitution of our country devolved this important duty" of marking off the boundaries of power between the Union and the states.[12] This remark underlines the tension between competing sovereignties as the source of the problem and the rule of law as the solution. Of course, nothing in the preceding lines explicitly justifies this generalization of Court sovereignty (independence and discretion) over the rule of law, but by this point the Court's judicial independence and discretion were well established, despite state sovereignty objections.

It has been said that "close scrutiny [of Marshall's generalities] may reveal little meaning."[13] But this misses the rhetorical functions of their ambiguities, which are full of tacit significance, particularly of the consequentialist kind. Thus James Boyd White argues, acutely, that Marshall's persuasiveness rests upon his skill in demonstrating that "the Court can offer the nation what no other branch can: the development, over time, of a self-reflective, self-corrective body of discourse that will bind its audience together by engaging them in a common language and a common set of practices. It is a claim to constitute a community and a culture."[14]

It is within the context of the Court's control of political and legal language that Marshall has the way to open up that ambiguous conflation of politics and the rule of law implicit in the expression "sovereign state." Here's how: if the Court, as a part of the tripartite whole that is the Union, has the sovereignty to arbitrate between competing legislative wills, then the whole (the Union) must perforce enjoy some kind of sovereignty over states as well. Thus, juxtaposed to Marshall's explicit reference to Maryland's status as a "sovereign state" is the reference to the role of the Court and Union indicating, in effect, a background and constituent precedent for the Union's rule of law sovereignty. Marshall's whole first paragraph, punctuated by the concluding sentence, provides a consequentialist choice: a community glued together by the Court's rendition of the rule of law, or the politics of war of all against all.[15]

This consequentialist Hobson's choice between order and chaos as the warrant for a rule of law version of sovereignty allows for no middle ground, and Marshall uses it at every crucial turn to vacate sovereignty arguments contrary to his. But simple as this logic is, it must still confront the conventional political and constitutional wisdom that "divided sovereignty" is a middle ground. Divided sovereignty embodies a distinction between the origin and extent of power: the origin of all power in the nation is "the people" and, as Madison put it, the "federal and state governments are . . . but different agents and trustees of the people, constituted with different powers, and designed for different purposes."[16] Advocates of state sovereignty contend that the shared origin of power for the Union and states implies that the extent of power, or sovereignty, is also shared between the two arenas. The tension between this middle ground of shared sovereignty and Marshall's logic belongs not peculiarly to McCulloch but is embodied in federalism. It is but another version of the political ambiguity surrounding sovereignty: how is the Union's authority augmented without destroying state sovereignty?

Marshall's solution to this dilemma is to weave other liberal conventions (about property and power), and their associated consequentialist considerations, into an attack on state sovereignty to show why divided sovereignty does not entail shared sovereignty. This weave is a strategy for moving back and forth between political and legal language and demonstrates that "the language of the Constitution, and hence the language of this opinion and law generally, is continuous with ordinary language and capable of the same richness, complexity and variation—indeed, of the same capacity for inconsistency."[17] This makes McCulloch more than the sum of its parts.

CONSTITUTIONALISM AND LIBERALISM IN McCULLOCH: THE GROUNDWORK

The groundwork for the attack on the consequences of state sovereignty is located in the defense of BUS's rule of law legitimacy. This defense begins with Marshall investing the BUS with considerable, albeit not total, legitimacy by recalling "the practice of the government."

The bill incorporating the bank . . . did not steal upon an unsuspecting legislature, and pass unobserved. After being resisted, first in the open field of debate, and afterwards in the executive cabinet . . . it became law. . . . It would require no ordinary share of intrepidity to assert that a measure adopted under these circumstances was a bold and plain usurpation to which the constitution gave no countenance.[18]

This appeal to plain politics generates three interrelated political claims. Overtly, it bestows on the BUS the same positive-law legitimacy denoted by the expression "sovereign state" assigned to Maryland. At the very least, this places the Bank on the same political footing as anything a "sovereign state" might promulgate. Second, and more subtle, is the implication that practices that pass as politics as usual are not "plain usurpations" of "the conflicting powers of the government of the Union and its members." It intimates a close (but not complete) connection between the plain politics (of incorporating the BUS) and rule of law authority. Finally, the remark about bold usurpations of power not going unnoticed signals the use of empirical claims as appropriate rejoinders to (Maryland's) theoretical state sovereignty claims.

In context, this appeal to plain politics appears common-sensical, yet it is as contentious as it is crowded with intimations. Remember, from the perspective of state sovereignty the Congress lacks authority to incorporate a bank, notwithstanding its promulgation. "Plain usurpation" or not, Maryland contends that the positive-law act of incorporation violates the rule of law. Moreover, if plain practices are a criterion of sovereignty, that criterion cuts both ways as a defense of the Maryland tax as well as the Bank: the Maryland tax did not "steal upon the scene" either. If both the BUS and the tax have a degree of legitimacy on the grounds of practices, then the criterion of practices suggests shared sovereignty. So, the appeal to practices does not, nor is it meant to, undercut state sovereignty directly; rather, it fulfills its purpose merely by shifting attention to plain politics.

Marshall uses this shift to practices to link references to fundamental liberal conventions (about property and power) with plain politics to integrate liberalism and the rule of law. By insisting that "[a]n exposition of the constitution . . . on the faith of which an immense property has been advanced, ought not to be lightly disregarded,"[19] Marshall makes explicit that upcoming appraisals of congressional capacity and sovereignty have plain economic consequences. This has the further effect of making political and economic considerations at least as central as abstract doctrines about sovereignty. Altogether, Marshall is suggesting that it is neither ideologically sound nor practical to "lightly disregard" the plain political fact that there would be no Bank if, in theory and practice, it did not serve the property interests of "the people." As a rhetorical package, appeals to practices, property, and the BUS connect up with the liberal convention that the public good arises out of the process of aggregating conflicting interests.

Marshall also admits what he must: that as political theory Maryland's conception of the rule of law out of state sovereignty is as compatible with the convention that public good arises out of the process of aggregating conflicting interests (with states as the units of aggregation) as popular sovereignty. This admission puts him in position to confront Maryland's own appeal to plain politics calculated to undercut popular sovereignty: that "the people" ratified the Constitution by virtue of their respective state delegations, and not as an undifferentiated public. Hence, the practice of state ratification is compatible with the liberal principle of power derived from the people and the theory of state sovereignty—whereas there is a gap between the actual politics of ratification and any other means by which the people could be expected to ratify the Constitution if popular sovereignty controlled.

Because state and popular sovereignty share the convention of power derived from the people, Marshall must undermine the claim that state sovereignty theory enjoys a closer fit with plain politics. He does this by linking that convention to the plain politics of political agency. Marshall insists that state delegations were merely the instruments of a political *process*: the Constitution was first submitted to the existing Congress, which in turn remanded it to state legislatures for ratification. In fact, Marshall says, "[n]o political dreamer was ever wild enough to think of breaking down the lines which separate the States, and of compounding the American people into one common mass."[20]

This rejoinder suggests that advocates of state sovereignty are guilty of a political fallacy to argue that popular sovereignty requires ratification by an undifferentiated mass; the voice of all the people *was* engaged simply by virtue of the fact that it is a *constitution* that was submitted to Congress. Thus, the rejoinder pushes the opinion deep into liberal questions about political agency: who acts fundamentally in politics, states or "the people"? Here Marshall depends on a reiteration of a Lockean version of the origin and extent of power:[21] not the states, but "the people," acting in "perfect liberty," constitute the political community through their "final" consent, a consent made conclusive by virtue of their independence and discretion.[22] This suggests popular sovereignty's superior fit with liberal conventions about the origin of power, "liberty," and the "consent of the governed" as well.

At the very least, and this is sufficient, this rejoinder makes Maryland's empirical claim to a better fit with practice at least arguable. That is because by virtue of this recitation state sovereignty theory is cast indirectly as rejecting the sovereignty of the people in its own name, whereas popular sovereignty is identified with both a liberal ideology about "the American people" as the agents of ratification and a role for sovereign states. In effect, no "political dreamer" considered destroying state lines, but advocates of state sovereignty would destroy the power, liberty, and consent of the people as specified by liberalism. The elegant twist of all this is that it makes popular sovereignty appear to be a compromise position, and state sovereignty an extreme and destructive doctrine!

Marshall backs this convention-bound conception of agency and politics with consequentialist criteria by indicating the three ends of consent (and their attendant liberal conventions): political stability ("to form a more perfect union"); political security and natural rights ("justice" and "the blessings of liberty"); and peace ("domestic tranquility"). Depending on the commonplace that the Articles of Confederation failed to secure those ends, and the equally common appreciation that it fell to the American people to solve the practical political problems created by divisive states, Marshall brings together popular sovereignty, liberalism, and plain political consequences to show why a Constitution "ordained and established" by "the people" must (by virtue of the consequences of state action) constitute the rule of law and bind the states.

From this plateau, Marshall ties his consequentialist account of the origin of the rule of law, seemingly free from the ambiguities of sovereignty that generated it, into the "universally admitted" (Lockean) convention that government is limited by enumerated powers. This convention, he allows, raises questions about the extent of powers that are "perpetually arising, and will probably continue to arise, as long as our system shall exist."[23] Marshall now admits that the character of power is fuzzy, and his explicitness about this lends an air of credibility to his account. (It also, as we shall see, commits constitutional interpretation to "the development, over time, of a self-reflective, self-corrective body of discourse.")

Marshall's next move is to link enumerated powers to sovereign positive-law authority. He points out that the "Union, though limited in its powers, is supreme within its sphere of action."[24] The effect of such talk is to picture American politics divided by rigid spheres of Union and state positive-law powers, each politically sovereign within its ambits.[25] While the extent of "limited government" may be contestable, the nature of the origin of the power of the Union's sphere is not: the Union is the government "of all; its powers delegated by all; it represents all, and acts for all." And it is supreme as long as it acts within its sphere.

The argument depends on the liberal convention about the origin of political power. Through it, Marshall transforms what is otherwise contestable about the extent of limited government, as it relates to the bigger issue of sovereignty, into an assertion of supremacy for that government that has the textual authority of the supremacy clause of the Constitution. Supremacy allows Marshall to play on the issue of agency: whereas the states act for themselves, the Union, though limited, has supreme power to serve "all of the people." That this is so allows Marshall to return to the plain political consequences of treating the states as if they were sovereign: any one state in the Union is willing to control the nation, but no one state is willing to let other states control it. Thus, the convention of limited government is a rhetorical instrument to contrast popular sovereignty, attached to a liberal picture of government that serves all, with state sovereignty and the politics of divisive states that run the risk of the war of all against all.

These repeated appeals to liberalism and consequentialist considerations are calculated to build up the tensions between state sovereignty theory and plain politics for creating and maintaining a "more perfect union." It is worth reiterating that the primary force of these arguments is political, not legal. The argument for the supreme authority of the Union depends on a liberal image of the birth and growth of power. A nation, an extraordinary political creation of "the people," born out of conflict and strife, endowed by the people with independence and discretion by them, struggles to survive the predictably destructive tendencies of state governments.

The conclusion to be drawn from this image of power is that the only way to preserve the Union ("to bind its parts") is to weigh competing theories of sovereignty on the basis of their compatibility with liberal conventions and practical consequences. It is this image of power that grounds Marshall's transformation of political language about agency into rule of law language about the supremacy clause: "this constitution, and the laws of the United States . . . shall be the supreme law of the land." With the recitation of the supremacy clause the groundwork of *McCulloch* has been completed. What follows is the transformation of this "mere reason[ing]" about politics to a rule of law defense of the Bank and an attack on the tax.

LIBERALISM AND CONSTITUTIONALISM: McCULLOCH AND THE BANK

Having argued for the rule of law supremacy of the Union, Marshall is now prepared to focus on how legislation is promulgated "in pursuance of the constitution."[26] The issue is cast in these terms: if incorporating a Bank is not among the enumerated powers, how can that act be said to be congruent with the Constitution? By answering this question Marshall is able to build up to a pragmatic conception of power embodied in the dictum that "it is a constitution we are expounding."[27]

The answer begins with the consequentialist observation that the explicit rejection of implicit or implied powers in the Articles of Confederation had proved politically disutile. Therefore, to avoid rigid explicitness, the new Constitution is not "prolix" like a legal code. Rather, its "great oulines [are] marked, its important objects designated, and the minor ingredients which compose those objects [can] be deduced from the nature of the objects themselves" with clarity and precision.[28]

Hence, the issue of incorporation, as a minor ingredient, is to be understood by a "deductive logic" that depends on "a fair construction of the whole instrument." Actually, the logic depends on the groundwork of conventions and pragmatic considerations (described above) to construct a network of political and legal premises for the means and ends of congressional power. Marshall's starting point is to note that the enumerated powers of the Union regarding revenues are "ample" to the extent that "[t]he sword and purse, all the external relations, and no inconsiderable portion of the industry of the nation [are] intrusted to its government." The justification for these ample powers is "happiness and prosperity" (that is, the consequentialist ends of stability, security and peace), and these ends require means appropriate for their execution.[29]

It is plain political sense, for Marshall, that given these ends, and given the power granted to the Union, "it is the interest of the nation to facilitate its execution."[30] This appeal to the plain politics of power leads to another consequentialist claim that constitutional construction would be unreasonable if it led to conclusions that obstructed the power necessary to manage the politics of revenue collection and expenditures. It follows that since implied and incidental powers are not explicitly excluded, constitutional construction requires the rule of law that powers required to secure the public good of enumerated ends include appropriate but unenumerated means.

Having situated the BUS in the wider context of the capacity of Congress to carry out its positive-law operations, Marshall creates an image of dire political consequences following upon a state sovereignty interpretation of the Constitution: an immense nation rendered helpless to manage its political exigencies because the government of "all the people" is constrained by a rule of law that limits congressional discretion over legislative means.[31] Behind this image is a plain political threat: if Congress does not have the power of incorporation, because it lacks sovereignty over such means, it could not long sustain the authority to pass other laws to accomplish its objects. Thus, where "the government has a right to do an act, and has imposed on it the duty of performing that act, [it] must according to the dictates of reason, be allowed to select the means. . . ."[32]

Using powerful liberal terms like "right" and "duty" cements the connection between positive-law power, sovereign authority, and the liberal principle of fiduciary government. To interpret the Constitution in such a way as to interfere with the duties of the Union violates the principle of delegated power and the cause of liberal government. Also, to interfere with the means of a fiduciary government is to risk having that government fail in its duty to secure stability, security, and peace. Marshall thinks this logic tight enough to insist that those who would argue a contrary view of the relation between means and ends for constituting a more perfect union "take upon themselves the burden of establishing the exception."[33]

Marshall completes this political reasoning with a conception of divided sovereignty to undercut shared sovereignty. First, he dismisses the idea that the extent of sovereignty is determined by whether the Union or state governments were formed first (since some states were formed before and others after ratification). Citing the supremacy clause, he asserts that the Union is sovereign within its sphere. Within the Union's (rigid) sphere of positive-law authority, incorporation can be an implied or incidental power because it is always a means toward some other end or object of government. Thus, within the ambits of congressional power, the act of incorporation is an act of sovereignty.

These remarks open up to a rejoinder to Maryland's rule of law claim that the necessary and proper clause was designed to restrict congressional power through enumeration for the sake of maintaining the integrity of the remainder of sovereignty not delegated to the Union. Maryland's reading is that the word "necessary" controls the clause as a restriction on power. Marshall refuses to get drawn into the issue at this level and reaches instead to "ordinary language," wherein "necessary" connotes that which is "convenient, or useful, or essential."[34] The word, he says, implies discretion over means incidental to ends; it is not used to express absolute exclusion but matters of degree determined by the subject, context, and intentions of actors. For this reason, any interpretation of the rule of law about congressional legislative means must be "intended to endure for ages to come, and consequently, to be adapted to the various crises of human affairs."[35]

Thus, the rule of law conclusion that "necessary" obtains to those means appropriate for executing sovereign powers, and that such means are "a right incidental to the power and conducive to its beneficial exercise," is crucial to a nation of citizens engaged by a common constitutional language and political practices.[36] The founders, Marshall recounts, intended "[t]hat any means adapted to the end, any means which tended directly to the execution of the constitutional powers of the government, were in themselves constitutional."[37] Now referring directly to the Constitution, Marshall observes how the clause appears in the context of the powers, not limitations, of Congress; how the form and effect of its words are not restrictive; and how, if the intention was to restrict congressional means, the convention would have done so explicitly. Ergo, the clause does not enlarge or restrict powers, it simply relates to powers incidental to enumerated ones.

The Union and the states then are separate spheres of divided power and sovereignty. A state sovereignty reading of shared sovereignty violates both the plain politics of legislative action and the rule of law regarding the supremacy of the Union to execute its fiduciary duties to the people within its sphere. Not that "any means" implies unbridled discretion. Marshall reiterates that the limits of government "are not to be transcended,"[38] specifying that rule of law for supremacy in the Union's sphere requires the conclusion that if "the end be legitimate . . . all means which are appropriate, which are plainly adapted to that end, which are not prohibited . . . are constitutional."[39] Given all that has come before it, "plainly" connotes plain politics: that which is politically reasonable or compatible with settled liberal expectations about what governments may do (including chartering corporations).[40] With this, the means-ends argument for the BUS is completed.

CONSTITUTIONALISM AND LIBERALISM: McCULLOCH AND TAX

Nothing in this political and legal means-ends defense of the BUS, in and of itself, yet excludes the legitimacy of Maryland's tax of out-of-state banks. As it stands, although Congress has the sovereign authority to incorporate the Bank, divided sovereignty leaves Maryland free to tax it within its rigid sphere. To void the tax, the rule of law argument for congressional plenary power and the Union's supremacy has to be positioned to bar the way against shared sovereignty without at the same time undermining divided sovereignty.

The assault on the tax begins indirectly, by way of analogy from the rule of law on imports and exports. Politically and legally, divided sovereignty leaves both the Union and states their share of respective sovereign powers of taxation. However, Marshall points to constitutional specifications where the power of taxation is withdrawn from state control. These instances, he says, are analogous to the supremacy clause principle that state sovereignty may be limited (even within its ambits) whenever it interferes with "necessary and proper" federal governmental activities.

Marshall recommends that within this context, the supremacy clause is an axiom for drawing lines between competing spheres of government, and generates two corollaries from it to distinguish between state and congressional functions. The first corollary is a plain political one out of positive law: Webster's famous dictum that "[t]he power to create is the power to preserve," and "the power to destroy in other hands is hostile to power to create and preserve."[41] This dictum summarizes all that has come before it. Power originates in the people, who, for the sake of stability, security, and peace, delegated power and consented to a Constitution that constitutes a Union. The power of this Union is fiduciary, and Congress has the right and duty to create and preserve itself in the name of the people. The power to destroy that unity comes from hostile and divisive states, which must be kept in check.

That check comes from the other corollary as a rule for constitutional construction: "the very essence of supremacy [is] to remove all obstacles to its action within its own sphere, and so to modify every power vested in subordinate governments, as to exempt its own operations from their own influence."[42] That is, shared sovereignty and the rule of law are incompatible, because the former prevents the Union from fulfilling its legislative duties by making it dependent on the states. Yet again, state sovereignty implies the theory and practice of war of all against all. Thus, only the rule of law of popular supremacy protects the Union from the states, and counters their odious use of political power.

Marshall, though, does not let the opinion rest here. Instead, he continues to work the internal logic of creating and preserving stability, security, and peace to achieve an even broader political defense of his version of federalism. Going beyond the supremacy clause to elaborate why states are subordinate reinforces the impression that the question of taxation is at least as important to federalism as the constitutionality of the BUS. This final assault then is an attempt to close out the shared sovereignty assertion that Maryland's absolute positive-law power of taxation is sufficient for the state to "exercise [its] acknowledged powers upon [the BUS]."[43]

To that end, Marshall exploits the logic of rigid political spheres to secure the distance between divided and shared sovereignty. Having acknowledged that the power of taxation is divided, Marshall takes pains to distinguish between the character of state and federal taxation relative to the kind of political sovereignty exercised. The power of each state, he asserts, arises from the people within it. The authority within each sphere is plenary and absolute because of the exigencies of government. He then reminds us, playing off of liberal anxieties over property and the abuses of power, that the only protection the people of a state have from "erroneous and oppressive taxation" is the "structure of government."[44] By "structure of government" Marshall means plain legislative politics.

The origin and extent of the taxation power of the Union is the same: its power arises from the people, its power is plenary within its sphere, and this power is subject to the same abuses. But the Union's politics is structured differently, by the power delegated to it as the government of all the people. This implies the plain politics of the separation of powers between the Senate and House, so that only a coordinate branch of the tripartite government, not the states directly, can control Congress's power of taxation.

With this argument Marshall has transformed the issue of sovereignty into a question of whether liberal conventions for the origin and extent of national government, with its separation of powers, are to be sustained in practice. Federalism, as a political and rule of law doctrine for divided powers, requires the conclusion that taxation sovereignty cannot be shared because no branch can extend its sovereign authority beyond the structural limits of its respective public and politics. The Bank is an instrument of the Union's taxation power, it serves national interests, and only the Union has the authority to protect or destroy it. Appropriately, it is "[o]n the supreme court of the United States [that] the constitution [ultimately] devolved this important duty" of policing the rigid spheres of taxation sovereignty.

The implications of this argument cannot be overemphasized. Apparently, neither implied power nor supremacy is sufficient to protect the interests involved. It is ultimately plain politics that dooms the tax. Daniel Webster, in another context, observed that to "confer . . . such immunities as may induce individuals to become stockholder, and to furnish . . . capital" is to control an economy.[45] The power to tax is a crucial exercise of political and economic power, and McCulloch is meant to ensure that states do not have the power, and privilege, to check the Union's independence and discretion over the development of capital in the nation. At bottom, consequentialist considerations about the plain politics of stability, security, and peace are behind McCulloch's conception of federalism.

CLS v. McCULLOCH: A DEFENSE

As we have seen, McCulloch's defense of national power and the Union's control of the economy depends on a pragmatic political theory of sovereignty (or will) and the rule of law (reason) to circumvent the theoretical and practical force of state (and shared) sovereignty without altogether undermining state power. A weave of liberal conventions and plain political claims, the theory uses the liberal convention of power derived from the people, and generalizations about the politics of liberal ends of government (the public good as stability, security, and peace), to confirm the political sovereignty (or will) of the Union. Consequentialist claims about the destructive effect of state machinations on rigid spheres of power drive a conception of the rule of law (or reason) for limited governments, with each sphere plenary within its own ambits and the Union supreme over all. In this political theory, the rule of law substantiates the (Lockean) principle of limits to the use of political power, which even sovereignty and positive law cannot set aside.

In *McCulloch*, sovereignty and the rule of law are coordinated to teach three general political lessons about federalism: (1) legal and political abstractions (like sovereignty) and political conventions (like "power derived from the people") create but cannot, by themselves, resolve concrete political and legal problems about the distribution of power; (2) pragmatic and consequentialist political judgments about the uses and abuses of power and the public good are necessary to resolve those problems; and (3) fact and value discretion alone, quite apart from the ambiguities of conventions like sovereignty, ensures that whatever image of politics arises from these convention-bound and plain politics arguments is always contestable.

The image of federalist politics that emerges is one of persistent and inevitable conflict over ideology—that is, over what governments may do. The fact that there is no formulaic solution for fleshing out what the public good is, or determining if the states or the Union should prevail, does not mean that anything goes. Federalism requires arguments about the fit between conventions and plain politics to integrate sovereignty and the rule of law; and we know from case law that that is always a matter of close calls. In turn, the ambiguity of controlling conventions and fact determinations entails that criteria for the distribution of power are intrinsically indeterminate. This indeterminacy ought not to be underestimated because it means that, in principle, arguments about power are never beyond rejoinder.

It means also that the indeterminacy of criteria can be a bulwark against taking the politics of divided sovereignty for granted. *McCulloch* in fact comes down to a skeptical way of thinking about power. Competing conventions provide the context within which advocates must be perpetually constructing their competing images of federalist politics. Pragmatism fulfills skepticism when, and if, sovereignty and the rule of law are constantly open to challenge and revision by competing interpretations of conventions and fact determinations. At this level, thinking along the lines of *McCulloch*'s jurisprudence should teach us to have an abiding skepticism about any use of political power.

But at another level, *McCulloch* teaches a CLS lesson. Pragmatism is arbitrariness fulfilled when case law fails to conform to its own criteria of justification. Despite its criteria, and general appeals to the war of all against all and divisive state action, *McCulloch* fails to provide "a careful examination of powers actually granted the Bank, . . . their relationship to the explicit powers of Congress, and . . . the degree to which they undermine the principle of limited powers."[46] *McCulloch* also fails to consider whether a nondiscriminatory tax on all banknotes would have been constitutional.[47] In failing to do so,

McCulloch subverts the rule of law by failing to meet its own plain political evidentiary criterion to address the specifics of the politics and economics of the BUS.

The salient question is, what to make of this failure? To be sure, fact and value discretion ensures that constitutional arguments always can be criticized for evidentiary gaps. Indeed, the lack of definitive criteria for how and when to draw the lines of power makes it difficult to be sure, on a case-by-case basis, whether an opinion is really grounded in pragmatic considerations or ad hoc policy decisions of the kind CLS complains about. It was no surprise that Marshall's adversaries read *McCulloch* as an aggrandizement of national hegemony; and it is easy to understand John Randolph's frustrated sentiment regarding Marshall's jurisprudence: "All wrong, all wrong, but not a man in the United States can tell why or wherein."[48] But dashed, and legitimate (in the full sense of the word), liberal expectations about state sovereignty do not provide sufficient grounds for concluding that *McCulloch* is fatally flawed.

To be so convinced we must be convinced that its gaps and other indeterminacies are inevitably caused by that liberal antinomy between the will and reason—or less metaphysically, by the inevitable incompatibility of federalism and the rule of law. We have to be convinced that its generalizations are inevitably and arbitrarily exploited to obscure actual political conditions; and that the lack of specific descriptions of plain politics is endemic to liberalism's failure to forestall the continuous aggregation of existing political and economic power. But to be convinced requires that we accept a metaphysical premise that reduces legal and political arguments, let alone politics, without remainder to virtually unintentional recapitulations of ideology and the existing social structure. This archimedean and deterministic perspective is literally at odds with *McCulloch*, which has been shown to be more than the sum of its conventional linguistic parts, and to have used those parts to reformulate as much as to mirror political beliefs and practices. In comparison, Tushnet's CLS appears to depend on the idea that citizens are shackled in a cave of liberal language, captured by a parade of shadow arguments and without real choices about what can be done with language and actual political conditions. This puts metaphysics in control of politics.

This presumes too much and ironically takes much of the political sting out of its critique. A manifestation of this flaw is the equivocal status of the critique's criteria of justification. If liberal metaphysics is hegemonic, and the critique is in any way internal to liberalism, then it suffers from the selfsame antinomies it purports to expose. Its complaints would be no more or less consistent or coherent than the liberal arguments it attacks, and rather than revealing liberal legalism's deep structural flaws, it could be passed off as nothing more than ox goring. Thus, the reduction that makes liberalism fatally flawed proves too much, leaving the critical tiger with much duller teeth.

One way to restore the bite of the critique is to contend that it is external to liberalism and transcends it on the basis of some alternative belief system (for example, socialism, marxism, nihilism, feminism, or even deconstructionism) and complementary economic schema. But while Tushnet denies being "committed to any level of liberalism,"[49] he also denies that CLS "has . . . a positive program" of its own;[50] it is fulfilled by attacking liberalism and making "pragmatic assessments . . . of who will be helped and who will be hurt by particular political actions," ostensibly "without a broader social theory."[51]

But, absent such a theory (or at least criteria of justification other than backing the losers over the winners), CLS's pragmatic instrumentalism appears to be even more arbitrary than the liberalism it attacks, which is at least constrained by its core conventions. Simply put, without explicit political criteria for assessing the validity of pragmatic judgments, there are no political grounds from which to say whether the CLS critique is valid or not.[52] It is all too easy, but nonetheless appropriate, to turn Tushnet's remarks against liberalism against him: "The arbitrary character of the [CLS] doctrine means that the sword of Damocles will drop, perhaps at random or perhaps for invidious political reasons, without having broader implications for the exercise of power generally."[53]

To be sure, these problems do not mean that liberal legalism is beyond the reach of the critique. In defense of *McCulloch* or against, its gaps have to be explained. But what is needed is a nonreductionist conception of language and politics that takes into account the constructive and constitutive role of political arguments. Such a view acknowledges that language is an instrument of political struggle, shaped not by metaphysical antinomies but by social practices in the context of concrete political determinations, that is, "situationally derived truths."[54]

A rhetorical analysis of the sort used here to test *McCulloch* takes us a considerable distance toward such a conception. It shows that the normal use of political and legal terms in constitutional reasons requires inventiveness and strategy; it demonstrates that political significance is not given, but is constructed by pragmatic integration of facts and values. It also demonstrates how and why the ambiguity of political language makes these pragmatic considerations possible, and how difficult it is to conclude (with Tushnet) that a political conclusion is necessarily wrong (or right, for that matter).

But rhetorical analysis alone is insufficient. We must go beyond the structures and functions of political and legal language for an independent empirical analysis of the political context within which arguments occur.[55] Empirical analysis raises political questions about whether the indeterminacies of practical language about the structure of American politics, the exigencies of the welfare state, and the jurisprudence of judicial review either expand or contract the reach of basic conventions to maintain or alter existing political practices.

These questions cannot be answered by argumentative analysis alone, any more than by metaphysical prescriptions.

Actually, CLS points up the need for this kind of explicitly political analysis, but retreats into metaphysics instead of delivering the goods. It is important to consider whether not only liberal but political reasoning in general is inclined toward incoherence. These are not philosophical considerations but contextual ones about the extent to which the control of political power, rather than ideology, accounts for the distortions in political arguments. Of course, competing ideologies provide conventions that structure arguments, and politics, in different and competing ways; but arguments, rather than stipulations, have to be made as to whether incoherence is to be attributed to ideology or to interests in maintaining power generally.

Tushnet's CLS critique disregards this kind of discussion of power and language. It does confront the inconsistencies, ambiguities, and equivocations that arise in liberal reasoning, and perhaps in all political choices. But when CLS fails to take seriously the inevitability of practical contextual considerations that give form and shape to political arguments, we need to go beyond CLS to return politics to theory. We must consider how all legal and political arguments are affected by the (unequal) distribution of power in actual, specific political contexts within which political arguments arise.

Considerations of this kind require an analysis of at least three ways in which political power, not liberalism per se, is the focus.[56] The first aspect is pluralism (or the lack of it). Pluralist politics require advocates to convince others to transfer their adherence and support for liberal conventions over to the policies that advocates seek to have implemented. To the extent that resource and demand constraints restrict political talk to elites, and therefore limit the range of interests articulated, it becomes necessary to differentiate between the extent to which it is resource and demand constraints, rather than liberal conventions (all by themselves), that constrain politics and policies. On the other hand, appraisals have to be made about the extent to which greater interest articulation, political participation, and conflict are either possible or desirable, independent of the unequal distribution of resources or the limits of liberalism.

The second aspect is the role of technology and bureaucracy. Here one must distinguish between how scientific and technological institutions, organizations, and managerial elites per se limit practical political arguments and policies. Is it liberalism or technology and bureaucracy that create and/or satisfy political, economic, and social demands, and therefore expand or contract discussions of power?

The third aspect is social class, which appears to be the sole concern of the CLS critique. Unequal resources and demand constraints do shape or privilege certain conceptions of conventions, and the problem is to characterize how conventions become objects of political struggle in the formation of the political agendas and the execution of policies. The issue here is the extent to which the control of agendas and the execution of policies result in arbitrary arguments, independent of liberalism.

In conclusion, the CLS critique is too abstract to conclude that *McCulloch*, and federalism, are fatally flawed. The virtue of *McCulloch* is its rhetoric: it takes liberal conventions and pragmatic considerations seriously. In so doing, *McCulloch* illustrates, independent of its specific doctrine, that the intrinsic indeterminacy of liberal legal reasoning provides the potential for the distribution of power to be understood in more than one way. At this level, that the Union prevailed in *McCulloch* is less important than the process of argumentation it reveals. As a model for transforming liberal political claims about power into the language of the rule of law, *McCulloch* is an exemplar of the self-reflective capacity of constitutional reasoning. The proof of that is the extent to which the issues of *McCulloch* remain alive in the evolution of federalism case law, both within and without CLS.

But to the extent that contemporary case law fails to fulfill the linguistic potential of *McCulloch* to both explore the plasticity of sovereignty and the rule of law, and to make earnest empirical investigations of actual political conditions (as *McCulloch* did), it can be expected that the momentum toward the aggregation of power will continue unchecked. *McCulloch* evidences both the potential strengths and weaknesses of liberal legal reasoning. CLS is right to remind us of the intimate connections between legal and political reasoning, and to warn us about how constitutional choices are political ones. It provides an important warning against simply presuming that liberal ideology is easily or always satisfactorily articulated in the law. However, until we are convinced that liberal ideology is uniquely given over to arbitrariness, the CLS attack extends only so far as to warn us of how political and legal arguments, despite their potential, fall prey to the pervasive and destructive effects of political power generally.

NOTES

1. Wheat. 415 (1819). Some of the material on *McCulloch* appeared in my *Political Philosophy and Political Action* 55, at 64–72, in WHAT SHOULD POLITICAL THEORY BE NOW? (J. Nelson ed. 1983).

2. I do not consider the extent to which Marshall's reasoning follows the legal and political strategies, let alone the prose, of Daniel Webster and William Pinkney.

3. Tushnet, *The Dilemmas of Liberal Constitutionalism*, 42 OHIO ST. L. J. 411, at 411–26 (1981). Also, Tushnet, *Critical Legal Studies and Constitutional Law: An Essay in Deconstruction*, 36 STAN. L. REV. 575 (1984); *Perspectives on Critical Legal Studies*, 52 GEO. WASH. L. REV. 238 (1984), and *Federalism and the Traditions of American Political Theory*, 19 GA. L. REV. 981 (1985).

4. It is generally acknowledged that the diversity of CLS doctrines (ranging from "super-liberalism" to feminism, socialism, deconstructionism, and anarchism) makes it

difficult to generalize about its debt to marxism. It appears that Tushnet's version owes at least an implicit debt to Marx and Mannheim in ideology.

5. Tushnet, *supra* note 3 Ohio St. L. J. at 412.

6. *Id.* at 415.

7. *Id.* at 421–22.

8. *See* R. Steamer, Chief Justice, Leadership and the Supreme Court 72 (1986). Also: R. Faulkner, The Jurisprudence of John Marshall (1986), for an excellent rendition of the commercial liberalism of Marshall. A salient difference between my account and Faulkner's is the emphasis given here to pragmatic and consequentialist considerations.

9. It should be noted that one of CLS's hermeneutic presumptions is that any careful reading of the text reveals the intrinsic incapacities of liberal legalism.

10. 4 Wheat. at 418.

11. The Federalist Papers, Nos. 33, 203 (J. Cooke ed. 1961).

12. 4 Wheat. at 418.

13. Steamer, *supra* note 8, at 69.

14. J. White, When Words Lose Their Meaning 251 (1984).

15. This motif mirrors that of the *Federalist Papers*, in which readers are asked to choose between anarchy, democracy, and a republic, where the first two guarantee disorder and only the third can break and control factions.

16. The Federalist No. 46, at 315.

17. White, *supra* note 14, at 260.

18. 4 Wheat. at 419.

19. Daniel Webster, in his oral arguments before the Court, brought attention to "the value of a vast amount of private property" implicated in the challenge to the BUS.

20. 4 Wheat. at 420.

21. *See* Faulkner, *supra* note 8, at 103–6.

22. 4 Wheat. at 420.

23. *Id.* at 421.

24. 4 *Id.*

25. This discussion of rigid spheres is adopted from remarks on *The Slaughterhouse Cases* in L. Tribe, American Constitutional Law 419–22 (1978).

26. 4 Wheat. at 421.

27. *Id.* at 422.

28. *Id.*

29. *Id.*

30. *Id.*

31. *Id.* at 422–23.

32. *Id.* at 423.

33. *Id.*

34. *Id.* at 426.

35. Marshall argues by analogy from oaths of office, punishment, and power to establish a postal service (4 Wheat. at 427–28) to illustrate legislative discretion over means not essential, but beneficial, to the exercise of power.

36. 4 Wheat. at 428.

37. *Id.* at 429.

38. *Id.* at 430.

39. *Id.*

40. By analogy to Article III, Section 4 (referring to the incorporation of territorial governments).

41. 4 Wheat. at 433.

42. *Id.* at 434.

43. *Id.*

44. *Id.* at 435.

45. Remarks of Daniel Webster, in a speech of July 1832, in response to President Jackson's veto of the BUS charter, quoted in E. WHEELER, DANIEL WEBSTER, THE EX-POUNDER OF THE CONSTITUTION 40 (1905).

46. Currie, *The Constitution in the Supreme Court: State and Congressional Powers, 1801–1835,* 49 U. CHI. L. REV. 887, at 933 (1982).

47. *Id.* at 167–68.

48. STEAMER, *supra* note 8, at 68.

49. Tushnet, *supra* note 3, STAN. 575, at 627.

50. Tushnet, *supra* note 3, GEO. WASH. L. REV. 238, at 241.

51. Tushnet, *id.* at 241–42.

52. *See also,* in another context, Wellman, *Practical Reasoning and Judicial Justification: Toward an Adequate Theory,* 57 U. COLO. L. REV. 45, at 52 (1985).

53. Tushnet, *supra* note 3, OHIO ST. L.J. at 422.

54. Poulakos, *Toward a Sophistic Definition of Rhetoric,* 16 PHIL. AND RHETORIC 35, at 42 (1983).

55. *See* McGuire, *The Structure of Rhetoric,* 15 PHIL. AND RHETORIC 146 (1982).

56. *See* R. ALFORD & R. FRIEDLAND, POWERS OF THEORY, CAPITALISM, THE STATE, AND DEMOCRACY 15–35 (1985).

8

Political Epistemology:
John Marshall's Propositions for
Modern Constitutional Law

JOHN BRIGHAM

Contemporary lore and literature on the founding has at least two shortcomings. Some of the material depicts the men of the period in a fashion that raises their genius to a superhuman level and, as a consequence, loses track of their politics. Another shortcoming is a consequence of depicting the contribution these men made to American politics as so inevitable that human creativity is difficult to discern. Thus a great deal of what constitutes legal politics is inevitably consumed by our notion of "the founding" with all the baggage that term must carry.[1] Yet, by the interpretation of fundamental texts American jurisprudence has created doctrinal referents emanating from the federal period to fit our conception of institutional authority.[2]

Both shortcomings can be seen in the scholarship on Chief Justice John Marshall, and they challenge our understanding of his historical place. In particular, there is the tendency of some Marshall scholars to leave the impression that the first among the great justices interpreted the Constitution rather matter of factly, perhaps even mechanically.[3] They acknowledge his creativity and his politics, but this picture is nothing like the one presented to an earlier generation influenced by Albert J. Beveridge's monumental biography.[4] Three opinions from John Marshall's pen, *Marbury v. Madison*, *McCulloch v. Maryland*, and *Gibbons v. Ogden* have become essential features of this historiography and have oriented modern constitutional discourse.[5] A fourth, *Barron v. Baltimore*,[6] though it has dominated constitutional law for a longer time than the others and then went into serious eclipse, may yet join the pantheon.[7] These cases are the place where the lore on interpreting the American Constitution is grounded.

This chapter describes the rhetorical character of John Marshall's greatest opinions in terms of the epistemic in ordinary politics. Thus, we tie his method of interpretation to the practical political labors of the founding generation and in this way we present a conception of a constitution being created as it was being interpreted. The exhortatory character of Marshall's opinions reveals his effort to impose his view on the new American polity, and in this sense they are particularly striking. In his exhortations, we consider John Marshall a practitioner in the politics of knowledge. At the same time that we celebrate his creative capacity with knowledge as an element in fashioning the American polity, we call attention to the interests served by the conceptions Marshall put forth. Thus, the interplay of symbol and interest helps us to understand an articulate politician who provided some important concepts that would later be used to bind the polity.

EPISTEMIC POLITICS

The four Marshall cases examined here define much of the modern constitutional landscape.[8] *Marbury* is the cornerstone of judicial review, *McCulloch* a key to federalism, *Gibbons* the linchpin of congressional power, and *Barron* determined the scope of the Bill of Rights for 150 years according to the framework Marshall set out. These cases add up to much of modern constitutional law. The emphasis one gets from looking at the cases is on "the first half" of the Constitution since what we consider the civil libertarian protections, the Bill of Rights and equal protection, did not develop until later. In this first half, covering separation of powers, the contemporary importance of these cases can not be overemphasized.

The four cases also spread across Marshall's thirty-five years as Chief Justice. *Marbury*, in 1803, is the earliest, and the situation from which it arises indicates that Marshall is just beginning to settle into his position. *McCulloch*, in 1819, is about the nature of a constitution and the nation itself. By 1824, when Marshall was sixty-nine years old, the issue of commerce led him to make the statement he did in *Gibbons*, while, at the end of his career, in *Barron*, 1833, we have Marshall handing us his most immediately accommodating decision and one that may see renewed interest as progressive students of the Constitution turn away from reliance on national power. It is not important to establish whether these cases are representative of the whole of his work. They are examined here because they constitute Marshall's most important contributions to contemporary constitutional discourse.

Scholarship on John Marshall is extensive, almost overwhelming in its historical scope and variety. Each generation has its Marshall, from the partisan factions of the founding period during which he was a force, to the contemporary sanctifiers of that period who look to Marshall as their law giver. The background for this chapter is a classic text written about the Chief Justice at the beginning of the modern era, *John Marshall and the Constitution*, by

Edward S. Corwin.[9] This work is compared with more recent scholarship treating Marshall and his opinions in contemporary constitutional law.[10]

Corwin's picture of Marshall has more blemishes than we tend to find today, yet elements of this picture have been the biographical force behind the credibility of claims for his authority in prior generations. The picture Hobbes painted of himself is offered by Corwin as a description of John Marshall, "that he made more use of his brains than of his bookshelves and that, if he had read as much as most men, he would have been as ignorant as they."[11] This man of will and ideas, a judicial activist in the modern nomenclature, for the first third of the nineteenth century would lay the foundations of contemporary constitutionalism in a basement chamber in the north wing of the new Capitol, said to have been dubbed by John Randolph "the cave of Trophonius," the master builder of antiquity.[12]

My approach looks at the Constitution as a language, although I feel some reluctance in using discourse terminology for two reasons. There has been so much around the academy for the last decade,[13] although the impact on the study of law has been more recent and is still somewhat less pervasive than the impact in a discipline like comparative literature.[14] And, most of the discourse analysis applied to the study of law and politics has had a relativist caste recently popular among those given to the study of multiple meanings.[15]

We begin with three related propositions. First, that John Marshall's decisions did not determine the future but were used by later constitutional scholars, particularly Thomas Cooley in the late nineteenth century, to support an emerging view of the past with federal judges distinctly more central to American politics than they had been in Marshall's time.[16] Second, as a correlative, that the words and arguments developed by judges such as John Marshall are materials given meaning by others. Their forms, their play on "reality," influences but does not determine how they can be employed. Third, the contemporary tone of Marshall's ideas about interpretation is due to his participation in the founding, something he did. But, the rootedness of his opinion in core structures of contemporary meaning that are now dominant in the American constitutional structure also gives them a tone. This was something others did.

A constitutional polity establishes specific ways of proceeding in politics.[17] The legacy of John Marshall is that his claims for sovereignty, the powers of Congress, the authority of judges, and the Bill of Rights have, for the most part, become part of our constitutional language. From his legacy, we have created possibilities and organized expectations. Marshall, the nineteenth-century partisan, has become the litmus test for constitutional understanding. For instance, in the hearings on the nomination of Robert Bork of the D.C. Court of Appeals to become a justice of the Supreme Court, when the nominee was asked what he thought was the most important case decided by the Supreme Court he said *Marbury v. Madison*. Bork passed this test. On one of the few times in the hearings that the committee was united in support of the nominee's views on the Constitution, heads on the Senate Judiciary Committee nodded in approving unison. Possibilities in constitutional language, like the case names appropriate for particular occasions, are the things that make sense for those who know the tradition. They determine the range of judicial action while giving that action meaning.[18] One of the issues to be explored here is the use of Marshall the partisan as the law giver.

Marbury

Generally *Marbury v. Madison* is the first case reported in nearly every major modern constitutional law text by law school professors and political scientists alike.[19] Although it is certainly not the first constitutional case or the first Supreme Court case, *Marbury* is where our conventions situate the beginning of constitutional law. This is because the convention requires establishing the centrality of the justices. The opinion begins with the Chief Justice acknowledging "[t]he peculiar delicacy of this case, the novelty of some of its circumstances, and the real difficulty attending the points which occur in it. . . ." Marshall's extreme sensitivity to nuance and politics is reflected in Corwin's portrait, one we can expect to be characteristic of thought about the Chief Justice in the last generation. The life of this opinion is a logic derived from the author's experience. Like the picture of the founding fathers we get in the same jurisprudence,[20] Marshall is a builder and his materials are the American experience. Construction of the opinion presents a picture of a rhetorically gifted judge. Although the politics of Marshall's involvement, where the judge is deciding on the legal standing of actions he took in an executive capacity, has been emphasized more recently, the conflicts in his interests have been interpreted as a way of adding to rather than detracting from the prevailing characterization.

The Chief Justice moves from an essentially political picture to the familiar legalistic query, with which he begins to try and impose a formal simplicity on the situation. In legal terms, he asks, "Has the applicant a right . . . ?" and "Do the laws of his country afford a remedy . . . ?" It seems obvious now that this talk of rights is an appropriate form of inquiry, but 200 years ago the legal foundations of the national Union were anything but certain and the Constitution was a relatively new mechanism for ordering the affairs of a people in the midst of the Americas.[21] Marshall engages in this discourse to which judicial authority is now traced without citing a single judicial authority as precedent.

In fact, Marshall states that "The government of the United States has been emphatically termed a government of laws, and not of men." We should take note of the exhortation behind what we might ordinarily suppose to be a rather matter-of-fact assertion. This is particularly true given the odd way in which the opinion is developed. As Corwin and others have noted, the Chief Justice ignores the tradition of judicial restraint in Blackstone and examines the jurisdictional question only after he has lectured the President on his "legal" obligations.[22] The often-quoted statement above is only the first of a number of places in the opinion where Marshall is emphatic about his picture of constitutional law ascending to the higher reaches of public authority. The Chief Justice seems to will his reading into the Constitution as a function of the personal authority by which he would soon come to dominate his colleagues.[23] Legal questions extracted from the melange of political interests such as, "Is he entitled to the remedy for which he applies?" are turned into simple findings offered with beguiling straightforwardness. "This, then, is a plain case for mandamus," asserts the Chief Justice before proceeding to the even more important claim, "a law repugnant to the Constitution is void." In holding "that courts, as well as other departments, are bound by that instrument," Marshall makes another obvious claim appear to be a finding that increases the authority of the Supreme Court.

The emotional pull will be translated into an expectation of guidance from higher authority. Marshall's Constitution in fact, from the earliest period, suggests an emphasis or source of authority that he wishes to transfer to somewhere else in order to put some compulsion behind his observation. He calls this compulsion "the law" and indeed subsequent jurisprudence, most notably that of Cooley mentioned above, placed the elevation of the law in the gift of Marshall's pen.[24] The tension at the time over what authority governed the political events at issue much less the meaning of "the law" is at least suggested by the fact that Secretary of State Madison had been ordered by the Court to justify not presenting the commission to Marbury and the secretary of state didn't respond.

The mid-twentieth-century view of Marshall's position is aptly captured by Robert K. Faulkner in Chapter 1.[25] Faulkner portrays *Marbury* as a decision that lays "the foundation of Supreme Court predominance over executive and legislative powers" and he makes the now-familiar claim that the decision established "judicial review as essential to the rule of a written constitution. . . ."[26] That Marshall claimed a capacity for judges to interpret the Constitution seems to be one of the things that is self-evident about that decision. The extent of that claim, whether Marshall meant specifically interpretation in cases before the Court or whether he meant more, such as interpretation that would bind other institutions, is unclear. The nature of the foundation is also unclear. There is no judicial precedent or learned source as has been indicated in the material already discussed. In addition, subsequent constitutional developments, while giving the case more authority, have constrained investigation into what it says.

It seems odd to characterize the decision in *Marbury* as establishing a power when the power is not used for another fifty years. It is even more peculiar since when it is used, In *Dred Scott v. Sandford*, the power of the judge to review an act of Congress has such disastrous consequences. The power of judicial review only becomes "ordinary practice," in the conventional sense, in the modern period beginning in this century, despite numerous protestations of the sort we inevitably associate with reliance on the work of John Marshall to the contrary. Thus, Marshall's rhetoric in *Marbury* with its *de novo* authority, its straightforward presentation, and its exhortations may have conned us into believing that the world of constitutional law is much simpler and judicial docrine less significant than it sometimes appears.[27]

McCulloch

This, an Error to the Court of Appeals for the State of Maryland involving a state tax on a federal bank, elaborates Marshall's view of the federal system. In Gerald Gunther's text, this case begins the second major section in his treatment of the Constitution, an inquiry into the structure of government that concerns the nation and the states. So, for the major treatise on the Constitution, Marshall is again the touchstone. The approach is in terms of a new structure instituted by Congress and bound to a Hamiltonian vision of the nation, the second Bank of the United States.

In examining Maryland's tax on the Bank, Marshall begins with a disquisition on the complexity and delicacy of the constitutional arrangements. He reminds us of the awesome power of interpretation falling upon the Court. The basis for the decision is an understanding of law not in terms of text and precedent but in terms of logic. The law that is laid down is John Marshall's logic. "The first question made in the cause is, has Congress power to incorporate a bank?" There is evidence for recognizing, even in the opinion, that the issue before the Court, federal-state relations, was anything but settled.[28] Although Marshall says the question is not open, it was bound to be relatively open less than a generation after the war for independence and the ratification of the Constitution. And, indeed, it is this relative openness that Marshall plays on in his pronouncement. His examination of the situation provides ample opportunity for subsequent commentary, like that of Gunther and Tribe and others, to teach the need for judicial authority.

Yet, in *McCulloch*, perhaps more jurisprudentially than in *Marbury*, we see Marshall incorporating the practices of a primitive political system through an expansive reading of the necessary and proper clause of the Constitution. Much of the discussion of this matter by the Chief Justice is an assessment of political considerations. The presence of the political is not surprising since in this case, Marshall sets out for courts, in general, what they might be able to handle based on the interpretation of clauses in the Constitution that stand in direct opposition to the conceptions of the same clauses offered by the President of the United States.[29] Marshall says, "It will not be denied that a bold and daring usurpation might be resisted, after an acquiescence still longer and more complete than this," speaking of a parameter linking the political and the epistemic. "But," he continues, "it is conceived that a doubtful question,[30] . . . if not put at rest by the practice of the government ought to receive a considerable impression from that practice." The basis of this ought is the transformative political compulsion to derive ought from is. Political philosophers have been debating the nature of such moves for over a generation,[31] wondering about the conditions under which they are possible. Here Marshall just asserts that the transformation has been accomplished.

This opinion is based on the extended oral argument of William Pickney, which lasted for three of the nine days allotted to defenders of the Bank.[32] According to Corwin the strength provided by Marshall's synthesis was "his scorn of the qualifying 'but's' 'if's' and 'though's' . . . [and] above all, his audacious use of the *obiter dictum*."[33] This style of discourse dominated with a clarity that dismissed the political context governing federal institutions. The discourse that dominated the Court in its day failed to dominate the nation until later. It has become Marshall's legacy.[34]

McCulloch has not been as popular nor as universally cited an opinion as *Marbury*. And, particularly problematic for conservatives, it does not quite fit with the element of modern conservatism associated with regional and local power, like that evident in the thought of those who would look to the Court as a bastion from which to resist federal legislative power. While Marshall's opinion in *McCulloch* has obvious attractions to those of any political persuasion who hope for a Court that will resist the assertion of local prerogatives, it may be that conservative control of the judiciary for the next generation will mean an increase in the popularity of *McCulloch* in conservative circles.

Gibbons

Gibbons v. Ogden is a most instructive indication of the epistemic claims in Marshall's politics and it is an opinion that is as hermeneutically *au courant* as the latest comp lit journal. In his opinion, the Chief Justice drew on the presentation of counsel Daniel Webster to refute arguments that it is said were originally developed by Chancellor Kent in 1812.[35] This grounds that analysis in the foremost jurisprudential thought of the period. The result is a reading of the constitutional text to serve Marshall's understanding of national interests and provide a coherent interpretation of that interest. Here again, of some interest to this inquiry into Marshall's epistemology, is a creative discourse neither as fixed in the mythology of discovery as later commentators would have us believe nor as instrumental as some reading of politics in law seem to want. Rather, it is a fine example of just what the Constitution as interpreted text is, politics and law, interests and ideas, timely determination and enduring ideology.

In twentieth-century America, the creativity of conservatives has too often been understated. The decision in *Gibbons* providing for a national marketplace and its creative commentary on the meaning of "commerce" is a fitting testament to the first of the great "law writers" to emerge after the Philadelphia Convention who would buttress the ideology of public policy determined through markets by reliance on judicial interpretation of the Constitution.[36] Many would follow a half century later.

The case, an Appeal from the Court of Errors of New York, was based on a grant of exclusive rights to operate a steamship. New York State gave a monopoly over ferry traffic on the Hudson to Ogden. Gibbons had been operating ferries licensed under federal law between Elizabethtown and New York City in violation of the state monopoly. He contended that the exclusive grant from New York was unconstitutional because it was "repugnant to that clause in the Constitution which authorizes Congress to regulate commerce."

In deciding how to interpret the Constitution and the reach of the power to regulate commerce, Marshall argues against what we now call strict construction. "It has been said," he said, "that these powers ought to be construed strictly." "But," he asks rhetorically, "why ought they to be so construed? Is there one sentence in the Constitution which gives countenance to this rule? What do gentlemen mean, by a strict construction?"[37] One gentleman on record in favor of such a construction was Kent, the distinguished jurist from New York whose *Commentaries* were a major source of law for the period. Kent's picture of the Constitution based the interpretive imperative of strict construction on the fact of a grant from sovereign states to establish the Union. Kent is not mentioned by the Chief Justice.

Moving from Marshall on the nature of language to a more text-oriented inquiry, we find that the political in Marshall's hermeneutic is as striking today as it is fashionable to talk about such things. "If, from the imperfection of human language," he begins, "there should be serious doubts respecting the extent of any given power, it is a well settled rule, that the objects for which it was given . . . should have great influence in this construction." Concluding this discussion on interpretation, John Marshall repeats the text and stakes out his ground by stating what must have been obvious, "The subject to be regulated is commerce." This becomes the basis for drawing on the contributions of Daniel Webster from oral argument: "our Constitution being, as was aptly said at the bar, one of enumeration, and not of definition, to ascertain the extent of the power, it becomes necessary to settle the meaning of the word," the Chief Justice points out in deceptively simple terms. Perhaps it is this surface simplicity and the exhortative power of his arguments that lead scholars to ground a "strict" interpretation of the Constitution in the work of this very creative jurist.

It is a puzzle, for if one looks beneath the surface, his logic and interpretive exegesis are far from simple. The limits on the application of the commerce power to "the exchange of commodities" and not navigation, presented by proponents of a limited congressional role" would restrict a general term, applicable to many objects, to one of its signification. Commerce, undoubtedly, is traffic, but it is something more: it is intercourse." Continuing, with emphasis, Marshall writes,

It has been truly said, that commerce, as the word is used in the Constitution, is a unit, every part of which is indicated by the term. If this be the admitted meaning of the word, in its application to foreign nations, it must carry the same meaning throughout the sentence, and remain a unit, unless there be some plain intelligible cause which alters it.

The subject to which the power is next applied is commerce "among the several States." The word "among," he says, means "intermingled with." Thus, with commentary and convention against him, Marshall read the words creatively, offering a gloss that would gain authority as the national interests it served grew in stature.

Barron

This is a case in a different context. In *Barron v. Baltimore* the spirit of the times was rising against John Marshall in the form of Jacksonian democracy as he confronted increasingly serious illnesses and the last years of his life. The decision was a concession to the powers being asserted in the states and as such it has, for the better part of this century, been eclipsed in significance by the earlier nationalistic rulings of the Chief Justice. Yet, Marshall's stature today is of such overwhelming proportions that this opinion too begins sections on the Bill of Rights, as a springboard to the modern formulations and a nod to the Chief.

Marshall opens his treatment of John Barron's claim that he has been deprived of his property due to actions by the City of Baltimore in his characteristically disarming way. He relies on the logic of the common lawyer, a discursive but primarily internal process, and the epistemological confidence of the philosopher to make the world appear inevitably to be the way he presents it. "The question is, we think, of great importance, but not of much difficulty," he opined. Thus, he dismissed difference in favor of certainty as he had all through his career and built from that certainty, a basis for how he believed the American government should develop.

Here the work of his colleagues in the founding generation, who labored in Philadelphia 201 years ago, gave Marshall the needed legal hook, the basis on which he was so adept at constructing. "The Constitution was ordained and established by the people of the United States for themselves, for their own government, and not for the government of the individual states," the aging Chief Justice pointed out.[38] The consequence, he said, with characteristic confidence, would *therefore* again appear to be obvious, "the fifth amendment must be understood as restraining the power of the general government, not as applicable to the states."[39]

In these cases, John Marshall's rhetoric does not just convince, if we take that term to mean a shifting of attitude or intention from one possible stance to another. The opinions in the four cases mentioned do not work on attitude or opinion much at all. The rhetoric that has become his legacy works on our understanding of how the world is. The logic in Marshall's opinions and his claims for experience have been used to shape that understanding and they have become the ideological basis for American institutions. The opinions confine by proposing ideological forms, such as "the Constitution as law," "commerce as intercourse," taxation as "the power to destroy," and the Bill of Rights as a bulwark of people against the federal government. From among these forms modern constitutionalists have shaped constitutional discourse. Ultimately, when these conceptions become social practices imbedded in the life and expectations of the polity, others will have accomplished the feats of nation building for which Marshall deserves some but not *all* the credit. The concluding section looks at meaning making with a great deal of respect for its capacity to constitute our political universe.

IDEOLOGIES OF AUTHORITY

Appellate judges do not have to obey a body of constitutional rules, but, like politicians and most everybody else, they need to make sense if they are going to have any impact at all. For over two decades the critique of positivism has called for attention to the constitutive force of social or "intersubjective" meanings and scholars have tried to draw attention from the individual instances of political choice, such as how a justice votes on a particular case, to the more enduring and determinative structures operating in public life, like judicial review, federal supremacy, and individual rights.[40] Theories of interpretation and discourse can help but they can also lead away into a hopeless relativism if they fail to acknowledge the power of communities that share a language and determine what makes sense. This compulsion to make sense is brushed aside too quickly in the work of some critical scholars.[41]

Marshall's reliance on logic and his experience was part of an emerging American juridical practice. Conventions, like the one that holds that only defendants can appeal from a trial verdict in a criminal case or that states have limited sovereignty are now well beyond the control of individual justices. When a case comes to the Supreme Court it is seen in terms of the conventions that draw on Marshall's language, like "due process" or "commerce." The knowledge that grounds these conventions is fashioned disproportionately from Marshall's opinions and holds a place for us that his experience held for John Marshall. With such a legacy, we are bound to creative processes very different from Marshall's.

If the conventions built on Marshall's opinions over two centuries were taken away, constitutional disputes would have no foundation. In this way, the language of law is constitutive due to the communities that accept its conventions. Three of John Marshall's opinions have this quality for contemporary constitutional law. All but *Barron* are dispositive of the ruling conventions in the law. There may even be a lingering authority surrounding *Barron* such that the incorporation of the Bill of Rights as governing state proceedings is not beyond examination.[42] Such examination, however, is likely to be within the panoply of Marshall and it will be *Barron* rather than the justice that gets edited.

Legal language is thus an influence that pushes human action toward uniformity.[43] In the sphere of constitutional law, action has come to be a function of professional practices drawing on Marshall's opinions as Marshall drew on his experience. The lawyers who speak to the courts today and the lawyers who sit on the bench have developed a special way of speaking about constitutional rights steeped in professional experience.[44] At the Supreme Court, the justices operate with the limited tools of any craftsmen or "bricoleur."[45] When they work with the Constitution, it is as legal doctrine, a system beyond conscious choice. For most of us, access to the tools is limited and respect for unlicensed bricolage is rare. Thus, contemporary constitutional tools are limited as a result of John Marshall's place and the practice, developed in his name, which teaches us to speak of the Constitution as "what the justices say it is."

Early in the twentieth century the Court and the Constitution became one under the conventions of "higher law" and Edward S. Corwin showed the American Constitution being elevated to the status of religion and institutionalized in the "artificial reason" of the legal profession. In constitutional law, Marshall's words and his language have become a touchstone for this artificial reason of increasing importance as the source has shifted away from the higher law toward the institution of the Supreme Court itself. For fifty years, the constitution as a set of judicial opinions has depended on judicial finality or deference to judicial authority in the constitutional arena. Since the New Deal, the Court has established its legitimacy through "process-based" justifications.[46] In these, the Court's place in the process (with John Marshall out front) has become the key to its authority. The attack on the "Four Horsemen" reconstructed institutional power for the justices appointed by Franklin Roosevelt and reached into the scholarly community demystifying the formalism and neutrality of constitutional law.[47] Now, judicial authority has shifted from the pole of expertise to the pole of institutional finality, although present controversies around judicial selection suggest the possibility of a new agenda.

Judicial pedestalism and the ideology of "the founding" have deprived us of appreciation for the creativity of John Marshall's enterprise, a creativity in which the political struggles of the nation are essential. In particular, contemporary scholars have slanted their reading of John Marshall's contribution in favor of modern beliefs about the power of judges. We should recognize that while institutionalization of Marshall's claims in *Gibbons* relative to commerce began to be clear rather early, in regard to federalism as in *McCulloch* it took the Civil War to get established, *Marbury* did not come until the twentieth century, and his picture of the limited application of the Bill of Rights in *Barron*, which dominated the nineteenth century and then went into dramatic eclipse, has recently been seen on the horizon. Good rhetoric can confine thought and build institutions when its conceptions are offered with both vigor and insight.[48] In this activity, which John Marshall so clearly represents, there is no distinction between ideas and interests. Thus, we can say with assurance that the legacy of John Marshall as well as the final word on the Constitution will be a political determination and a legal one.

NOTES

1. Much of course has been gained, such as H. ARENDT's ON REVOLUTION (1963), which explored the act of founding in a new way that allows us to see the significance of the period on mythology.

2. The interpretive approach, where the focus is on the symbolic and it consequences for politics, has also been cavalier with history, losing even more.

3. Wolfe, *John Marshall and Constitutional Law*, 15 POLITY 5–25 (1982); THE RISE OF MODERN JUDICIAL REVIEW (1986).

4. A BEVERIDGE, THE LIFE OF JOHN MARSHALL (1916).

5. 1 Cranch 137 (1803), 4 Wheat. 316 (1819), 9 Wheat. 1 (1824).

6. 7 Pet. 243 (1833).

7. *See* testimony of Robert Bork, September 1987, before the Senate Judiciary Committee.

8. The fact that *Barron* is often left out in favor of more typically Federalist opinions like *Fletcher v. Peck* and *Dartmouth College v. Woodward* is one indication of the contemporary influence of his nationalism. *See* Wolfe, *John Marshall and Constitutional Law*, *supra* note 3, at 12.

9. E. CORWIN, JOHN MARSHALL AND THE CONSTITUTION (1919).

10. Wolfe, *John Marshall and Constitutional Law*, *supra* note 3; Faulkner, *The Marshall Court and the Making of Constitutional Democracy* [*infra* Chapter 1].

11. CORWIN, *supra* note 9, at 42.

12. *Id.* at 54. Trophonius built the temple at Delphi.

13. S. FISH, IS THERE A TEXT IN THIS CLASS? (1980); J. CULLER, THE PURSUIT OF SIGNS (1981); F. JAMESON, MARXISM AND FORM (1971).

14. J. Brigham, Constitutional Language: An Interpretation of Judicial Decision (1978); C. Sumner, Reading Ideologies (1979); O'Neill, *The Language of Equality in a Constitutional Order*, 75 Am. Pol. Sci. Rev. 626 (1981).

15. L. Carter, Contemporary Constitutional Lawmaking: The Supreme Court and the Art of Politics (1985); J. White, When Words Lose Their Meaning (1984).

16. Marshall could be considered responsible for the failure of the future to unfold as he tried to dictate it, as with the response to *Barron* in the twentieth century.

17. W. Murphy, J. Fleming, and W. Harris, American Constitutional Interpretation (1986).

18. See J. Brigham, Civil Liberties and American Democracy (1984) on this point for further examples.

19. See G. Gunther, Constitutional Law (1986); M. Freeley & S. Krislov, Constitutional Law (1985); *but see* S. Goldman, Constitutional Law (1987). Goldman reports *Marbury* as the second case.

20. See Rossiter's introduction to the widely available edition.

21. J. Agresto, The Supreme Court and Constitutional Democracy (1984) at 70.

22. Corwin, *supra* note 9, at 64. Corwin also points out that in *Marbury* Marshall's reading of the thirteenth section of the Act of 1789 as in violation of Article III is questionable due to the Chief Justice's urging that the words of the Constitution "must be given an exclusive sense or they have no operation at all."

23. See D. Morgan, Justice William Johnson (1944).

24. See G. Haskins & H. Johnson, Foundations of Power (The Oliver Wendell Holmes Devise History of the Supreme Court of the United States vols. 3-4).

25. Faulkner, *supra* note 10.

26. *Id* at 8.

27. Thomas Shevory helped to explain this point to me drawing on the panel discussion for the John Marshall Symposium (Marshall University, Huntington, W. Va., Nov. 23-24, 1987).

28. "It has been truly said that this can scarcely be considered as an open question, entirely unprejudiced by the former proceedings of the nation respecting it. . . ."

29. *Supra* note 9, at 126.

30. "One on which human reason may pause, and the human judgment be suspended, in the decision of which the great principles of liberty are not concerned, but the respective power of those who are equally the representatives of the people are to be adjusted. . . ."

31. Searle, *How to Derive 'Ought' from 'Is'*, in Theories of Ethics (P. Foot ed. 1967).

32. A speech of which Justice Joseph Story wrote, "I never in my whole life heard a greater speech." Corwin, *supra* note 9, at 129.

33. *Id.* at 137.

34. The theme of community is the basis on which James Boyd White examined this case and points out the foundational nature of Marshall's interpretation. White, *supra* note 15, *passim* 231-74.

35. Corwin, *supra* note 9, at 137.

36. See C. Jacobs, The Law Writers and the Courts (1954); B. Twiss, Lawyers and the Constitution (1942).

37. See Wolfe (1986) *supra* note 3, at 7. "There is no word in any of Marshall's writings or opinions, nor even a first- or second-hand report of his conversations, that encourages judges to adapt the Constitution."

38. *See* Wolfe (1986) *supra* note 3, at 44 for a discussion of the sue of grammatical context in this argument.

39. "If in every inhibition intended to act on state power, words are employed which directly express the intent; some strong reason must be assigned for departing from this safe and judicious course in framing the amendments, before that departure can be assumed."

40. P. WINCH, THE IDEA OF THE SOCIAL SCIENCE (1958); Taylor, *Interpretation and the Science of Man*, 25 REV. METAPHYSICS 3–51 (1971).

41. D. KAIRYS, THE POLITICS OF LAW (1982). *See also* CARTER, *supra* note 15.

42. *See* E. Meese, *The Law of the Constitution*, speech at Tulane University (Oct. 21, 1986).

43. Schwartz, *A Proposed Focus for Research on Judicial Behavior*, in THE FRONTIERS OF JUDICIAL RESEARCH 490 (J. Grossman & J. Tanenhouse eds. 1969).

44. O'Neill, *supra* note 14.

45. G. GARVEY, CONSTITUTIONAL BRICOLAGE (1971).

46. Tribe, *The Puzzling Persistence of Process-Based Constitutional Theories*, 89 YALE L.J. 1063 (1980).

47. Lerner, *The Supreme Court and American Capitalism* in ESSAYS IN CONSTITUTIONAL LAW (R.G. McCloskey ed. 1957).

48. Slocum, *On the Indeterminacy Crisis: Critiquing Critical Dogma*, 54 U. L. REV. 462–503 (1987); Stone, *From a Language Perspective*, 90 YALE L.J. 1149–205 (1981).

9

John Marshall and the Interpretation of the Constitution

James E. Lennertz

[W]e must never forget that it is a *constitution* we are expounding.[1]

Justice Frankfurter described Marshall's pregnant statement of the matter as "the single most important utterance in the literature of constitutional law—most important because most comprehensive and comprehending."[2] This chapter explores the meaning of Marshall's statement as the basic premise of his model of constitutional construction.

In 1987 President Reagan's nomination, and the ultimate rejection by the Senate, of Robert H. Bork to be an associate justice of the United States Supreme Court was an unanticipated and vitriolic component of the national celebration of the bicentennial of the Constitution.[3] This controversy dramatized enduring issues raised by Bork's theory of constitutional construction, issues that centered on what Bork has identified as "the seeming anomaly of judicial supremacy in a democratic society."[4] Bork, equating democracy with majoritarian rule through representative political institutions, sees the Court as having a critical role in preventing majority and minority tyranny. Yet, authority exercised in this "undemocratic" way can only be legitimate, that is, presumed to be by societal consent, if the Court adheres to a process of principled constitutional interpretation: the Court must demonstrate "in reasoned opinions that it has a valid theory, derived from the Constitution, of the respective spheres of majority and minority freedom."[5] Bork insists that judges must derive and define, as well as apply, constitutional principles with neutrality.[6] By this he means only those principles specified in the text or indicated by history to have been personally intended by the framers.[7] Bork identifies this mode of interpretation as "interpretivist" and harshly criticizes much current constitutional decision making and scholarship as "non-interpretivist."[8] What is particularly provocative about Bork is his conviction that his approach is not only superior to others but that it is the one true and objective appreciation of some determinate constitutional reality.[9]

A notable contemporary contrast to Bork's approach is presented by Ronald Dworkin, who suggests that all judges, indeed all people trying to understand complex social phenomena, are "interpretivists."[10] Dworkin identifies three stages of interpretation. In the first, or "preinterpretive," stage, the interpreter tentatively identifies the elements of the object of interpretation. In the second, or "interpretive," stage, the interpreter develops a coherent and consistent justification of the principal elements identified in the preinterpretive stage. In the third, or "postinterpretive," stage, the interpreter reforms the elements required in the object of interpretation in light of the justification that was developed.[11]

Creative interpretation thus rests upon two assumptions: first, that the object of interpretation has value because it serves a purpose, or has a point, which can be identified independently of the object of interpretation and, second, that this purpose should shape the development of the object of interpretation.[12] Indeed, the priority of purpose shifts the anchor of constancy from the particular conceptualization, as Bork would have it, to the general concept.[13] This converts judicial interpretation from a mechanical to an organic enterprise and requires the interpreter to "see" the object of interpretation "in its best light," that is to say, illuminated by its overriding purpose.[14] This is not to say that the interpreter is unencumbered by the text or its history, for these factors limit the range of acceptable interpretations. Unlike for Bork, however, these factors do not completely determine the "real" interpretation for Dworkin.[15]

Dworkin identifies the basic requirement as the "virtue of political integrity," which he closely associates with coherence and consistency.[16] These concerns direct the judge always to be attentive to two factors: first, the relationship between the particular decision and the whole of the law and, second, the relationship of the past to the present and the future. By the first concern Dworkin means that the judge must seek to reconcile the demands of the case with the purposes of the law as a complex enterprise. By the second Dworkin means that intent is important as a "*formal* structure for all interpretive claims," which guides the interpreter's inquiry into purpose.[17] Dworkin would agree that historical research is part of this process of inquiry;[18] indeed, he would claim that certainty—with its relationship to consistency and therefore integrity—is the strongest claim of Bork and the historicist school.[19] Yet Dworkin would disagree for two reasons with Bork's complete identification of this inquiry with the attempt to discover the contemporaneous expectations of the historical persons involved in the development of the text. First, certainty is only one of several values involved in integrity, and it is less important in constitutional matters than in others.[20] Second, to Dworkin, the question of what "it"—the practice or text—means as an emergent social reality must be distinguished from what "they" meant by their participation.[21]

It is precisely the appeal to "what the Constitution *really* means" that is at the heart of the enduring dilemma of constitutional interpretation. A strictly literal construction may be inadequate to resolve ambiguity and respond to emerging issues, and a construction not adequately rooted in the text may permit unwarranted extension of constitutional values.[22] Marshall clearly appreciated this problem of constitutional construction.[23] One must acknowledge that legal and constitutional concepts are realities at least in the sense that "they are forms of thought with a vitality and validity of their own."[24] Moreover, one can see interpretations as joining the rational and the imaginative within the context of the text.[25] The dilemma can, perhaps, best be managed by recognizing the distinction between an epistemological and an ontological approach, that is to say, more progress may be made if one concentrates upon how one can know what the Constitution means rather than what it means.[26] By such an epistemology the judge would self-impose a set of interpretive rules that would "constrain the interpreter *and* accommodate creativity by allowing the interpreter to interact with the text and build bridges between it and man's other intellectual endeavors in the humanities."[27] Dworkin and others have considered the relationship between constitutional interpretation and approaches to knowledge in literary, artistic, and scientific fields,[28] noting the common concern for simplicity, elegance, and verifiability.[29]

Thomas Kuhn also suggests the commonality of scientific and jurisprudential paradigms in his seminal work, whose basic thrust posits a dynamic of theoretical development.[30] "Normal" science, and ostensibly "normal" jurisprudence, involve a patterned explication from "accepted" premises that shape the prevailing paradigm. These paradigms, however, have a life cycle, emerging from periods of "revolutionary upheaval," controlling a period of mature vitality, and disintegrating under the press of new facts, new questions, and new circumstances. Indeed, it is just such a cycle, driven by the adversary process and inductive, comparative reasoning, that Levi describes.[31] This dynamic perspective—and the notion of a living constitution—also relates to concerns over popular participation in constitutional development.[32]

Marshall's approach to constitutional interpretation will be explored by examining his opinions in major cases that confronted the problems of federalism and the contract clause.[33] These two lines of cases address the major themes of Marshall's constitutional jurisprudence: the national union and vested rights.[34] While judicial review and other formative matters also raised novel questions, the establishment of a coherent paradigm for managing the dispersion of public authority in a federal republic was a central difficulty of the new nation.[35] The contract cases represent early constitutional consideration of vested rights and as such constitute the civil rights cases of the period.[36] Moreover, there are strong relationships between the contract and federalism cases.[37]

In *Fletcher v. Peck* Fletcher sued for breach of a covenant for land purchased from Peck in 1803.[38] Peck's line of title originated with a grant in 1795 by the state of Georgia. In 1796 Georgia passed an act declaring the 1795 act null and void as founded upon the corruption of certain legislators. Marshall delivered the opinion of the Court, which ruled that the 1796 act, which had annulled conveyances pursuant to the 1795 act, was an unconstitutional impairment of the obligation of contract. Marshall first declared the 1795 grant to be a contract. Relying upon equitable principles, he then rejected the assertion that the corruption involved in the first act made it appropriate for the later Georgia legislature to repeal it, thereby invalidating its own obligations and annulling the rights of innocent third parties. Marshall indicated that, while natural law principles might be sufficient to prohibit Georgia from so acting if it were a single sovereign power,[39] Georgia's membership in the Union imposed upon the state additional limitations through the U.S. Constitution, which "may be deemed a bill of rights for the people of each state."[40] Marshall declared that the words of the contract clause apply generally to all contracts—executory and executed—and that the state's participation as a party to the contract does not shield it from application of the constitutional limitation.

In *Sturges v. Crowninshield* the Supreme Court considered issues certified to it by the circuit court regarding an action on two promissory notes, both dated March 22, 1811, at New York.[41] The defendant had pleaded his complete discharge of the debts pursuant to an April 3, 1811, act of the New York legislature for the benefit of insolvent debtors and their creditors. The plaintiff demurred to this plea on the grounds that the New York statute was unconstitutional either because it was a law of bankruptcy, which power was granted exclusively to Congress,[42] or because it impaired the obligation of contracts.

Chief Justice Marshall delivered the opinion of the Court. While the presence of express prohibitions on state power in certain areas—such as making treaties—indicates the sense of the founders that an affirmative grant of power to Congress did not categorically imply a prohibition on the states, the obverse—that the absence of an express prohibition implied concurrent power—may not be presumed.[43] Marshall proceeded to consider the relation between insolvency and bankruptcy laws, concluding that, although there was substantial overlap, it would be "inconvenient" to deny states their traditional authority over the protection of insolvents (most particularly regarding imprisonment of debtors). Moreover, it would not be a "violent construction of the constitution" to permit such state relief in cases beyond federal reach. Indeed, Marshall set forth a broad theory of concurrent powers, indicating that it was not the mere existence but rather the actual exercise of national power in a conflicting way that produces a constitutional issue of federalism.[44]

One should note that, after this preliminary discourse on the critical federalism issue of exclusivity/concurrence, Marshall declined—as "totally unnecessary"[45]—the opportunity to determine whether some actual inconsistency exists. Instead, he proceeded to the "great question"[46]—whether the New York statute impaired the obligation of contract. Marshall declared this clause to be as "plain and simple" as it is "sacred."[47] A total discharge by act of state law of a contractual debt—indeed, even a partial release—impairs the obligation and violates the Constitution. Such was the unequivocal command of the provision, and argument directed to the spirit of the document as evidenced by the particular concerns that may have been in "the mind of the convention" is only appropriate to resolve ambiguity or contradictions with other clauses or to prevent patent absurdity or injustice.[48] Although the state retained the authority to adjust matters related to public remedies, such as imprisonment of debtors and statutes of limitations, the discharge of the debt by the New York statute violated the inviolability of contract and was therefore unconstitutional.

In *McCulloch v. Maryland* the U.S. Supreme Court considered an appeal from a state court judgment against McCulloch, the cashier of the Baltimore branch of the Bank of the United States.[49] The Maryland judgment sought to recover statutory penalties for the bank's nonpayment of a state tax upon the issuance of bank notes by banks operating in Maryland but not chartered by the state. After acknowledging the serious conflict and asserting the unique authority of the Court, Marshall posed first the question of Congress's power to incorporate a bank. Marshall reasoned that federal power flowed from the people and not the states and that, being a government of all, it "is supreme within its sphere of action."[50] Admitting that the national government is one of enumerated powers and that establishing a bank or corporation is not explicitly enumerated, Marshall nevertheless argued that incidental or implied powers are not excluded by the nature or the words of the document. Indeed, this ambiguity requires "a fair construction of the whole instrument."[51] Marshall analyzed the necessary and proper clause and concentrated upon the range of usage of the word *necessary*, accomplishing the following *tour de force*: "A thing may be necessary, very necessary, absolutely or indispensably necessary."[52] Opting for the first sense of the word, Marshall concluded that appropriate and unprohibited means to legitimate ends are constitutional.

The second question concerned the constitutionality of Maryland's tax. Admitting that the taxing powers are concurrently held by the federal and state governments, Marshall reasoned that the security of the whole and its legitimate public institutions and policies should not be subject to the discretion of any part. Marshall concluded by declaring the tax unconstitutional, though acknowledging the validity of nondiscriminatory state taxes.

In *Dartmouth College v. Woodward* the original trustees sought control over the records, seal, and property of the college after the passage by the New

Hampshire legislature of acts that amended the charter to provide for public control.[53] The trustees argued that those acts impaired the obligation of contracts. Marshall's opinion for the Court first considered the appropriate breadth of the concept of *contract*. The critical distinction is to be drawn between public and private relationships—between political arrangements represented in the form of civil institutions and "contracts which respect property, or some object of value, and confer rights which may be asserted in a court of justice."[54] Mutual obligations of the former type are not protected by the contract clause, while those of the latter type are. After deciding that the funds and officers of the college were private, the Court considered whether the act of public incorporation invests the college with a public character, asking rhetorically whether the state's grant in the charter of special corporate privileges entitles the state to change the terms of those privileges. Marshall next rejected the defense's argument that the trustees, having only a legal and not a beneficial interest, have no standing. Neither did the donors retain nor did individual students have an interest. Marshall's answer was that the corporation is the repository of all rights. And as to this extraordinary concentration of authority in the trustees, the authorizing public retains no power of amendment.

It remained to decide whether the statutes impaired these obligations. Marshall reasoned that the contract spoke not merely to general educational ends but also to the means specified as the college governance system. The donor's expectation of immutability being critical,[55] the state's "intrusion" into the college governance system impaired the obligation of contract and must fall. Marshall's decision in this case has been described as activist in the modern tradition.[56]

In *Cohens v. Virginia* the defendants were convicted of violating a Virginia statute that prohibited the sale of lottery tickets.[57] Defendants sought a writ of error, claiming that they acted pursuant to acts of Congress authorizing the municipal organization of the District of Columbia. Virginia challenged the jurisdiction of the U.S. Supreme Court. Marshall's introduction characterized Virginia's argument most dramatically. Assuming for purposes of argument that Virginia's prosecution violated federal statute or constitutional law, Virginia's advocates asserted that the federal judiciary could not review the judgment of the Virginia courts.[58] Marshall accepted the general proposition that states, since they retain sovereignty, cannot be sued except upon their consent; nonetheless, such consent need not be particular but may be expressed generally in the federal Constitution, which sets out the distribution of authority in the federal system. To accept Virginia's argument would have granted each member of the Union a veto over the will of the whole. Even if unequivocal defiance was improbable, a multiplicity of "gradations of opposition" would have caused debilitating obstruction to the legitimate operation of the

Union. Given the intentions and the realistic expectations that Marshall presumed the founders to have had, the Constitution had to be interpreted to have established the means to protect itself.[59] The basis of federal jurisdiction here was the subject matter of the claim and not the character of the parties. Indeed, the "case or controversy" language of Article III expressed a limit upon the federal judicial power.

Virginia next argued that the Eleventh Amendment specifically precluded federal judicial power as to suits between a state and citizens of another state. Marshall answered that Virginia had read the clause too broadly. The federal judicial power explicitly extends to actions wherein states are parties. The amendment, growing out of concerns at the time of the founding regarding the prosecution of individual debts against states in federal courts, specifically speaks to actions commenced by individuals against states. This case involved a constitutional defense by an individual in a suit by a state against an individual and therefore falls outside of the letter and spirit of the Eleventh Amendment exception. More generally, the words of the Article III grant of appellate jurisdiction, "the necessity of uniformity, as well as correctness in expounding the constitution and laws of the United States, . . ."[60] the contemporaneous position of *The Federalist*, and the action of the first Congress in its explicit provision for federal appellate jurisdiction from specified judgments of state courts all supported the validity of this exercise of appellate jurisdiction. Almost as a footnote, the Court considered the merits and affirmed the judgment of the Virginia court, finding that the defendant's authority to sell lottery tickets was limited to the District and did not extend to states with contrary laws.

In *Gibbons v. Ogden* the New York legislature had granted to Livingston and Fulton an exclusive right for a term of years to navigate steamboats in New York waters.[61] Ogden held that right by assignment and was awarded an injunction by the New York courts against Gibbons, who had been operating two steamboats between New York and New Jersey. Gibbons was licensed under a federal statute relating to vessels engaged in the "coasting trade." Gibbons's appeal asserted that the New York laws that granted the exclusive right to Ogden violated the commerce clause.[62]

Marshall's opinion for the Court began with rejection of Ogden's claim that the national powers enumerated in the Constitution be "construed strictly."[63] Marshall then proceeded to define expansively the key terms of the commerce clause: *commerce* includes navigation but also extends broadly to all manner of "commercial intercourse";[64] *among* includes commerce that crosses state or national boundaries but also extends broadly to "commerce which concerns more states than one";[65] and *the power to regulate* includes the authority to facilitate but also extends broadly and is plenary.[66]

Marshall acknowledged the argument by the parties relative to the exclusivity/concurrence problem, but he declined to decide the issue.[67] He reasoned that, whatever the authority of New York to regulate interstate commerce in the absence of federal exercise, here Congress had exercised the power. Having legitimately exercised that power, federal law is supreme without regard to the appropriate authority of the state with respect to matters of domestic trade or the police power. Before announcing the reversal of the New York court, Marshall sarcastically apologized for the tedious demonstration of propositions "which may have been axioms."[68] He closed, as he began, with comments on "strict construction."

In *Ogden v. Saunders* Saunders had sued for nonpayment on bills of exchange accepted by Ogden in New York in 1806.[69] Saunders responded to Ogden's reliance on an 1801 New York statute for the relief of insolvent debtors by contending that the law was an unconstitutional impairment of the obligation of contracts. After being stalemated for several years, the Court rejected Saunders's attack on the statute, holding that prospective application of such laws was constitutional. Marshall, joined by Justices Story and Duvall, dissented. Marshall began with a summary of what he had thought was the consensus on the principles of constitutional construction. Marshall, while admitting that the words of the contract provision do not clearly resolve the question, then used his integrative, commercial conception of the Union as the basis for opening the possibility of general prohibition. He considered other restrictions upon the states, noting the explicit retroactive scope of the limits on *ex post facto* laws and bills of attainder and the more general reach of elements that relate "to the civil transactions of individuals."[70] Marshall then launched into a treatise on the nature of contract rights and society, finding these rights to be natural and anterior to society.[71] He distinguished society's legitimate authority to prescribe contractual prerequisites and remedies.[72]

Note the formative nature of Marshall's time and judicial enterprise. Not only was the Constitution a "virgin document,"[73] but also the notion of a comprehensive, written constitution as foundational law was novel.[74] The legal tradition, however, was rich with canons of interpretation of instruments such as wills, deed, contracts, and statutes.[75] In *Ogden* a frustrated Marshall summarized what he had thought to have been the consensus on constitutional construction.

To say that the intention of the instrument must prevail; that this intention must be collected from its words; that its words are to be understood in that sense in which they are generally used by those for whom the instrument was intended; that its provisions are neither to be restricted into insignificance, nor extended to objects not comprehended in them nor contemplated by its framers, is to repeat what has already been said more at large, and is all that can be necessary.[76]

Marshall, being a contemporary of the framers, often presumed what must have happened from general principles that he believed were self-evident and consensual rather than controversial.[77] The case marked a generational as well as a political transition for the Court.[78]

Marshall adhered to the prevailing legal and philosophical conventions with respect to intent. While this tradition allowed for consideration of the entire document and its purposes, it put primary emphasis on the text.[79] It did not generally give emphasis to the personal intentions of the framers.[80] While Marshall was attentive to the specific text in each of the cases examined, he consistently asserted that particular words and provisions must be construed within the context of the whole document. For Marshall this meant a construction grounded upon a unified conception of the purposes of the Union, including the liberal conception of a national commercial system.[81] The key was always *purpose*[82] drawn from a consideration of the whole document.[83] And this purpose was not to be subverted by overly narrow construction of the text.

> Powerful and ingenious minds, taking, as postulates, that the powers expressly granted to the government of the Union are to be contracted, by construction, into the narrowest possible compass, and that the original powers of the States are retained, if any possible construction will retain them, may, by a course of well digested, but refined and metaphysical reasoning, founded on these premises, explain away the constitution of our country, and leave it a magnificent structure indeed, to look at, but totally unfit for use.[84]

Marshall often proceeded "without that helpful but obfuscating crutch of the law, precedent."[85] But Marshall's opinions were consistent with a common law sense that cases were important primarily as exemplary of principles.[86] And his opinions were comprehensive, even approaching "the treatise."[87] Still, as in *Fletcher* and other cases, there was often a surprising "leap" from the past precedent; yet, this is the essence of the landmark case.[88] Marshall's reliance upon natural law, especially in his opinions on the contract clause, was gradually transferred to reliance upon the written Constitution, although his dissent in *Ogden* suggests that he retained a basic commitment to these principles throughout.[89]

In the end much of the debate over Marshall's constitutional jurisprudence revolves around the question of whether his decisions were political or legal.[90] Indeed, this was close to the heart of the distinction between Federalist and Jeffersonian Republicans with respect to the constitutional jurisprudence. The Jeffersonian Republicans believed that critical constitutional issues ought to be resolved in accordance with the will of the people, while the Federalists held to a realm of law beyond majority preference.[91] Many, including Beveridge, clearly concluded that Marshall's actions were more political than legal.[92] Indeed, Marshall regularly arranged the order of consideration of issues to engage in "legally unnecessary" discourses upon the broadest issues. And he seemed perfectly prepared, as in *Cohens* or even *Marbury*, to lose the battle in order to win the war.

And yet, one should not assume that value-laden choice made his decisions exclusively political.[93] The foundation for interpretation of the constitutional is a constitutional theory, a system of ideas about "what the constitution is or *ought* to be."[94] One should not be surprised that Marshall's opinions so explicitly articulate and strongly rely upon his model of constitutional theory.[95] In all of his actions as Chief Justice, Marshall sustained the sense that he was working within the legal perspective. He believed that it was possible to resolve the tension between majoritarian and legal realms by sharply separating them.[96] Marshall did not think judicial review to be undemocratic, although Bickel thought that Marshall was merely "sliding over this ineluctable reality."[97] Founded upon contractarian notions, the Constitution was, with the possible exception of the allocation of power among the governmental units, less a positive enactment than a declaration of natural principles.[98] While acknowledging an appropriate realm for majoritarian political choice, Marshall, and many with him, believed that neutral, consensual principles, pronounced via legal means, should not submit to electoral majorities.[99]

Whatever respect might have been felt for the state sovereignties, it is not to be disguised that the framers of the constitution viewed, with some apprehension, the violent acts which might grow out of the feelings of the moment; and that the people of the United States, in adopting that instrument, have manifested a determination to shield themselves and their property from the effects of those sudden and strong passions to which men are exposed. The restrictions on the legislative power of the states are obviously founded in this sentiment: and the constitution of the United States contains what may be deemed a bill of rights for the people of each state.[100]

Indeed, Marshall would probably have agreed with Ackerman's distinction between normal and revolutionary politics, which gives a special role of the courts: to prevent "normal" political institutions and politics from presuming that they authoritatively and definitively spoke for the people.[101] Marshall believed that he was acting legally,[102] particularly in the area of vested rights and the contract clause.[103] In part this was due to the special circumstances of the founding when some governmental functions were still not perceived as political.[104] In part this was due to Marshall's approach, which carefully elaborated a legal method that was faithful to common law traditions and that expressed a "magisterial reverence" for the law that accentuated its distinction from normal politics.[105]

Inevitably, constitutional law is both legal and political.[106] The question then is not whether Marshall was acting legally or politically but whether he acted with integrity to reconcile the political and the legal dimensions of his responsibilities.[107] It is in this regard that Frankfurter, himself cognizant of the interaction of law and politics, called him the only statesman-judge.[108] Newmyer also emphasized this quality. "Marshall's genius, . . . was not that he abandoned the framework of the law, but that the legal framework allowed discretion and choice sufficient for statesmanship. The message is that the Supreme Court can affect politics without ceasing to be a court of law; . . ."[109]

It remains to relate elements of Bork's and Dworkin's perspectives to Marshall, particularly to his decisions in the cases examined. Bork would indicate that Marshall certainly worked within a constitutional theory rooted in the text. Yet he would be troubled with Marshall's expansive use of the concept of purpose and his presumptions about discerning intent, although Marshall's contemporaneous knowledge of and strong adherence to enduring liberal principles would probably reassure Bork.

Although on balance Dworkin would evaluate Marshall favorably, he would have two initial difficulties.[110] First, Marshall's conception of interpretation would appear too static and therefore resistant to Dworkin's stages of interpretation.[111] Second, Marshall's commitment to primary emphasis on the text for the identification of purpose would be in tension with the assumption of creative interpretation, which calls for the identification of purpose independent of the particular object of interpretation. Dworkin, however, would see circumstances that at least mitigate these concerns. Marshall must be evaluated within the context of his time; he was operating within a particular "interpretive community," which constrained both the form and substance of his reasoning.[112] Moreover, Dworkin would credit Marshall's strong commitment to purpose, broadly conceived, as substantially consistent with the assumption of creative interpretation. Brief reference might also be made to two qualities of good theories, namely simplicity and elegance, which Marshall's constitutional theory is thought to have.[113]

Dworkin would, with two important qualifications, evaluate Marshall positively with respect to the basic requirements of integrity. Marshall's constitutional theory is generally coherent and his decisions were generally consistent. Marshall's model of American society and the U.S. Constitution, particularly as expressed through the concepts of federalism and the contract clause, represents a comprehensive application of liberal Lockean principles.

The first qualification is that Marshall repeatedly left the exclusivity/concurrence issue of federalism without clear resolution. Breadth of construction and consistency of application can be seen in the federalism cases. Note particularly the establishment of implied powers in *McCulloch* and a broad conception of the commerce power in *Gibbons*. Note as well in *Cohens* how resolutely Marshall presents two critical assumptions: first, that the states implicitly consented to surrender significant elements of their sovereignty by entry into the Union and, second, that the founders intended to completely insulate the national government from the risk of state diversity or deviance. Yet Dworkin would be concerned, particularly given the increasing sectional division during that period, with Marshall's unwillingness or inability to articulate a general model that clearly and reasonably defined secure realms of state power.

The second qualification is that Marshall never compellingly clarified the contract clause distinction between impairment and legitimate state regulation of prerequisites and remedies. The contract clause cases demonstrate the power and risk of simple and broad definition. Indeed, note that Marshall's openness to a wide range of relationships as contractual—see *Fletcher* and *Dartmouth College*—and a wide range of state regulation as impairment—see *Sturges* and *Dartmouth*—led to his frustration in *Ogden* when he was trapped politically by a contrary Court majority and logically by the inconsistencies of his model. Dworkin would probably indicate that a Marshall who had been more sensitive to the interrelationships among the stages of interpretation might have been able to work through this area more effectively.

While Justice Holmes damned Marshall with faint praise[114] and Crosskey portrayed him as a tragic hero,[115] few would deny that "his was the pen through which history wrote."[116] Perhaps the key is to appreciate that constitutional development is a vital national seminar within which occurs dialogue or discourse with its interplay of descriptive analysis and creative synthesis.[117] In this we are not doomed to uncritical relativism, for the seminar develops over time "some universe of discourse, some system of meaning, some institutional epistemology, . . ."[118] Perhaps Marshall was the great first seminar leader not because he invariably got the right answers but because he often asked the right questions.

NOTES

1. McCulloch v. Maryland, 4 Wheat. 316, 407 (1819).

2. Frankfurter, *John Marshall and the Judicial Function* 69 HARV. L. REV. 217, 219 (1955).

3. *Senate Consideration of the Nomination of Robert H. Bork to be an Associate Justice of the U.S. Supreme Court*, 100th Cong., 1st Sess., 133 CONG. REC. S15,011 (daily ed. Oct. 23, 1987).

4. Bork, *Neutral Principles and Some First Amendment Problems*, 47 IND. L.J. 1, 2 (1971); *see also* A. BICKEL, THE LEAST DANGEROUS BRANCH 16–17 (1962); *but see* Ackerman, *Discovering the Constitution*, 93 YALE L.J. 1013, 1016 (1984) (who attempts to "dissolve" rather than solve the difficulty).

5. Bork, *supra* note 4, at 3.

6. *Id.* at 7; *see also* Wechsler, *Toward Neutral Principles of Constitutional Law*, 73 HARV. L. REV. 1 (1959); *see also* Chaudhuri, *F.S.C. Northrop and the Epistemology of Science: Elements of an Objective Jurisprudence*, 12 S. DAK. L. REV. 86, 92 (1967); *but see* Tushnet, *Following the Rules Laid Down: A Critique of Interpretivism and Neutral Principles*, 96 HARV. L. REV. 781, 806 (1983) (who contends that neutrality is only a valid criterion with respect to application).

7. Bork, *supra* note 4, at 17. Bork also identifies rights granted secondarily to the individual "for the sake of a governmental process that the Constitution outlines and that the Court should preserve."

8. Bork, *Styles in Constitutional Theory*, 1984 SUPREME COURT HISTORICAL SOCIETY YEARBOOK 53, 55, 59; *but see* Tushnet, *supra* note 6, at 784–85 (who contends that interpretivism and neutral principles implicitly presume communitarian assumptions about shared meanings that contradict the individualistic liberal premises that prompt the search for interpretivism and neutral principles).

9. Bork, *supra* note 8, at 53: *See also* Bork, J., dissenting in Barnes v. Kline, 759 F.2d, 21, 71 (D.C. Cir. 1985); Bork, *supra* note 4, at 6.

10. R. DWORKIN, LAW'S EMPIRE, 359–60 (1986).

Academic scholarship has recently explored a different distinction: this divides justices into interpretivist and noninterpretivist camps. These labels are also highly misleading, however. They suggest a distinction between judges who believe constitutional decisions should be made only or mainly by interpreting the Constitution itself and others who think they should be based on extraconstitutional grounds. This is an academic form of the crude popular mistake that some judges obey the Constitution and others disregard it. It ignores the philosophical character of law as interpretive. Every conscientious judge, in either of the supposed camps, is an interpretivist in the broadest sense: each tries to impose the best interpretation on our constitutional structure and practice, to see these, all things considered, in the best light they can bear. They disagree about what the best interpretation is, but it is an analytical error, a localized infection left by the semantic sting, to confuse this with a disagreement about whether constitutional adjudication should be interpretive at all. The great debates of constitutional methods are debates within interpretation, not about its relevance. If one justice thinks the intentions of the framers are much more important than another does, this is the upshot of a more foundational interpretive disagreement. The former thinks that fairness or integrity requires that any sound interpretation match the framers' state of mind; the latter does not.

11. *Id*. at 65–66.

12. *Id*. at 47.

13. *Id*. at 71.

14. *Id*. at 47. "Once this interpretive attitude takes hole, the institution of courtesy ceases to be mechanical; it is no longer unstudied deference to a runic order. People now try to impose *meaning* on the institution—to see it in its best light—and then to restructure it in light of that meaning."

15. *Id*. at 52, 360.

16. *Id*. at 166–67.

17. *Id*. at 58–59.

18. *Id*. at 167.

19. *Id*. at 365.

20. *Id*. at 367.

21. *Id*. at 63; *see also* Powell, *The Original Understanding of Original Intent*, 98 HARV. L. REV. 885, 895 (1985); *see also* McIntosh, *A Poetic for Law: Constitutional Theory as Metaphor*, 30 How. L.J. 355, 400 (1987).

22. Keckeissen, *On the Possibility of an Epistemological Approach to Constitutional Interpretation*, 91 DICK. L. REV. 747, 749 (1987).

23. Gibbons v. Ogden, 9 Wheat. 1, 188 (1824).

What do gentlemen mean by a strict construction? If they contend only against that enlarged construction which would extend words beyond their natural and obvious import, we might question

the application of the term, but should not controvert the principle. If they contend for that narrow construction which, in support of some theory not to be found in the constitution, would deny
to the government those powers which the words grant, as usually understood, import, and which
are consistent with the general views and objects of the instrument; for that narrow construction,
which would cripple the government and render it unequal to the objects for which it is declared to
be instituted, and to which the powers given, as fairly understood, render it competent: then we
cannot perceive the propriety of this strict construction, nor adopt it as the rule by which the constitution is to be expounded.

24. Corwin, *Constitution v. Constitutional Theory*, 19 AM. POL. SCI. REV. 291, 299
(1925).

25. McIntosh, *supra* note 21, at 362–63. "What makes the Constitution as a whole
metaphoric is less the expressive quality of its constituent semantic units, than the way it
functions metaphorically. It does not simply refer to reality; it constructs it, and at once
presents a perspective on that reality."

26. Keckeissen, *supra* note 22, at 749; *see also* Kellogg, *Learned Hand and the Great
Train Ride*, 56 AM. SCHOLAR 471, 476 (1987). *But see* McIntosh, *supra* note 21, at 373.

27. Keckeissen, *supra* note 22, at 750.

28. DWORKIN, *supra* note 10, at 53; *see also* Keckeissen, *supra* note 22, at 758; *see also*
Northrop, *The Epistemology of Legal Judgements*, 58 Nw. U.L. REV. 732 (1964); *see also*
Chaudhuri, *supra* note 6; *but see* McIntosh, *supra* note 21, at 359 (who contends that constitutional interpretation is closer to literary than natural scientific inquiry); *but see also*
West, *Adjudication Is Not Interpretation: Some Reservations about the Law-As-Literature
Movement*, 54 TENN. L. REV. 203 (1987) (who contends that the distinction between
literature as an expressive work of art and law as an imperative command backed by
sanctions makes the application of literary interpretation inappropriate for effective
jurisprudential criticism).

29. DWORKIN, *supra* note 10, at 53; *see also* Keckeissen, *supra* note 22, at 753 (whose
model presents five criteria for evaluating the process of "enlightened guesswork" by
which beliefs or interpretations are developed: [1] conservatism, [2] simplicity, [3] modes-
ty, [4] generality, and [5] refutability).

30. T. KUHN, THE STRUCTURE OF SCIENTIFIC REVOLUTIONS 23 (1970).

31. LEVI, AN INTRODUCTION TO LEGAL REASONING 8–9 (1948).

The first stage is the creation of the legal concept which is built up as cases are compared. The
period is one in which the court fumbles for a phrase. Several phrases may be tried out; the misuse
or misunderstanding of words itself may have an effect. The concept sounds like another, and the
jump to the second is made. The second stage is the period when the concept is more or less fixed,
although reasoning by example continues to classify items inside and out of the concept. The third
stage is the breakdown of the concept, as reasoning by example has moved so far ahead as to make
it clear that the suggestive influence of the word is no longer desired.

32. Tushnet, *supra* note 6, at 787. "For about thirty years, roughly from 1940 to
1970, interpretivism had a bad reputation, largely because, allied as it was to politically
conservative positions, it seemed too vulnerable to external critique. That critique is captured by counterposing 'the dead hand of the past'—interpretivism—to the need for 'a

living Constitution.'" *See also* Ynetma, *Constitutional Principles and Jurisprudence*, 25 GEO. L.J. 577, 580 (1937); *see also* Corwin, *supra* note 24, at 302.

33. U.S. CONST. art. I, §10. "No State shall . . . pass any . . . law impairing the obligation of contracts, . . ."

34. Broderick, *From Constitutional Politics to Constitutional Law: The Supreme Court's First Fifty Years*, 65 N.C.L. REV. 945, 951 (1987).

35. DWORKIN, *supra* note 10, at 185–86.

36. Corwin, *The Basic Doctrine of American Constitutional Law*, 12 MICH. L. REV. 247 (1914), in 1 SELECTED ESSAYS IN CONSTITUTIONAL LAW 101, 127 (1938). *But see* Kainen, *Nineteenth Century Interpretations of the Federal Contract Clause: The Transformation from Vested to Substantive Rights against the State*, 31 BUFFALO L. REV. 381, 480 (1982). *See also* Morgan, *Marshall, the Marshall Court, and the Constitution*, in CHIEF JUSTICE JOHN MARSHALL: A REAPPRAISAL 168, 176 (W. Jones ed. 1956).

37. Kainen, *supra* note 36, at 425; *see also* Corwin, *The Doctrine of Due Process of Law Before the Civil War*, 24 HARV. L. REV. 366, 460 (1911), in 1 SELECTED ESSAYS IN CONSTITUTIONAL LAW 203, 214–15 (1938).

38. 6 Cranch 87 (1810).

39. *Id.* at 136; *see also* Lynch, *Fletcher v. Peck: The Nature of the Contract Clause*, 13 SETON HALL L. REV. 1, 14 (1982).

40. 6 Cranch 138.

41. 4 Wheat. 122 (1819).

42. U.S. CONST. art. I, §8 [4].

43. 4 Wheat. 193 (1819).

44. *Id.* at 196.

45. *Id.* at 197.

46. *Id.*

47. *Id.* at 200.

48. *Id.* at 202. Note Marshall's frame of reference not to the minds of the framers but to "mind of the convention."

49. 4 Wheat. 316 (1819).

50. *Id.* at 405.

51. *Id.* at 406.

52. *Id.* at 414.

53. 4 Wheat. 518 (1819).

54. *Id.* at 629.

55. *Id.* at 647–48 (Marshall's discussion of human nature in this regard).

56. Campbell, *Dartmouth College as a Civil Liberties Case: The Formation of Constitutional Policy*, 70 KY. L.J. 643, 706 (1981–82).

57. 6 Wheat. 264 (1821).

58. *Id.* at 377.

59. *Id.* at 387.

[A] constitution is framed for ages to come, and is designed to approach immortality as nearly as human institutions can approach it. Its course cannot always be tranquil. It is exposed to storms and tempests, and its framers must be unwise statesmen indeed, if they have not provided it, as far as its nature will permit, with the means of self-preservation from the perils it may be destined to encounter.

60. *Id.* at 416.

61. 9 Wheat. 1 (1824).

62. U.S. CONST. art. I, §8 [3]. An alternative argument was based upon the progress of science and the useful arts clause. U.S. CONST. art. I, §8 [8].

63. 9 Wheat. 188 (1824).

64. *Id.* at 189.

65. *Id.* at 194.

66. *Id.* at 196–97.

67. *Id.* at 222. Justice Johnson concurred separately on the grounds that the commerce power is exclusive.

68. *Id.* at 221.

69. 12 Wheat. 214 (1827).

70. *Id.* at 336.

71. Isaacs, *John Marshall on Contracts: A Study in Early American Juristic Theory*, 7 VA. L. REV. 413, 421 (1921).

72. R. FAULKNER, THE JURISPRUDENCE OF JOHN MARSHALL 17–19, 27–28 (1968). Faulkner argues that Marshall's staunch protection of certain contract rights is compatible with his willingness to allow state action within the realms of creation and remedies flows from his conception of the nature of liberal society with the preeminence of productive rights and the consequent arrangement of political power appropriate to sustain and nurture commercial development on the Lockean model.

73. Frankfurter, *supra* note 2, at 218; *see also* F. FRANKFURTER, THE COMMERCE CLAUSE 12 (1964).

74. Powell, *supra* note 21, at 894; *see also* DWORKIN, *supra* note 10, at 380.

The Constitution is foundational of other law, so [the best] interpretation of the document as a whole, and of its abstract clauses, must be foundational as well. It must fit and justify the most basic arrangements of political power in the community, which means it must be a justification drawn from the most philosophical reaches of political theory. Lawyers are always philosophers, because jurisprudence is part of any lawyer's account of what the law is, even when the jurisprudence is undistinguished and mechanical. In constitutional theory philosophy is closer to the surface of the argument and, if the theory is good, explicit in it.

75. Powell, *supra* note 21, at 894.

76. Ogden v. Saunders, 12 Wheat. 332 (1827).

77. Isaacs, *supra* note 71, at 423.

78. *Id.* at 425.

79. Powell, *supra* note 21, at 903–4.

Although the Philadelphia framers certainly wished to embody in the text the "most distinctive form of collecting the mind" of the convention, there is no indication that they expected or intended future interpreters to refer to any extratextual intentions revealed in the convention's secretly conducted debates. The framers shared the traditional common law view—so foreign to much hermeneutical thought in more recent years—that the import of the document they were framing would be determined by reference to the intrinsic meaning of its words or through the usual judicial process of case-by-case interpretation.

80. *See* Sturges v. Crowninshield, 4 Wheat. 202 (1819); *see also* Powell, *supra* note 21, at 942.

81. Frankfurter, *supra* note 2, at 218.

82. FAULKNER, *supra* note 72, Preface at xiii.

83. McCulloch v. Maryland, 4 Wheat. 407 (1819).

A constitution, to contain an accurate detail of all the subdivisions of which its great powers will admit, and of all the means by which they may be carried into execution, would partake of a prolixity of a legal code, and could scarcely be embraced by the human mind. It would probably never be understood by the public. Its nature, therefore, requires, that only its great outlines should be marked, its important objects designated, and the minor ingredients which compose those objects be deduced from the nature of the objects themselves.

See also FAULKNER, supra note 72, at 82. "It is the combination of modest ends and pervasive means which underlies Marshall's interpretation of the 'great powers' corresponding to the Preamble's 'great purposes.'"

84. Gibbons v. Ogden, 9 Wheat. 222 (1824); *see also* Crosskey, *John Marshall and the Constitution*, 23 U. CHI. L. REV. 377, 378–79 (1956).

85. FAULKNER, *supra* note 72, Preface at viii; *see also* Gertz, *John Marshall: Molder of the U.S. Constitution*, 6 DECALOGUE J. 3, 6 (1955).

86. Goebel, *The Common Law and the Constitution*, in CHIEF JUSTICE JOHN MARSHALL: A REAPPRAISAL 101, 108 (W. Jones ed. 1956).

87. FAULKNER, *supra* note 72, at 220.

88. Lynch, *supra* note 39, at 18.

In every landmark case, as in *Fletcher*, there is a hesitation that reveals the gap to be leaped, the Kierkegaardian leap which once accomplished lands you in another world, one of the opinion's making. The case is a landmark precisely because the outposts of the past did not lead to its placement. They lead to a place infinitely short of it. The rules and rationale of precedent cannot get you there. What is needed is a new creation, a numinous principle that breaks the bonds of past precedent and present provision, elevates the law and moving it by transcendental force places it on the other side. Once accomplished, there is no return. The past is effaced. The future will start from that point. That is what a landmark is. The law has been renewed. Thus, in *Fletcher* the contract clause was construed, broadened in construction, and state power was substantially limited.

89. Dorfman, *John Marshall: Political Economist*, in CHIEF JUSTICE JOHN MARSHALL: A REAPPRAISAL 124, 131 (W. Jones ed. 1956); *see also* Sherry, *the Founder's Unwritten Constitution*, 54 U. CHI. L. REV. 1127, 1168 (1987). *But see* Frankfurter, *supra* note 2, at 225 (who described Marshall's natural law references as "literary garniture").

90. *See* Nelson, *The Eighteenth-Century Background of John Marshall's Constitutional Jurisprudence*, 76 MICH. L. REV. 893 (1978).

91. *Id.* at 928–29.

92. Beveridge, *Maryland, Marshall and the Constitution*, THE MARSHALL READER 45, 46–47 (E. Surrency ed. 1955). "[T]hese opinions of the great Chief Justice were not legal documents; they were great State papers. Not one of them was addressed to the case before the Court; all of them were addressed to profound and determinative economic and social conditions, national in extent."

93. Chaudhuri, *supra* note 6, at 86.

94. Corwin, *Supra* note 24, at 294. [emphasis added].

95. *Id.* at 293.
96. Nelson, *supra* note 90, at 901–2.
97. *See* BICKEL, *supra* note 4, at 16–17.
98. Sherry, *supra* note 89, at 1146. *See also* McIntosh, *supra* note 21, at 386–87.
99. Nelson, *supra* note 90, at 926.
100. Fletcher v. Peck, 6 Cranch 87, 137–38 (1810).
101. Ackerman, *supra* note 4, at 1029–30.

Given the danger that normal government will be captured by partisans of narrow special interests, Publius proposes to consolidate the Revolutionary achievements of the American people through the institution of judicial review. When normal representatives respond to special interests in ways that jeopardize the fundamental principles for which the Revolutionaries fought and died, the judge's duty is to expose them for what they are: merely "stand-ins" for the People themselves. . . . Rather than trying to immobilize the People, the Supreme Court's task is to prevent the abuse of the People's name in normal politics. The Court's job is to force our elected representatives in Washington to engage in the special kind of mass mobilization required for a constitutional amendment if they hope to overrule the earlier achievements of the American Revolution.

102. Nelson, *supra* note 90, at 935–36. *See also* FAULKNER, *supra* note 72, at 194.
103. *See* Kainen, *supra* note 36, at 406.
104. Nelson, *supra* note 90, at 954.
105. *See* FAULKNER, *supra* note 72, at 218–19.

The Chief Justice's mode of construction, "adhering to the letter of the statute, taking the whole together," also tended to engender close respect for law. And the style of his writing had a similar effect. . . . The gravity of the Chief Justice's style is proverbial. . . . Marshall rose to a kind of magisterial reverence when he treated the fundamental law. By no means, his whole manner indicated, was the the Constitution to be confused with the hurly-burly of politics. It was to be venerated, not controverted. It seems, as the more flippant and unreflective commentators have not hesitated to point out, that Marshall dealt not merely with a constitution framed by unusual men, but with a sacred law made by sainted men.

106. *Id.* at 194–95.

Perhaps the resolution is by now obvious. The Americans' fundamental law, to which Marshall deferred, embraced a particular kind of politics. The Constitution of rights and powers reflected the prescriptions of liberal jurisprudence, the great means, with political economy, of applying Lockean enlightenment. Modern scholars may view this as one among several kinds of politics. Hence we see the judges' interpretation of the fundamental law, in the light of that politics, as involving not only discretion but will or bias. What we now see as but one variety of politics appeared to Marshall, however, as the private law, and the public law, dictated by nature itself. Marshall viewed the Lockean political understanding as the true political perspective. From that point of view courts simply follow the law, or at least guide their discretion according to the appropriate "general principles of law."

See also Nelson, *supra* note 90, at 899 (for an analysis of Frankfurter's important perspective). *See also* DWORKIN, *supra* note 10, at 378, 397–98.

107. Newmyer, *On Assessing the Court in History: Some Comments on the Roper and Burke Articles*, 21 STAN. L. REV. 540 (1969)

There are, however, some special problems facing the historian who attempts to put law in a cultural context. The Supreme Court lives in the world, to be sure. Judges make law, not find it.

When they do they are swayed by ordinary human passions and are inclined to political, social, and economic predilections deriving from their own background and experience. Yet there is an important qualification. The Court is not a legislature. Its procedures and intellectual assumptions are not those of Congress. Judges have biases that shape policy decisions, but they also have commitments to the institutional tradition of the Court and to the methodology of the law. However much the Court is part of the real world of interests and political power, it does not cease being a court of law. The obligation of the constitutional historian is twofold in this regard. He must go beyond the narrow, formal view of the law into the realm of politics, economics, and intellectual history. At the same time, he must do justice to the legal side of the Court; he must show *how*, within the limits of unique legal institutions, the Justices accomplish their cultural mission.

108. Frankfurter, *supra* note 2, at 218.
109. Newmyer, *supra* note 107, at 546.
110. DWORKIN, *supra* note 10, at 356–57.

Marshall has often been accused, in the long debates that continue yet, of begging all the important questions. That charge is easy to sustain under the plain-fact picture of law we considered and rejected early in this book, the picture that insists on a firm analytical distinction between legal questions about what the law is and political questions about whether the courts should enforce the law. If this distinction were sound, then of course we could not drag any conclusion about what any court should do from the proposition that American law includes the Constitution, which is only a statement about what the law is. Law as integrity, on the contrary, supports Marshall's argument. He was right to think that the most plausible interpretation of the developing legal practices of the young country, as well as of its colonial and British roots, supposed that an important part of the point of law was to supply standards for the decision of courts. History has vindicated the substantive dimension of that interpretation. . . . His decision was accepted, at least in that abstract form, and subsequent constitutional practice has coagulated firmly around it. No interpretation would fit that practice if it denied the powers Marshall declared. Even those who think he made a mistake concede that almost two centuries of practice have put his position beyond challenge as a proposition of law, and the constitutional wars are now fought on the terrain it defines.

111. FAULKNER, *supra* note 72, at 196–97.
112. DWORKIN, *supra* note 10, at 67–68.

We can now look back through our analytical account to compose an inventory of the kind of convictions or beliefs or assumptions someone needs to interpret something. He needs assumptions or convictions about what counts as part of the practice in order to define the raw data of his interpretation at the preinterpretive stage; the interpretive attitude cannot survive unless members of the same interpretive community share at least roughly the same assumptions about this. He also needs convictions about how far the justification he proposes at the interpretive stage must fit the standing features of the practice to count as an interpretation of it rather than the invention of something new. . . . [T]here cannot be too great a disparity in different people's convictions about fit; but only history can teach us how much difference is too much. Finally, he will need more substantive convictions about which kinds of justification really would show the practice in the best light, . . . These substantive convictions must be independent of the convictions about the fit just described, otherwise the latter could not constrain the former, and he could not, after all, distinguish interpretation from invention. But they need not be so much shared within his community, for the interpretive attitude to flourish, as his sense of preinterpretive boundaries or even his convictions about the required degree of fit.

113. Frankfurter, *supra* note 2, at 218. Faulkner, *supra* note 72, at 220.

114. O. W. Holmes, *Speech on John Marshall*, The Holmes Reader, 114 (1955) *But see* Faulkner, *supra* note 72, at 227–68.

115. Crosskey, *supra* note 84, at 396–97.

His greatness, clearly, was not that of triumphant victory. It was a greatness that consisted in devoting half a lifetime to a cause in which he profoundly believed; in faithful service to that cause in the face of overwhelming odds; in unflagging courage in the face of those odds, and in the face of constantly recurring defeats. There can be no doubt, moreover, that John Marshall, in spite of the conditions in which he worked, accomplished much in the way of minimizing damage; . . .

116. Gertz, *supra* note 85, at 4; *see also* Fairman, *John Marshall and the American Judicial Tradition*, in Chief Justice John Marshall: A Reappraisal 77, 83 (W. Jones ed. 1956). *See also* Seddig, *John Marshall and the Origins of Supreme Court Leadership* 36 U. Pitt. L. Rev. 785, 815 (1975).

117. Tushnet, *supra* note 6, at 785–86. "It may be that we live in a world of tension, in which no unified social theory but only a dialogue between liberalism and conservatism is possible." *See also* McIntosh, *supra* note 21, at 363. *See also* Ackerman, *supra* note 4, at 1072.

118. McIntosh, *supra* note 21, at 379.

10

Epistemology and Hermeneutics in the Constitutional Jurisprudence of John Marshall

Michael Zuckert

My title indicates a desire to summon John Marshall before the bar of contemporary scholarship and compel him to testify regarding our conflicts over the nature of the judicial function. Today we most commonly raise that issue in terms of the categories of interpretivism versus noninterpretivism—"the former indicating that judges should confine themselves to enforcing norms that are stated or clearly implicit in the written Constitution, the latter the contrary view that courts should go beyond that set of references and enforce norms that cannot be discovered within the four corners of the document."[1]

Scholars have, for the most part, viewed Marshall as a consummate political judge, and therefore as some sort of noninterpretivist. They differed in how they understood the category "political judge." But they shared the thought, sometimes only implicitly, that ends and undertakings more or less extrinsic to the Constitution itself shaped Marshall's interpretations of the Constitution. Christopher Wolfe, in his recent *The Rise of Modern Judicial Review* (although not he alone), shifted the focus: Marshall's constitutional judgments are best understood as an effort to give effect to the Constitution itself. As Wolfe said, "Both the theory and practice of early American judicial review demonstrated the possibility of a non-legislative form of judicial review," a form that Wolfe understands as embodying "judicial objectivity."[2]

But neither Wolfe nor Marshall himself held that the text or bare words of the Constitution were perfectly clear, or better, clearly determinative of the myriad issues posed to it. Questions might arise that were not within the contemplation of the drafters of the text, and even where the drafters may have considered the matter, the text might not obviously settle one correct answer from a range of more or less plausible textual readings.

Wolfe recognizes textual lacunae, yet holds that the Constitution may nonetheless settle an issue. "The starting point" for appreciating how Marshall's approach might produce nonlegislative, that is, objective or correct, interpretations is "the fact . . . that some principles may be implicitly in a constitution, though not explicitly so."[3] Wolfe here puts his finger on *the* problem of constitutional (or other) hermeneutics: How can something not be in a text and yet be in it?

Wolfe's answer is to identify a series of "rules of interpretations" that in effect allow Marshall to fill in constitutional meanings in a nonlegislative manner. These rules themselves are not of Marshall's own fashioning, but are methods for interpreting legal texts that had evolved over centuries of common law adjudication in England and then America. Wolfe puts much weight on the fact that those rules were codified by Blackstone, and given pride of a very early place in his *Commentaries on the Laws of England.* Wolfe finds much evidence for "the widespread acceptance of [such] rules of legal interpretation during the period in which the Constitution was framed and put into effect."[4]

He thus suggests that the rules supply objective or correct readings of the text, because the text was constructed originally with such rules in mind. To overstate the point, perhaps, it is as though the rules were a kind of code, which initially were used to encode the text, and later employed again to decode it. Wolfe thus defends a strong view of "objectivity in interpretation"—that Marshall gives us the "thing itself," that is, the true and accurate meaning of the text.[5]

Because of the strength and subtlety of his argument, I wish to take Wolfe's discussion as a point of departure for a reconsideration of Marshall's interpretive practice. More than anything, that practice reveals the ultimate inadequacy of the interpretivist/noninterpretivist dichotomy. When all is said and done, I shall argue, Marshall's practice points us toward a version of interpretation in which the interpretive act is recognized as more like what noninterpretivists describe, but in which that fact does not thereby foreclose the result from being an authentic expression of "fidelity to the law." For reason of space I limit myself to one area of Marshall's jurisprudence only. I recognize the resulting limit of the base of my conclusions and concede the need to extend my discussion to encompass more of Marshall's practice.

My intent is not so much to challenge Wolfe's reading of Marshall's hermeneutics—although I shall do that—but to use this discussion as a vehicle for sketching the outlines of a general account of the nature of (Marshall's) constitutional interpretations. This account proceeds in terms of a number of concepts that can be briefly identified here, but need to be discussed more fully in their proper place. (1) *Text*—by text I mean the narrow set of words immediately under interpretation. For constitutional cases, this will typically be some clause or other of the Constitution, for example, the necessary and proper clause, or the contracts clause. (2) *Context*—by context I mean the (relatively narrow) textual context in which the text under consideration occurs. For example, the necessary and proper clause occurs in the context of a list of other enumerated powers; the contracts clause in a list of other limitations on state powers. (3) *Transtext*—transtexts are the textlike constructs that are deployed in intermediate stages of the interpretive process in order to deal with the openness of text and context. Among the most important transtextuals are rules that establish how one ought to take certain juxtapositions of text and context, as well as how to deploy context in order to make sense of text. (4) *Pantext*—every interpretation is ultimately governed by a conception of the whole, of the meaning, character and point of the whole. This whole, the pantext, is strictly speaking not in the text, but it governs what is found there. (5) *Pretext*—as H. G. Gadamer emphasized in his theory of interpretation, the model of interpretation that has the interpreter begin with a clean slate and be simply open or receptive to what is there is false to the phenomenon. Instead readers approach texts with expectations, with forestructures of meaning. As Gadamer and Martin Heidegger before him emphasized, these forestructures involve a range of pre-positions, from language rules to generic expectations.[6] In constitutional interpretation the most important pretextual elements are expectations or preprojections of meaning at the transtextual and pantextual levels.

Pretext is not quite the same as premise, however, in that the relationship between pretextual and (so to speak) posttextual elements is dialectical rather than deductive as in the model of the premise. Precisely because pretext is dialectically related to posttext I demur from the conclusion to which Heidegger and Gadamer seem driven by their uncovering of the pretextual: that no approach to the "text-in-itself," no "objective" interpretation is possible, for there is no text-in-itself, but rather only an interpretive event between text and pretext.

MARBURY v. MADISON: A DISSENTING OPINION

Marshall's interpretive practice in *Marbury* (and elsewhere) would have stood out much more clearly, I suspect, had he been less successful in controlling dissent on his Court. Of course, what his colleagues on the Court would not do, modern scholars have somewhat made up for.[7] Nonetheless, and with a generalized debt to these scholars, I think it will be helpful to our attempt to interpret Marshall's interpretive practice if we construct a hypothetical dissenting opinion in *Marbury*, so as to have a basis of comparison from which we might draw some conclusions about interpretive procedure. I focus attention almost exclusively on that part of Marshall's opinion that considered the constitutionality of Section 13 of the Judiciary Act of 1789.

JUSTICE JURIST (concurring in part and dissenting in part):

"Only with great reluctance do I dissent from the reasoning of my distinguished colleague and chief, Justice Marshall. I am all the more reluctant to enter a dissenting voice because I agree entirely with his disposition of the first two issues raised in this case—viz. that 'applicant has a right to the commission he demands,' and secondly, that 'the laws of his country afford him a remedy.' I reject only his holding that 'a writ of mandamus issuing from this Court' is not an appropriate remedy. The part of his reasoning on that last question that I cannot accept is his conclusion that Congress has not the power under the Constitution of the United States to grant this Court the power to issue writs of mandamus in exercise of its original jurisdiction in a case of this sort. Lest my position be misunderstood, let me say at once that I have no reservations at all regarding the power—or rather the duty—identified in the Court's opinion not to give effect to laws unwarranted by the Constitution.

"Mr. Marshall appears to rest his decision on three claims: (1) the text of Article III, Section 2 provides that the Supreme Court 'shall have' original jurisdiction in certain named classes of cases, and 'shall have' appellate jurisdiction in all other cases within the grant of judicial powers; (2) no words in the Constitution are to be taken as 'mere surplusage,' that is, 'entirely without meaning'; and (3) the case at hand is not among those identified by the Constitution as belonging to this Court's original jurisdiction. Therefore, he concludes, Congress, not being free to reassign what the Constitution has assigned, is not permitted to provide this Court with original jurisdiction in this case.

"Respectfully, I must say there is hardly a shred of support for this construction of the Constitution.

"Regarding the distribution of jurisdiction between original and appellate in Article III, Section 2. Let us look at the text: 'In all Cases affecting [a list of parties], the Supreme Court shall have original Jurisdiction. In all other Cases before mentioned, the Supreme Court shall have appellate Jurisdiction . . . with such Exceptions as . . . the Congress shall make.' Now I would ask Mr. Marshall why he failed to note the grant of power to Congress to make 'exceptions'? Perhaps he might attempt to weasel out from under my question by saying the exceptions have to do with other things. I say that is surely an insupportable reading of the text, for what are the exceptions, exceptions to? They must be exceptions to what the Constitution has just said or done—they must be exceptions to the totality of allocation that has just been set forth. The exceptions clause must mean nothing less than that Congress has power to reshuffle the distribution of cases as just listed!

"Ah, but Mr. Marshall replies that nothing must be read so as to be without meaning or point—that nothing in the text must be read so as to make it 'mere surplusage.' (But who is Mr. Marshall to talk—he himself makes the exceptions clause such surplusage—he almost reads it out of the Constitution!) But, implies he, reading the exceptions clause so as to authorize congressional reassignment of cases between original and appellate jurisdiction makes the constitutional allocation meaningless, surplusage.

"But does it? Even if the exceptions clause authorizes Congress to reshuffle all cases between both jurisdictional categories it would not be mere surplusage: it would supply a rule for distribution unless and until Congress acts to provide otherwise; it supplies an allocation that Congress would do well to keep to unless it had good reasons to depart from it. Article I, Section 4, Clause 2 provides good precedent for such a reading: 'The Congress shall assemble . . . on the first day in December, unless they shall by law appoint a different day.'

"But there is no need to read the exceptions clause so loosely. Most likely it means to give Congress power to transfer cases from this Court's appellate to its original jurisdiction; but not to authorize transferral in the opposite direction. That is why the exceptions clause is attached to the sentence that directs the allocation to the appellate jurisdiction.

"Congress may transfer cases from appellate to original, but may not transfer original to appellate; nothing is therefore mere surplusage, neither the initial distribution nor the power to make exceptions to it. Such an interpretation not only coheres best with the text, including the phrasing and punctuation of the section, but a readily ascertainable principle makes perfect sense of the constitutional presumption as thus understood. The Constitution reserves cases of special delicacy, those involving parties of special dignity—ministers of foreign nations and the states of our nation—for original hearing in the highest tribunal known under the laws and Constitution of the United States. Such an honor, or rather such a saving from the dishonor of appearing before lower tribunals, comports with the honor owed by a nation aware of its own dignity to its member states, of equally high dignity, and to our honorable sister states in the great human family of nations.

"I had said earlier that the Court has almost read the exceptions clause out of the Constitution. Were it only true. Better to fail to give effect to part of the Constitution, than by misinterpretation to give a pernicious effect. God forbid I should ever countenance a misreading of the text, but I would sooner throw my inkwell into the Potomack River than to destroy the most precious parts of the Constitution, as the Court has begun to do today.

"The exceptions clause remains in the Constitution—and what must it mean in the light of today's decision? It cannot now mean Congress may make exceptions in the sense of the shifting classes of cases from appellate to original jurisdiction; it must therefore now be taken to allow Congress to make exceptions to the appellate jurisdiction—not so as to shift such cases to the original jurisdiction, but so as to deny the Court's jurisdiction altogether. Under such a misguided construction, Congress might be deemed empowered to strip the Court of all its jurisdiction, except the relatively minor original jurisdiction.

"A glance at several other clauses of the Constitution readily shows how incorrect such a result would be. According to Section I of Article III, 'the judicial power of the United States, shall be vested in one Supreme Court, and in such inferior Courts as the Congress may from time to time ordain and establish.' Congress may, in other words, opt not to create 'inferior Courts,' in which case the United States judicial system would consist only of the Supreme Court. And if Congress may at the same time strip the Supreme Court of some or all of its appellate jurisdiction, then that much of the judicial power of the United States would not be vested in any court of the United States. But Article III says the judicial power 'shall be vested. . . .' And there can be little doubt that 'shall' in this clause is meant in a mandatory sense, for in the next clause Congress is granted discretionary authority to establish lower courts in very different language: 'as the Congress *may* . . . establish.' Indeed, in the next sentence in that article 'shall' is thrice used in the nondiscretionary or mandatory sense: 'the Judges . . . *shall hold* their offices during good Behavior. . . .' Can this mean judges will hold their office at the discretion of Congress? And the judges 'shall' . . . receive for their Services, a Compensation, which *shall* not be diminished during their Continuance in Office.' Can this mean that Congress may if it chooses deny the judges a compensation? Or diminish it? Only fear of tiring my readers prevents me from further documenting the use of 'shall' in the Constitution. Is the use of 'shall' in the judicial article different from that everywhere else in the Constitution? Is the judiciary of lesser import than the other parts of the governmental system? Is it to be served up on a cross of gold to the legislative or executive branches? May I throw my inkwell into the Potomack before I allow such a conclusion without protest.

"The pernicious reading that turns 'shall be vested' into 'may be vested' runs counter to every principle of our constitutional system. Our system is marked by two chief features—a new and special kind of federalism and a new kind of republicanism, marked, by among other things, a carefully poised system of checks and balances ultimately aimed to achieve the greatest degree of security for the rights of individuals.

"Let us see what the interpretation sponsored by our esteemed Chief Justice does to these two principles. Our federalism breaks new ground in its provision for the construction and operation of the general government and state governments independent of each other. Unlike the government under the Articles of Confederation, our new government does not require the interaction of agencies of the states to carry out its policies. It has its own executive and judicial establishments to carry out its own laws directly on its citizens. But what happens to the judicial system of the United States under the construction adopted today? There now may constitutionally prevail a situation in which no court of the United States is vested with the major part of the judicial power, leaving the laws of the United States to be enforced—if enforced they would be—entirely in the Courts of the States, without even the supervisory power of the federal judiciary via its appellate jurisdiction. This result surely clashes with every principle of our new system.

"The Chief Justice's interpretation also violates the character of the republicanism to which the Constitution is committed. Mr. Marshall himself has given a very adequate account of one feature of this republicanism—the placement in our written Constitution of limits on the powers of the legislature in the interests of the rights of individuals. And, as the majority opinion so aptly argues, it falls to this Court to enforce those rights. But how can this Court enforce limits on the powers of Congress if Congress is armed at every moment with the threat of the power to remove the appellate jurisdiction from this Court? Imagine the following very clear instance, which Heaven forbid, no American Congress would ever dare attempt. But it is, I submit, perfectly constitutional under the holding of this case, Article I, Section 9 secures for all citizens that great charter of our liberties, the writ of habeas corpus, 'unless when in cases of Rebellion or Invasion the public Safety may require' its suspension. Yet suppose an unscrupulous Congress were to suspend the writ without the justifying circumstances named in the text? And what if, at the same time, it were to pass a law stripping the Supreme Court of its jurisdiction to hear cases challenging that suspension? Can our constitutional system long be considered safe under such possibilities as these?

"What the Chief Justice did today is a short step for a man, but a long step back toward the days of Stuart tyranny, which those of us who were. . . ."

Let us leave the splenetic Justice Jurist here. He surely will find much to go on about, but we have had as much from him as we require. Those familiar with the literature will realize that Justice Jurist has hardly said anything novel, but the point of this long dissenting opinion is not so much to find new grounds to berate Marshall on, but rather to supply a concrete basis for a more analytic discussion of Marshall's interpretive practice in *Marbury*.

Different as their outcomes are, Marshall and Jurist share much as interpreters. Both, for example, have a heavy textual component. Justice Jurist makes heavy appeal to context as when he sets the distribution of jurisdiction into the larger context of Article III. Marshall, interestingly, is rather weak on context in this case. Both deploy transtextual considerations in important places in their opinions. Marshall appeals to the "no mere surplusage" rule, a rule that is certainly not in the text, but that provides a way of "taking" what is there, that is, a way of giving meaning to text. Marshall also speaks of "the solicitude of the convention, respecting our peace with foreign powers" as an account for why the text singles out the few cases that it does for original jurisdiction. Justice Jurist employs that same "surplusage" rule, and also relies on either transtextual dimensions; for example, he draws out a rationale for the settlement of the jurisdictional question as he believes the Constitution settles it.

While there are differences in the quality and quantity of the various factors of text, context, and transtext (usually, I must say, to the advantage of Justice

Jurist), the most noticeable difference between the two occurs at what I have called the pantextual level. Justice Jurist devotes the whole last part of his opinion to pantext, reaching that level with a crescendo of invective and self-righteousness inspired by his confidence in the pantextual correctness of his interpretation. Chief Justice Marshall, on the other hand, devotes no space to pantext, certainly not in that part of his opinion concerned with the constitutional question we are now considering. (Justice Jurist correctly points to Marshall's discussion of judicial review itself as containing considerations of a pantextual sort, but he also attempts to show that Marshall's holding is incorrect on the basis of Marshall's own pantext.) Marshall, in other words, makes no explicit effort to note, or even to show the consistency of his reading of Article III, Section 2 with a pantext.

I would like to explore the possibility, however, that there is a pantext implicit in Marshall's opinion, a pantext that coheres, at some level, with his reading of the text.

MARSHALL'S PANTEXT—FROM CONSTITUTION TO CONSTITUTIONAL LAW

Justice Jurist puts Marshall's achievement in *Marbury* in a rather different light from the ordinary. He emphasizes how much Marshall gave up for the Court, how potentially dependent, even subordinate he made the Court to Congress. That emphasis fits with another part of Marshall's opinion that Justice Jurist might also have taken exception to had it led to a result he disagreed with. I refer to Marshall's discussion of the question of whether the judiciary could serve legal orders like a writ of mandamus on executive officers like the secretary of state—or the President. Although Marshall answered that question in the affirmative he carefully hedged it around with a discussion of the limits of that power. The chief limit is what came to be known as the "political questions" doctrine: "Questions in their nature political, or which are, by the Constitution and laws, submitted to the executive, can never be made in this Court."

Admittedly, Marshall's description of the political questions limitations on the Court is vague and of uncertain boundaries. What are "questions in their nature political," so far as they are something different from a question "submitted by law or Constitution, to the executive"? He speaks elsewhere of cases where executive discretion is to be exercised, or where the officer is "the mere organ of executive will" as instances where judicial scrutiny is inappropriate. Vague as the boundary may be, however, it is significant that Marshall insists on it, and that it stands as a potential limitation—according to Marshall, a constitutionally mandated limitation—on the power and ability of the Courts to control the executive. That is, *Marbury* sets major limits on the Court's relation to the executive via the political questions doctrine, and its relation to the legislature via Marshall's reading of the execptions clause.

Justice Jurist's emphasis suggests then that we should see *Marbury* in almost the reverse of the way we normally tend to do. He sees the case as weakening or limiting the Court; we tend to see it as the great assertion, sometimes even usurpation, of the power of judicial review. Our perspective is shaped, it seems, by a background sense that the Court left *Marbury* stronger than it entered; Justice Jurist was convinced it left the case weakened.

The long-run central issue was whether the Court went into *Marbury* with a reasonable case for possessing its power of powers, the power of judicial review. If not, then the assertion of that power in *Marbury* was surely a gain for the Court; but if so, then perhaps the perspective of Justice Jurist is roughly correct.

Few historical questions have elicited so much scholarly attention and, not surprisingly, the results have been less than conclusive on the issue of whether the Supreme Court was intended to have the power of judicial review. The most recent extensive review of the question, Raoul Berger's *Congress v. The Supreme Court*, is unhesitant in affirming that "proponents and critics of judicial review both expected the Courts to have the 'final' word on constitutional limitations."[8] John Agresto's recent rereview of the evidence, less exhaustive, but extremely thoughtful, concluded in a similar vein: "That the founders intended judicial review is relatively clear."[9] And yet, other recent writers remain unpersuaded.[10]

I have no intention of presenting yet one more review of the evidence, but I do wish to report my own sense that those who hold back from accepting the conclusion that judicial review was originally intended are overscrupulous. At the Constitutional Convention all who spoke on the topic indicated they recognized judicial review to be part of the Constitution they were preparing—even though not all favored it. At ratifying conventions the same recognition emerged frequently, but here the enthusiasm for the institution seemed even greater than at Philadelphia. In the First Congress, the debate over the Bill of Rights promoted affirmation of the power. The premise of Section 25 of the Judiciary Act of 1789 is the existence of the power. Even Justice Gibson in *Eakin v. Raub*, generally admitted to be the ablest opponent of Marshall's argument on judicial review, concedes that "a right to declare all unconstitutional acts void . . . is generally held as a professional dogma." Admittedly Gibson's testimony is from 1825, two decades after *Marbury*, but if the issue were really in such doubt might we not expect sufficient lingering doubts that Gibson would not have the sense of coming into a wholly new and unknown land when he found reason to reject the reasoning in *Marbury*?

In light of the evidence, therefore, what was remarkable about *Marbury* was not the assertion of a power that was intended and expected to belong to the Court, but the careful drawing of limits and bounds around the Court's power.

While that aspect of Marshall's opinion is frequently discussed in terms of the political imperatives the Chief Justice faced in his struggle with the executive (and the Republicans),[11] I propose an alternative approach—that Marshall was attempting to present or develop a coherent constitutional doctrine of judicial review at the pantextual level, and that this is what led him to the weakening of the constitutional status of the Supreme Court he effected in *Marbury*.

Judicial review as it made its way into the Constitution represented the uneasy convergence of two rather separate lines of constitutionalism. One line we might call legalist constitutionalism; the other political constitutionalism. We in the twentieth century tend not to see the existence, much less the difference, between the two lines, because for us the Constitution has so deeply become identified with constitutional law. That development is at once a profound falsification of the nature of the original American Constitution and a natural development or expression of it. The obscurity of the distinction, however, shields us from appreciating the emergence of constitutional law out of the Constitution, or the triumph of the legalist constitution over the political constitution.

The legalist constitution takes the shortest and most direct route to the institution of judicial review. It is largely to the legalist understanding of the Constitution that Marshall appealed in his classic argument for judicial review in *Marbury*. The legalist constitution is a set of fundamental rules, and especially of limits, directly commanding the various agencies of government and securing the rights of citizens. Legalist constitutionalism was particularly a device favored by those who distrusted government and had confidence in pronouncements to control them. It is, in other words, the perspective favored especially by antifederalists at the time of the debate over the Constitution, and by those who put great stock in bills of rights, although these partisans did not alone favor judicial review as a corollary to their legalist constitutionalism. But, as John Agresto and others who have traced the history of this brand of constitutionalism have shown, judicial review attached itself to it rather easily once the Constitution came to be conceived as law, more fundamental, but otherwise like any other.

James Madison was the leading sponsor in the founding generation of the alternative political understanding of constitution. Instead of viewing a constitution as a set of legal rules, directly aiming to produce (or prevent) some governmental outcomes or other, Madison saw a constitution as a way of structuring institutions, the structure of which would produce (or prevent) the desired outcomes. Thus Madison says in *The Federalist* No. 51 the way to secure the separation of powers is not by putting decrees demanding the requisite separation into the Constitution, but rather "by so contriving the interior structure of the government as that its several constituent parts may, by their mutual relations, be the means of keeping each other in their proper places."

The chief security for minority rights in Madison's political constitution is not a bill of rights, enforced by the Supreme Court, but the kind of political structure outlined in *The Federalist* No. 10.

Madison's political constitution coheres much less readily with the practice of judicial review. Indeed, it is not clear that judicial review is any essential part of it. In *The Federalist* No. 51, for example, where Madison speaks of the institutional devices on which he puts greatest weight in maintaining the separation of powers, he neglects to mention the Supreme Court and judicial review. Rather he refers to legislative bicameralism and the executive veto.

Madison thinks constitution as political constitution, and that thinking pervaded his initial drafts for constitutional reform, which eventually made their way into the Virginia Plan. The Virginia Plan was from start to finish a political, not a legalist proposal. One way to describe the course of the convention is in terms of a transformation of the Virginia Plan into a partly legalist constitution—but only partly legalist. The limits of the transformation can be seen at a glance by comparing *The Federalist* with any standard treatise on constitutional law. *The Federalist*, except for a few places, is still clearly and decisively political science, not constitutional law.

Madison's preconvention thinking, however, led him to a number of novel insights that ultimately had the greatest significance for the emergence of constitutional law. He had one such major insight with respect to each of the three great areas of innovation in the Constitution—federalism, republicanism, and rights. Madison at a stroke reconceived the nature of federalism and pioneered a new approach to the issue. One of the most important aspects of his new approach was a full recognition of the problem of encroachments. It is not enough, he recognized, merely to divide authority between the state and general governments and enshrine the division in a written document. The division itself can hardly be made adequately, given the insufficiencies of the human mind and of human language. Moreover, political bodies have a natural tendency to encroach on the powers of each other even when lines of authority are perfectly clear. Most past federal systems had not recognized much less solved the problem of encroachment, with disastrous results: "The want of some such provision seems to have been mortal to the ancient Confederacies, and to be the disease of the Modern." Some body was needed, in other words, to serve as policeman of the federal system, noting and acting to correct encroachments.[12]

The solution Madison proposed, as contained in the Virginia Plan's sixth resolution, was to arm the national legislature with a power "to negative all laws passed by the several States, contravening in the opinion of the National Legislature the articles of Union." The details of this solution are not needed here, nor the reasons for the convention's ultimate rejection of this cure for the disease of encroachments; but we must note that Madison would have armed the national legislature with the power to, in effect, enforce the Constitution here. And he did so out of a sense that the national legislature was, of all the available bodies, the body best structured to produce the right resolution to conflicts of authority that might arise.[13]

Madison had a similar insight with respect to republicanism in the Constitution. The republican character of the constitutional scheme resided in two main features, the "electoral connection" between the people and the government, and the "auxiliary precautions" of the separation of powers. Schooled by Montesquieu, Madison and most of the other framers saw a proper separation of powers as essential to the securing of liberty in their new system.[14] But Madison saw that separation of powers schemes, relying on the same device of dividing up powers, were beset by the same problems as were federal schemes. That is, the problem of encroachments was a serious problem here as well, and one, we have already noticed, for which Madison rejected the legalist solution of "parchment barriers." Failure to provide adequately for securing the separation of powers could lead to a situation Madison pronounced "the very definition of tyranny"; namely, "the accumulation of all powers, legislative, executive, and judiciary, in the same hands. . . ."[15]

Madison's solution here could not be the same, however, as the solution to the problem posed by federalism, for in the republican system to be established in the Constitution, the legislature was the body most to be feared as likely to centralize powers in its own hands. In the Virginia Plan, therefore, he proposed a Council of Revision as the device to safeguard the separation of powers: the council was to be composed of the executive together with "a convenient number of the National Judiciary." They would have the power to negative all laws passed by the legislature, including its negative on state laws. The negative could be overridden, however, by special majority in the legislature. Since the discussions of judicial review that occurred at the convention occurred in the context of discussion of the Council of Revision, the story of the rejection of this council has been told many times, and need not be repeated here, other than to note that one major reason for the rejection was the concern that because of judicial review the judges would possibly and awkwardly pass on laws twice.[16] While the evidence seems plain that neither Madison nor the others saw the council of Revision as a complete substitute for judicial review, it is clear that many of them put much greater weight on the council, partly because they believed it would have a much greater weight than the courts alone—more of Madison's political approach to the Constitution.

Finally, Madison built into his planning one other feature that proved ultimately central to the emergence and development of judicial review. He was concerned not only with the possibility that the general government could be oppressive to its citizens, but even more concerned the states would be. He was therefore most eager to build into the structure of the general government a device that would supply protection of rights for citizens of the states against oppressive action by the states. Madison saw his recognition of this problem, the problem of majority faction, as his deepest insight. And he saw his solution to the problem, a solution built wholly on republican principles, as his most ingenious political idea. And that solution was not a bill of rights enforced by the Supreme Court, but rather a proposal to vest in the legislature of the general government a power to "negative all laws whatsoever" passed by the states. Such a power, Madison insisted, using his argument on the effects of majority formation in an extended republic, would work to safeguard the right of all Americans against the degradation of the state governments. This solution also was rejected by the convention—Madison could not even persuade his Virginia colleagues to include it in their plan, so radical a departure was it from prevailing political practices.[17]

The three solutions to the three problems Madison identified had in common the fact that they were essentially political devices that were to operate in a political, not a legal, way—and that all three were replaced by the Supreme Court. The convention rejected the legislative system, and instead provided the system of enumerated powers as the basis for a delimitation of the spheres of the different levels of government, as well as a firm specification of various acts the states may not perform, all to be enforced by the courts.

The Council of Revision's task of securing the constitutional separation of powers broke into two parts. The executive negative remained the political check, and the judiciary retained the judicial review function, which had been understood to belong to them in all discussions of the council. Madison, at least, apparently continued to see the executive negative as the more important of the two, judging by his discussion in *The Federalist* No. 51.

Finally, for Madison's beloved universal negative aiming to secure private rights in the states, the Constitution substituted explicit limits against state actions violative of rights, which are contained in Article I, Section 10. These specific limits, some of which were also secured against the general government in Article I, Section 9, were to be taken custody of by the courts.

The Supreme Court then was the heir, so to speak, of Madison's three insights and of his failed effort to work out political solutions to them. The convention adopted instead a mode of solution from the legalist tradition, a dimension of the Constitution that was enlarged first in the Bill of Rights, and then to an even greater degree by the post–Civil War amendments. The choice of the Court as the body to enforce these three sets of limits, instead of Madison's more political devices, was the decisive move that has led to the triumph of constitutional law.

But these legalist constitutional features were grafted onto a Constitution that in chief inspiration and dominant character remained political. And the resulting hybrid contained many anomalies, which is suggested, I think, by

Madison's career-long vacillation on the question of judicial review. Most of the time he grudgingly accepted or admitted its existence, but he never quite believed in it. He surely preferred the political constitutionalism he had sponsored, and I do not believe his hesitation about judicial review represented mere petulance on his part.

A review of some of the reasons Madison held back from judicial review points to the problem Marshall was grappling with in *Marbury*. He seems to have had four such reasons for preferring political route over judicial review. In the first place, it was more reliable. He never thought "parchment barriers" worth much and he worried that the Court would lack the weight to make constitutional limits effective.

The device of the Court, moreover, was an option for a device Madison suspected—the device of "a will independent of society," the device of a philosopher king, a race of men in whom Madison never believed. He did not trust modes of rule in which power was given to largely irresponsible people who were told to go out and do good with it. The Court was the model of "above-it" politics; Madison saw greater effectiveness and security in well-constructed institutions.

Third, Madison saw the result of judicial review as judicial supremacy, and that result he found genuinely perplexing. How can one supposedly coequal branch have particular authority to lay down the law for the other branches? And that branch was, moreover, the least responsible to the people, a virtue in some respects, but ultimately deeply troubling to Madison as well. Madison's own solution would not have led to these paradoxical results. No one body would have been in the position of supremacy because the three tasks were broken up to be done by two different bodies—the legislature, itself divided in two, acting to negative the laws of states, and the Council of Revision, composed of the other two branches and overrideable by the legislature acting to negative the acts of the legislature. Madison's would be a baroque system of mutual interactions in which no clear supremacy could ever be asserted anywhere. And every part of it involved bodies that were themselves responsible bodies.

Finally, the Madisonian system would operate in a political rather than a legalistic way. The legislature and the council would openly act on the basis of prudence and policy. Those bodies would consider matters more in the way the Constitutional Convention, for example, did its work, than in the manner of a court of law. The legislature, sitting in its capacity as reviewer of the laws of the states, would have the incentive as officers of the general government to protect the prerogatives of that government against encroachments from the states. And as representatives from so many states, the legislators would have sufficient neutrality to protect the states from encroachments by each other. And the Council of Revision would have the benefit of the legal perspective. "How much good . . . would proceed from the perspicuity, the conciseness, and the systematic character which the code of laws would receive from the Judiciary talents."[18] Yet the council would not operate as a court of law—limited to the specific facts of a particular case before it, bound by precedent and legal fictions, capable of judging only the constitutional dimensions of the laws they were reviewing. At the same time, the judiciary would be joined by the executive, who would bring to bear an entirely different set of considerations—considerations of practicability and efficacy, matters to which courts are not always well attuned. For as Marshall insisted in *Marbury* the main business of courts is the protection of "vested rights" and "the question whether a right has vested or not, is, in its nature, judicial, and must be tried by the judicial authority."[19] That is, the focus of judicial inquiry is important, but narrow, and different from the range of issues that a broader political perspective would bring into view.

My point is not so much to defend Madison's political constitution, however, but rather to bring out the fact that the Constitution moves in both directions at once. The convention overlaid on Madison's constitution this other, rather different constitution, and indeed gave over to the legalist constitution, the Court, and judicial review those three central functions from Madison's political constitution. Two types of constitutions juxtaposed, without clarity on how the two related to each other—that is the situation of the original constitution, magnified somewhat by the Bill of Rights. How, for example, does the political thrust of most of the Constitution relate to the legalist thrust of the rest? How does the legalist constitution respond to the considerations brought forth above as telling in Madison's mind against it?

Now the task that drove Marshall in *Marbury* was how to supply an interpretation of the two constitutions that the convention had achieved. Marshall was seeking, we might say, the constitution behind the Constitution; the true pantext is the version of the Constitution that produces the most coherent overall constitution. In this case that meant seeking for the constitutional understanding that would allow scope for the political constitution within the legalist solution that judicial review represented. Marshall differed from Justice Jurist just here—in attending to the yet more comprehensive constitution that embodied both political and legal constitution. Jurist's constitution, it is clear, is the legalist constitution through and through.

Marshall, it is true, did not speak explicitly of the talk we have posited as his, but his achievement in *Marbury* makes perfect sense if seen as a response to the problem of the relation between the political and the legalist constitutions. The task was twofold—to articulate the relationship of the two constitutions to each other, and to show how the composite constitution so described can respond to the problems of the legalist constitution that Madison voiced. Marshall's version of the Constitution, strong as it was in asserting a niche for the legalist constitution, and therewith for the courts, nonetheless carefully carved out an autonomous and in a certain sense ultimately supreme political constitution. The executive retained the large sphere of discretionary or political authority, free from court supervision and free to respond to nonlegalist imperatives; the legislative, Marshall established in later cases, retained a very large scope of discretionary power independent of Supreme Court supervision; and finally, Congress now possessed a very powerful political check against the Court—the power to control the Court's appellate jurisdiction. Surely Marshall neither expected nor desired that Congress exercise this power frequently, or perhaps not at all, but it would serve as a standing warning to the Court that it could not take the legalist constitution too far nor assert its supremacy in a too-galling way.

Marshall's pantext in *Marbury* does not respond to all the concerns that Madison had about the legalist constitution, but it makes a beginning. The political questions doctrine, for example, draws a line around the sphere of the Court's concern and leaves the political constitution free play outside that sphere. "The province of the court is, solely, to decide on the rights of individuals, not to inquire how the executive, or executive officers, perform duties in which they have a discretion."[20] Thus there may be some degree of judicial supremacy, but Marshall circumscribes its scope and attempts to give breathing space to the Madisonian constitution.

His reading of the exceptions clause clearly coheres with this construction of the pantext. It responds, for example, to Madison's persistent puzzlement over the paradox of judicial review—that through it one coequal branch somehow becomes more than equal. If that is true, it is also true that the congressional control of the Court's appellate jurisdiction returns the Court to a parity with the other branches that the legalist constitution seem to destroy. And the Court's vulnerability via this congressional power allows or requires the Court to be caught in the play of political forces that work through the whole constitutional system. Without destroying the Court's character as a court of law, it would guarantee that the Court keep in mind the limits of its position, and ultimately, the fact that the legalist constitution, of which it is the especial guardian, must coexist with (and even to some degree be subordinate to) the political constitution. That, I submit, is the pantext of Marshall's opinion in *Marbury v. Madison*.

MARSHALL'S HERMENEUTICS: THE PRIMACY OF PANTEXT

Now that we have taken this long detour to piece together Marshall's pantext we can turn to our chief task, the discussion of the hermeneutic question in constitutional interpretation. We must note the limits of the discussion at the onset, however. First, I focus almost exclusively on *Marbury* and therefore whatever conclusions I draw need to be tested and adjusted by analysis of other instances of Marshall's interpretive practice. Second, and perhaps more significant, I am proceeding to discuss Marshall's interpretive practice on the basis of at least two elements I have constructed. Neither Justice Jurist's dissenting opinion, nor, more importantly, Marshall's pantext as I have outlined it in the previous sections is present in the text in the same way as, for example, Marshall's own discussion of the distribution of original and appellate jurisdiction. That means of course, that the interpreter of interpretive practice faces precisely the same situation as the initial interpreter of a text, that is, facing a text, in need of interpretation. Since the focus of my attention here is Marshall's hermeneutics and only in the service of Marshall's composite constitution, I shall not pursue further the attempt to establish conclusively that the pantext I have attributed to Marshall was his own. I merely insist that the construct that I have put forward is a plausible reading of Marshall's view, coherent with what is most explicit in *Marbury*, and that it can serve as a basis for my more central task of explicating Marshall's interpretive practice.

It will be convenient, and I hope not too forced, to consider his practice in terms of our own categories of text, context, transtext, and pantext. These do not differ that much in fact from the categories of "the rules of legal interpretation" that Wolfe finds systematized in Blackstone and echoed in Marshall: words (text), context (context), subject matter, the effects and consequences (transtext), and the spirit and reason of the law (pantext).

Blackstone's list differs in one important respect (apart from details within the categories) from the set of categories put forward here. Blackstone and Marshall apparently see the list in something like a lexicographical order; an item further down the list only comes into play when the item above it on the list somehow fails. According to Blackstone, context, for example, "is to be used only 'if the words happen to be still dubious.'" According to Wolfe, Marshall's principle is the same. "If the words of the document are clear, then the judges are bound and can do no more than apply them." The interpreter is to follow "a determinate order . . . of moving from words to context to subject matter."[21] Our categories, by contrast, contain no necessary commitment to any particular temporal ordering for their deployment.

Text.   Marshall and Jurist have a clear disagreement over the meaning of the text, although it is not the sort of disagreement that might spring to mind when one thinks of disagreement over words. They have no difficulty in understanding the words in the same way. They both recognize that the Constitution in Article III, Section 2 distributes different cases between the Supreme Court's original and appellate jurisdiction. The meaning of these words apparently gives them no difficulty. In constitutional interpretation this is not always true. In *McCulloch v. Maryland*, for example, the very meaning of "necessary" is contested; in *Fletcher v. Peck* and *Dartmouth College v. Woodward* the scope of "contract" or in *Ogden v.*

Saunders "obligation." But in *Marbury* none of these more common or obvious textual problems occurs. It would seem then a good instance of a case where Blackstone-Marshall rules could produce a determinate result at their first waystation, the words of the text.

And yet Marshall and Jurist disagree. One way to state the character of that disagreement is to state it concerns the puzzling question: just what is the text? Marshall identifies the relevant text as the parts that establish the distribution of jurisdiction; Jurist adds to that the suggestions clause. What the relevant test is, is itself a question or issue. If the text is not self-giving or self-identifying, as it is not, it is difficult (at the least) to work with a model of interpretation that begins with—and, in its lexicographical principle—would even, when possible, end with the text. The text does not have absolute priority in the interpretation, but itself seems (somehow) to be an artifact of the interpretation itself.

Another way to state the character of the disagreement between Marshall and Jurist is to state that it concerns the bearing of the text. They agree it distributes jurisdiction, but that in itself does not answer the question of whether Congress may redistribute it differently. In this case there is thus a certain openness about text, at the level of bearing, even when there is no particular problem at the level of primary meaning (that is, grammar and semiosis). One wonders whether there isn't always or in principle such an openness of bearing in any text, such that the text itself never (hardly ever?) can settle the question of meaning—if we take meaning to include at least primary meaning and bearing.

Context. This last point remains obscure to me, but it is easier to see what both judges do in order to respond to the openness of the text in the double sense we have identified thus far (that is, the nongivenness of the text, and the openness of bearing and therefore of meaning): they have recourse to other conceptual levels of the interpretive process. In this case Marshall passes over context almost entirely and takes up transtext as a way to establish bearing. Jurist, by contrast, moves most emphatically to context as a way to settle text, and therewith to settle bearing.

Let us follow Jurist in his turn to context. Now Wolfe in his fine discussion of context is especially sensitive to the variety of contexts, and thus much of what I have to say may agree with him, but, it seems to me, the general thrust of his discussion points toward a relatively specific sense of context.[22] The objectifying possibilities on context, that is, the ability of context to supply a determinate reading when text fails to do so, would seem to depend on the existence of a more or less specific or closed context. There would seem to be *a* or *the* context for a given text.

Jurist appeals to context—the exceptions clause if we consider that context instead of text, the rest of Article III, some other specific clauses of the Constitution, the general character of the constitutional scheme (which last is so abstract that it is probably just as well not classed as context, but instead dealt with as transtext or pantext). The first conclusion we may draw, however, is that just as there is an openness as to what the text is, so there is no clear line between text and context. And beyond that there is an openness of context generally as well. For Jurist Article I, Section 4 is context for Article III, Section 2, whereas for Marshall it is not. What is context for each is already determined (in part?) by what each takes the text to be. There is an interaction and mutual determination of the dual openness of text and context. Context therefore cannot operate in the manner of the official Blackstone-Marshall theory, any more than text can.

Transtext. Marshall, on the other hand, appeals to transtext, the "no mere surplusage" rule, in order to establish the bearing of text. The transtext to which Marshall appealed was an interpretive rule. Transtextuals however can be quite varied in character. History of the "intention of the law giver" sort, judicial precedent, consideration of historical and political context are all transtextuals. (I classify political and historical context with transtext rather than context, out of a desire to restrict the latter to intratextual features brought to bear in as interpretation; transtextuals are interpretive elements that go beyond or transcend the text.)

Marshall's transtextual appeal in *Marbury* suggests the limits of the transtext as well, however. Marshall uses the surplusage rule as a way to establish the bearing of the text. As Jurist points out in his blistering attack on Marshall, there is great ambiguity in the bearing of the surplusage rule on the question of bearing; Jurist suggests two other readings that conform to the surplusage rule, neither of which is evidently inferior to Marshall's reading. That is, the question of bearing seems to arise once again at the next level of the bearing of the transtext. And that difficulty is magnified by the further indeterminacy that appears when we notice that Marshall's surplusage rule is by no means of universal application. For example, in *McCulloch* he treats the Tenth Amendment as in effect "mere surplusage," an interpretive move for which he could surely offer a defense, but the point is that some other or further knowledge of meaning or bearing must guide the interpreter in knowing which kind of transtext, which rule should be applied and when.

That point can be appreciated even better if we extend our net and consider not only Justice Jurist's approach in *Marbury*, but consider other opinions that might have been constructed with a central appeal to quite other transtextual elements than either Marshall's or Jurist's. An opinion might have been constructed, for example, by Justice Historian, that appealed to historical precedent in favor of a reading different from both Marshall's and Jurist's. Justice Historian might canvas English history and notice that even though the judiciary there is considered independent, nonetheless Parliament exercises power to assign jurisdiction to courts far beyond what Marshall concedes to Congress. Perhaps most decisive would be Justice Historian's appeal to the actions of the first Congress, which in the Judiciary Act of 1789 assumed an understanding of Article III, Section 2 that seemed to agree with neither the Chief Justice nor his critic. On the one hand, Congress failed to vest the full range of federal judicial power in the Supreme Court (which Marshall's interpretation supports), but on the other reshuffled jurisdiction (which Jurist's supports). Because of the special authority of the first Congress, its nearness to the moment of drafting and ratifying the Constitution, and the great overlay of membership between Congress and the constitutional convention, the testimony of the Judiciary Act would be worth a great deal. There was even a lower court case, *United States v. Ravara*, which suggested that Congress had great latitude in how it treated the jurisdiction of the Courts, a latitude that even included the power to reassign the constitutionally assigned original jurisdiction.[23]

Justice Jurist thus appeals to a wholly different set of transtextuals, and they seem to support a wholly different decision of the issue at hand.

We have thus far omitted from our discussion one transtextual that played a very prominent part in Justice Jurist's opinion, and a somewhat more subdued part in Marshall's opinion as well—the attempt to establish bearing through the attempt to establish point. Jurist appealed to a certain account of what the point would be of providing for the distribution of jurisdiction in the Constitution that he says was provided for. This is not an appeal to actual historical actors, although in principle it could be. (Justice Historian might well have made the appeal to point in a more historical manner.) For Jurist, it is an appeal to a construct of what a rational, or perhaps better, a sensible person might have been attempting to achieve in establishing the legal provision in question. This is, in other words, the kind of transtextual appeal that has tended to dominate recent discussions of common law interpretation methods in early constitutional law.[24]

But point cannot in fact resolve the problem of nongivenness of text and context, for at best it can lead the interpreter toward a point for the text-context as identified, but it cannot of itself authenticate the text-context complex so tested.

Pantext. We come then to the final category, pantext, and my chief claim: the interpretive practice of both Justice Jurist and Chief Justice Marshall reveals not the Blackstone-Wolfe theory of interpretation, but rather the (dialectical) domination of pantext. Pantext is that view of point and meaning not for this or that specific part of the text, but for the text as a whole. In Jurist's case the pantext is the twin first principles of the Constitution as establishing a certain kind of federal union and a certain kind of republican separation of powers scheme. That pantext validates, or even determines, the text-context-transtext complex he elucidates in his opinion. His affirmation of the validity of his reading of the text derives from the coherence of that reading with the pantext he identified; and his rejection of Marshall's alternative reading rests on the incompatibility of that reading with the pantext.

Marshall's pantext is more subtle and complex. Judging from other opinions of his we must conclude he was aware of Jurist's pantext, but saw that text as embedded in yet a larger whole. And it was his perception of that pantext that in turn produced his reading of text in *Marbury*. It was in light of his understanding of the whole, the peculiar blend of the legalist and the political constitution, that Marshall rendered the text as he did.

The role of pantext in Marshall means that Marshall's interpretive practice is very different from the model put forth by Blackstone and by Wolfe on behalf of Marshall himself. The differences are threefold: (1) pantext is universally implicated in interpretation and not merely intermittently so; (2) pantext is prior and not posterior to textual interpretation; (3) interpretation proceeds according to a dialectic between interpretive levels rather than lexicographically. Interpretation is not a foundationalist activity.

The openness of bearing and the nongivenness of text point always to the place of pantext. Never are the bare words sufficient because one must always ask, are these the right bare words? And what bearing do these bare words have? As we have seen, interpreters deploy context and transtext in an attempt to answer those questions, but they always implicitly point toward pantext. That is, one rests satisfied with the givenness and bearing of the text only when some coherence with a pantextual construct is present. The interpreter may be only dimly aware of pantext and may have a confused notion of what his or her pantext is, but interpretation always requires some fit with the interpreter's sense of what the whole is all about.

Pantext thus is not some appeal reserved only for extra hard cases where the lower levels of interpretation have somehow failed. Interpreters are constantly driven to pantext because meaning always exists contextually. Something "means" only when fittable into some context. As Schleiermacher long ago emphasized, interpretation is essentially a matter of wholes and parts. A part cannot be a part without reference, more or less explicit, to its whole. A different fit, that is, a different relation between a part (a text-nugget) and a whole modifies meaning, even if, physically speaking, the text remains the same. Meaning thus unfolds: One can always modify meaning, by coming to a different sense of the whole. Thus pantext is prior to text. Pantext serves as what we have called pretext. Some interpretation of the whole is at work from the outset shaping the interpreter's sense of the parts.

At the same time, pantext is not merely imposed from the top, so to speak, onto the text such that pantext simply determines and shapes text, much as some recent theories in the area of philosophy of science claim theories do vis-à-vis observations or data. The relationship is dialectical; both text and pantext are open to redefinition in the interpretive process as the interpreter moves back and forth between the levels. Confrontation with text can lead to revision of the pretextual pantext, because the aim of interpretation is overall coherence between text and pantext. Text has sufficient independence of pantext that it is able to resist mere imposition of any pantext—not any pantext can successfully work with a text; the text is not simply an artifact of the interpretation.

On the other hand, however, the parts of the text do not have the character of pregiven building blocks from which an even larger whole can be built. Interpretation is not foundationalist in the sense that one can move from given nugget and then on up. The latter is more or less the Blackstone model of interpretation. It corresponds to epistemology in the world of knowledge: Proper identification of the given parts (the data), and proper inference from them on the basis of established rules of legal reasoning (method) will produce valid results (scientific knowledge). The title of our panel, therefore, should be "interpretation" or "epistemology." The testimony of Marshall's practice says: "interpretation."

The dialectical character of interpretation clearly implies the illegitimacy of dispensing with text in favor of pantext. A judge no longer would be interpreting if he or she took a conception of pantext and directly derived results from it, by passing text altogether. Such a procedure would imply that pantext is given in a way that we have just argued text is not. But the fact is that text is more given than pantext, that pantext is always construct. Indispensable and centrally important construct, but construct nonetheless. Every such construct is tentative subject to being reconsidered and reformulated in the light of coherence with the text, context, and transtext that it brings along with it, in the specific query posed in any given case.

Moreover, it is not for courts to translate pantext into text—that is the task of legislators. The court's job is "to say what the law is," which requires that it engage in the kind of interpretive process I have described. The involvement of pantext is necessary to finding meaning; legislation from pantext is not. There is no reason to expect only one determinate textual embodiment of pantext, especially given the fact that pantext exists at a very general and very abstract level. Text and pantext mutually light each other up. Neither can be deduced from the other. Thus the understanding of interpretation suggested by Marshall's interpretive practice does not give aid and comfort to the noninterpretivist conception of a legislative role for the courts.

Marshall's testimony therefore on the question of our time favors not only the legitimacy and desirability, but the possibility, of interpretivism, albeit he requires us to think of interpretivism differently from the way we usually do. His interpretive practice in some respects points to a method of interpretation that gives great weight to all the kinds of indeterminacies of text to which noninterpretivists frequently appeal. The dominance, priority, and dialectical role of pantext do not imply that valid interpretation is not possible. Indeed, pantext only really comes to view if one engages in *interpretation*, that is, the strenuous effort to grasp the meaning of the text. To substitute one's preference for text is not interpretation; to substitute implementation of evolving societal values for text is not interpretation; to be primarily results-oriented is not interpretation.

Marshall's mode of interpreting the Constitution retains the aspiration to correct interpretation, so far as it actually *is* interpretation. But he requires of us that we reconsider what we mean by correct or valid interpretation. We most often think of correctness on the foundationalist model of the Blackstonian theory, a theory Marshall himself on occasion endorsed, although I suspect never quite to the degree Wolfe attributes to him. The foundational method appeals to us because of its closeness to the scientific/epistemological model of knowledge and because it therefore promises, or seems to, the certainty of meaning that we seek. We are especially prone to seek such certainty in legal interpretation, because, unlike literary interpretation, for example, the stakes are very high. Under usual circumstances, the authoritative and coercive powers of the state come into play to enforce the judicial interpretation. The average literary critic can only wish for such aid.

Given that desire for certainty it is surely understandable that the foundational model should achieve a certain popularity among lawyer and layperson alike, and even find expression in the prose of judges and legal theorists who know better. But if the foundational theory is an error, it is a salutary error, for the most part, for it keeps at the center of judicial awareness the imperative to find the correct meaning. It serves as a worthwhile shorthand for the public, whose experience of interpretation is not extensive enough to lead to understanding of the true nature and necessity of the enterprise, and to judges who need to be reminded that their only legitimate activity is interpretation.

The inaccuracy of the foundational theory is less than salutary when partially thought-through analysis of the nature of the interpretive activity exposes the inadequacies of the foundational theory, but does not go so far as to lay bare the true nature of interpretation. The result—legal realism, and noninterpretivism of various kinds. Noninterpretivism, for all its apparent sophistication, remains caught within the foundationalist model. Noninterpretivism is merely the negative of foundationalism. It has not yet grasped interpretation.

NOTES

1. J. ELY, DEMOCRACY AND DISTRUST 1 (1980). The terminology seems to have been invented by Grey, *see Do We Have an Unwritten Constitution?* 27 STAN. L. REV. 703 (1975).

2. C. WOLFE, THE RISE OF MODERN JUDICIAL REVIEW 14, 40, 41, 61 (1986).

3. *Id.* at 37.

4. *Id.* at 42.

5. For an alternative view *see* Fiss, *Objectivity and Interpretation*, 34 STAN. L. REV. 739 (1982).

6. H. GADAMER, TRUTH AND METHOD (1975).

7. Consider Van Alstyne, *A Critical Guide to* Marbury v. Madison, DUKE U. L. REV. 1 (1969).

8. R. BERGER, CONGRESS VS. SUPREME COURT 188 (1969).

9. J. AGRESTO, THE SUPREME COURT AND CONSTITUTIONAL DEMOCRACY 63 (1984).

10. Consider Gunther, *Judicial Review*, in ENCYCLOPEDIA OF THE AMERICAN CONSTITU-TION 1055-56 (1986), and Levy, *Judicial Review, History, and Democracy: An Introduction*, in JUDICIAL REVIEW AND THE SUPREME COURT (L. Levy ed. 1967).

11. On the political view of *Marbury*, *see* e.g. Levy, *supra* note 10; and D. DEWEY, MAR-BURY V. MADISON (1970).

12. For a more extended discussion of the problem of encroachments, see Zuckert, *A System without Precedent: Federalism in the American Constitution*, in THE FRAMING AND RATIFICATION OF THE CONSTITUTION 142-45 (L. Levy and D. Mahoney eds. 1987).

13. For a more extensive view of the political dimensions of the partial negative, *see* Zuckert, *Federalisms and the Founding*, 48 REV. POL. 166-210.

14. *See* THE FEDERALIST No. 47.

15. *Id.*

16. *See*, for example, BERGER, *supra* note 8.

17. For a fuller account of the universal negative, *see* Zuckert, *supra* note 13, at 187-97.

18. NOTES OF DEBATES IN THE FEDERAL CONVENTION (June 6).

19. Marbury v. Madison, 1 Cranch 137, at 166 (1803).

20. *Id.*

21. WOLFE, *supra* note 2, at 18, 43, 47, 51.

22. *Id.*

23. *Id.* at 44-48.

24. *See id.* at 48-49 and Powell, *The Original Understanding of Original Intent*, 98 HARV. L. REV. 885 (1985).

Select Bibliography

Adams, Henry. *History of the United States of America during the Administration of Thomas Jefferson*. New York: Library of America, 1986 edition.

Adams, John S., ed. *An Autobiographical Sketch by John Marshall*. Ann Arbor: University of Michigan Press, 1937.

Bailyn, Bernard. *The Ideological Origins of the American Revolution*. Cambridge: Belknap Press of Harvard University, 1967.

Baker, Leonard. *John Marshall: A Life in Law*. New York: Macmillan Co., 1974.

Banning, Lance. *The Jeffersonian Persuasion: Evolution of a Party Ideology*. Ithaca, N.Y.: Cornell University Press, 1978.

Beveridge, Albert J. *The Life of John Marshall*. Four volumes. New York: Houghton Mifflin Co., 1916.

Boyd, Julian. "The Chasm that Separated Thomas Jefferson and John Marshall." In *Essays on the American Constitution*, edited by Gottfried Dietze. Englewood Cliffs, N.J.: Prentice-Hall, 1964.

Boyd, Julian, ed. *The Papers of Thomas Jefferson*. Twenty-one volumes to date. Princeton, N.J.: Princeton University Press, 1950–.

Broderick, Albert. "From Constitutional Politics to Constitutional Law." *North Carolina Law Review* 65 (1987).

Campbell, Bruce A. "*Dartmouth College* as a Civil Liberties Case: The Formation of Constitutional Policy." *Kentucky Law Journal* 70 (1981–82).

"Chief Justice John Marshall: A Symposium." *The University of Pennsylvania Law Review* 104 (1955).

Corwin, Edward D. *John Marshall and the Constitution: A Chronicle of the Supreme Court*. New Haven, Conn.: Yale University Press, 1921.

Cotton, Joseph P., Jr., ed. *The Constitutional Decisions of John Marshall*. New York: G. P. Putnam's Sons, 1905.

Crosskey, William W. *Politics and the Constitution in the History of the United States*. Two volumes. Chicago: University of Chicago Press, 1953.

Curtis, George T. *Constitutional History of the United States from the Declaration of Independence to the Close of the Civil War*. Two volumes. New York: Harper and Bros., 1897.

Diggins, John. *The Lost Soul of American Politics*. New York: Basic Books, 1984.

Dillon, John N., ed. *John Marshall: The Complete Constitutional Decisions*. Chicago: Callaghan and Co., 1903.

Dumbauld, Edward. "John Marshall and Treaty Law." *American Journal of International Law* 50 (1956).

Faulkner, Robert K. *The Jurisprudence of John Marshall*. Princeton, N.J.: Princeton University Press, 1968.

Flanders, Henry. *The Life of John Marshall*. Philadelphia: T. and J. W. Johnson and Co., 1904.

Frankfurter, Felix. *The Commerce Clause under Marshall*. Chapel Hill: University of North Carolina Press, 1937.

Frisch, Martin. "John Marshall's Philosophy of Constitutional Republicanism." *Review of Politics* 20 (1958).

Gertz, Elmer. "John Marshall: Molder of the U.S. Constitution." *Decalogue Journal* 6 (1955).

Gunther, Gerald, ed. *John Marshall's Defense of* McCulloch v. Maryland. Stanford, Calif.: Stanford University Press, 1969.

Haines, Charles G. *The Role of the Supreme Court in American Government and Politics, 1789–1855*. New York: Russell and Russell, 1944.

Hamilton, John C. *History of the Republic of the United States of America First Traced in the Writings of Alexander Hamilton and His Contemporaries*. New York: D. Appleton, 1857–64.

Isaacs, Nathan. "John Marshall on Contracts: A Study in Early American Juristic Theories." *Virginia Law Review* 7 (1921).

Johnson, Herbert A. *Foundations of Power: John Marshall, 1801–15. Volume 2: History of the Supreme Court of the United States*. New York: Macmillan Co., 1981.

Johnson, Herbert A., and Charles T. Cullen, et al., eds. *The Papers of John Marshall*. Five volumes to date. Chapel Hill: University of North Carolina, 1977–.

Jones, William M., ed. *Chief Justice John Marshall: A Reappraisal*. Ithaca, N.Y.: Cornell University Press, 1956.

Konefsky, Samuel J. *John Marshall and Alexander Hamilton: Architects of the American Constitution*. New York: Macmillan Co., 1964.

Kutler, Stanley I., ed. *John Marshall*. Englewood Cliffs, N.J.: Prentice-Hall, 1972.

Lerner, Max. "John Marshall and the Campaign of History." *Columbia Law Review* 39 (1939).

Loth, D. G. *Chief Justice: John Marshall and the Growth of the Republic*. New York: W. W. Norton and Co., 1949.

McDonald, Forrest. *Novus Ordo Seclorum*. Lawrence: University of Kansas Press, 1984.

McLaughlin, Andrew C. *A Constitutional History of the United States*. New York: D. Appleton-Century, 1935.

Magruder, Allan B. *John Marshall*. New York: Houghton Mifflin Co., 1917.

Marshall, John, *The Life of George Washington*. Five volumes. Fredericksburg, Va.: The Citizen's Guild of Washington's Boyhood Home, 1926 edition.

Mason, Frances N. *My Dearest Polly: Letters of Chief Justice Marshall to His Wife.*
    1779–1831, New York: Garret and Massey, 1961.
Matthews, Richard K. *The Radical Politics of Thomas Jefferson: A Revisionist*
    View. Lawrence: University of Kansas Press, 1984.
Mendelson, Wallace. "John Marshall's Short Way with Statutes." *Kentucky Law*
    Review 36 (1948).
Nelson, William E. "The Eighteenth Century Background of John Marshall's
    Constitutional Jurisprudence." *Michigan Law Review* 76 (1978).
Newmyer, R. Kent. *The Supreme Court under Marshall and Taney.* New York:
    Crowell, 1968.
Oliver, A. *The Portraits of John Marshall.* Charlottesville: University of Virginia
    Press, 1976.
Palmer, Benjamin W. *Marshall and Taney: Statesmen of the Law.* Minneapolis:
    University of Minnesota Press, 1939.
Parrington, Vernon L. *The Romantic Revolution in America.* New York: Harcourt,
    Brace and Company, 1927.
Phillips, Isaac Newton. *John Marshall: An Address Delivered before the Graduates*
    of Chicago-Kent College of Law. St. Paul, Minn.: West Co., 1901.
Platt, Horace G. *John Marshall and Other Addresses.* San Francisco: Argonaut Co.,
    1908.
Pocock, J.G.A. *The Machiavellian Moment.* Oxford: University Press, 1975.
Rhodes, Irwin S. *The Papers of John Marshall: A Descriptive Calendar.* Two vol-
    umes. Norman: University of Oklahoma Press, 1975.
Riethmuller, Christopher J. *Alexander Hamilton and His Contemporaries; or, The*
    Rise of the American Constitution. London: Bell and Duddy, 1864.
Roche, John P., ed. *John Marshall: Major Opinions and Other Writings.* New
    York: Bobbs-Merrill Co., 1966.
Services, John A. *A Bibliography of John Marshall.* Washington, D.C.: U.S. Com-
    mission for the Celebration of the 200th Anniversary of the Birth of John Mar-
    shall, 1956.
Severn, William. *John Marshall: The Man Who Made the Supreme Court Supreme.*
    New York: McKay, 1969.
Siegel, Adrienne. *The Marshall Court: 1801–1835.* Milwood N.Y.: Associated Facul-
    ty Press, 1987.
Smith, William R. *History as Argument: The Patriotic Historians.* The Hague:
    Mouton and Co., 1966.
Stites, Frances. *John Marshall: Defender of the Constitution.* Boston: Little,
    Brown and Co., 1981.
Surrency, Erwin C., ed. *The Marshall Reader: The Life and Contribution of Chief*
    Justice John Marshall. Dobbs Ferry, N.Y.: Oceana Publications, 1955.
Sutherland, Arthur E. *Constitutionalism in America: Origin and Evolution of Its*
    Fundamental Ideas. New York: Blaisdell Co., 1965.
Sutherland, Arthur E. *Government under Law.* Cambridge: Harvard University
    Press, 1956.
Swindler, William F. *The Constitution and Chief Justice Marshall.* Dodd, Mead
    and Co., 1979.

Thayer, J. B. *John Marshall*. New York: Houghton Mifflin Co., 1911.

Von Holst, Hermann E. *Constitutional and Political History of the United States*. John J. Lalor and Alfred B. Mason, trans. Chicago: Callaghan and Co., 1889.

Warren, Charles. *The Supreme Court in United States History* (Boston: Little Brown, 1924).

White, G. Edward. *The Struggle for Nationalism: The Marshall Court, 1815–1825; The Challenge of Jacksonian Democracy: The Marshall Court, 1826–1835; Volumes 3 and 4: History of the Supreme Court of the United States*. New York: Macmillan Co., 1987.

Wills, Garry. *Inventing America: Jefferson's Declaration of Independence*. Garden City, N.Y.: Doubleday and Co., 1978.

Wood, Gordon. *The Creation of the American Republic, 1776–1787*. Chapel Hill: University of North Carolina Press, 1969.

Ziegler, Benjamin M. *The International Law of John Marshall: A Study of First Principles*. Chapel Hill: University of North Carolina Press, 1939.

Table of Cases

Index

Ackerman, Bruce, 182
Adams, Henry, 17, 22
Adams, John, 98, 100, 128
Agresto, John, 201, 202
Alien and Sedition Acts, 15, 104
American Revolution, 96
The Antelope, 29
Antifederalists, 202
Arendt, Hannah, 127
Aristotle, 79, 82

Baker, Leonard, 36
Bank of the United States: congressional power to establish, 147, 149, 150, 164–65; immunity from tax, 139; Jefferson's view, 118; political lesson of, populist resentment, 23–24, 152–53; state sovereignty issue, 143–44, 177. *See also McCulloch v. Maryland*
Bankruptcy law, in the states, 36–51
Barber, Benjamin, 119
Barron v. Baltimore, 159–60, 167–68, 169, 170
Beard, Charles, 91
Behavioral jurisprudence: advantages of, 57–58; assumptions of, 58–59; Marshall Court analyzed with, 66–67; model of, 59–70; psychological components, 68–69; statistical procedures related to, 60–63, 66–67
Berger, Raoul, 201
Beveridge, Albert, 76, 119, 159
Bicentennial of the U.S. Constitution, 1
Bickel, Alexander, 182
Bill of Rights: bicentennial of, 2; debate over, 201; importance of, for Jerfferson, 122–24; importance of, for today, 161; Madison's views on, 205, 207; Marshall's treatment of, 27, 167–68, 170. *See also Barron v. Baltimore*
Blackstone, William, 194, 209, 210, 211, 213, 214, 215
Bloc analysis, 66
Bonaparte, Napoleon, 22, 30–31
Bork, Robert, 161–62, 173–74, 183
Brandeis, Louis, 61, 62
Brennan, William, 61
Brown v. Board of Education, 65
Brown v. Maryland, 101
Brown v. United States, 30
Burr, Aaron, trial of, 21–22

Canon, Bradley, 64
Chase, Samuel, 15, 17

Contributors

JOHN BRIGHAM is professor of political science at the University of Massachusetts, Amherst. He studies legal ideologies and institutions and is the author of several books on these subjects, including most recently, *The Cult of the Court* (1987).

RICHARD A. BRISBIN, JR., is assistant professor of political science, West Virginia University. He specializes in constitutional law, judicial politics, and public administration. He has written extensively on the Supreme Court of various historical periods. His current work includes an analysis of the records of recent conservative justices.

ROBERT K. FAULKNER is professor of political science at Boston College. He is a leading scholar of John Marshall's constitutional thinking. He has published widely in the field of political theory. His most enduring contribution to Marshall studies is undoubtedly *The Jurisprudence of John Marshall* (1968), which dominates interpretation of Marshall's political thought.

HERBERT A. JOHNSON is professor of history and law at the University of South Carolina, Columbia. He is a leading contemporary scholar of the Marshall Court and era. He served on the staff of *The Papers of John Marshall* and was editor of volumes 1 and 2. He coauthored *Foundations of Power: John Marshall 1801–1815* (1981), which forms volume 2 of the *History of the Supreme Court of the United States*, published under the auspices of the Permanent Committee on the Oliver Wendell Holmes Devise. He has published many other works on early American legal history.

JAMES E. LENNERTZ is associate professor of political science at Lafayette College. He specializes in and writes about issues relating to public law and constitutional theory. He is centrally concerned with the relationship of scientific to legal epistemologies.

RICHARD K. MATTHEWS is associate professor of political science at Lehigh University. He specializes in political theory, especially American political thought. He is the author of a variety of works on political theory; his publications include *The Radical Politics of Thomas Jefferson* (1984). He is currently writing a book on James Madison's "politics of fear."

THOMAS C. SHEVORY is assistant professor of politics at Ithaca College. He specializes in public law, public policy, and political theory. He has published articles relating literary interpretations to political practices and political interpretations to policy practices. He is currently writing a book on John Marshall's political theory.

JOHN STOOKEY is professor of political science at Arizona State University. He has published extensively on judicial decision making, court process, and aspects of the judiciary. Much of his work has dealt with the Supreme Court, and he is currently engaged in a project to analyze historical practices of litigation in the southwestern United States.

IRA L. STRAUBER is professor of political science and philosophy at Grinnell College. He specializes in political theory and constitutional law. He is the author of numerous articles interpreting legal interpretation and reasoning from the perspective of political theory. Most recently, his article "The Rhetorical Structure of Freedom of Speech" appeared in the fall 1987 issue of *Polity*.

GEORGE WATSON is professor of political science at Arizona State University. He specializes in judicial politics and political science methodology. He has published extensively in both of these areas.

MICHAEL ZUCKERT is professor of political science at Carleton College. He specializes in political and constitutional theory and has written widely in these areas. His recent publications include "Federalism and the American Founding" in *The Constitution: A History of Its Framing and Ratification* (L. Levy & D. Mahoney eds. 1987) and "Self-Evident Truths and the Declaration of Independence" in *Review of Politics*, Summer 1987.